Self and Identity in Indian Fiction

INDIAN ENGLISH Literature

Self and Identity in Indian Fiction

S.P. SWAIN

Prestige

an international publishing house

Published by
Prestige Books
3/28, East Patel Nagar
New Delhi 110 008
Ph. 9818755529

ISBN: 81-7551-162-1

Printed at Chaman Offset Press, New Delhi 110 002

Contents

Introduction:
Random Thoughts on Identity
9

Quest for Identity: A Study of
Anita Desai's *Bye-Bye, Blackbird*
17

Hugo, the Nowhere Man: A Study of
Anita Desai's *Baumgartner's Bombay*
34

Theme of Fragmentation:
Salman Rushdie's *Midnight's Children*
47

Problems of Identity: A Study of
Bharati Mukherjee's *Desirable Daughters*
56

The Crisis of Identity:
V.S. Naipaul's *A House for Mr. Biswas*
64

V.S. Naipaul's *The Middle Passage*:
Centre and Marginality
76

Self and Society: A Study of
Bhabani Bhattacharya's *So Many Hungers!*
82

The Alienated Protagonists in
Bhabani Bhattacharya's *So Many Hungers!* and
***Music for Mohini*: A Comparative Study**
91

Sindi Oberoi:
Arun Joshi's Alienated Hero
97

The Problem of Alienation and the Quest for Identity in Joshi's Novels
107

Search for Identity: A Study of Raja Rao's *The Serpent and the Rope*
115

The Theme of Marriage in Raja Rao's *The Serpent and the Rope*
124

Myth in Raja Rao's *Kanthapura*
130

Khushwant Singh's *Train to Pakistan:* A Thematic Analysis
148

The Novels of R.K. Narayan and Indian Reality
158

Nirad Chaudhuri's *The Autobiography of an Unknown Indian*: A Critique
169

The Quest for Meaning: A Study of Amitav Ghosh's *The Shadow Lines*
180

Gandhi and Indian Novel in English
188

Acknowledgements

I thankfully acknowledge to the editors of the following journals/ anthologies in which my articles appeared: *Commonwealth Novel in English*, Virginia (US), *The Atlantic Literary Review*, *The Journal of Indian Writing in English*, *The Vikram Journal of English Studies*, *New Quest*, *The Quest*, *Indian Journal of English Studies*, *The Indian PEN*; *Indian Women Novelists*, *Nirad C. Chaudhuri*, *Khushwant Singh*, *The Novels of Amitav Ghosh*, and *Indian Literature Today*, ed. R.K. Dhawan; *Encyclopedia of Literatures in English*, *Indian Writing in English*, *Commonwealth English Literature*, ed. M.K. Bhatnagar; *V.S. Naipaul: Critical Essays*, ed. Mohit K. Ray; *Amitav Ghosh's The Shadow Lines*, ed. Novy Kapadia; *The Novels of Bhabani Bhattacharya*, ed. Monika Gupta; *Indian Writing in English*, ed. Syed Mashkoor Ali; *Critical Explorations and Indian Novelists in English: Critical Perspectives*, ed. Amar Nath Prasad; *Indian Fiction in English*, ed. A.N. Shukla. The author also acknowledges his indebtedness to Dr P.M. Nayak with whom he co-authored the articles on Anita Desai's *Baumgartner's Bombay* and *Gandhi and Indian Novel in English*.

Introduction: Random Thoughts on Identity

A non-descript term, identity suggests our thoughts and feelings, our psychic presence, our place of habitation, and even our longings, dreams and desires. The individual identity, like the national identity, is formed through a series of random and frequently bizarre accretions. In the formation of the individual identity, several factors come into play. One is the cumulative offspring of all these diverse and divisive forces. A formative and not an innate product, one's identity is determined by three factors. Firstly, childhood impressions and aspirations play a vital role in deciding it. An individual has to break off most of his reliance on his parents, and become free enough to leave home and develop ideas and aims of his own which will give him a distinct identity. How strong the rebelliousness in each individual is, and what form it takes, is the second element in determining identity. The third element is the zeitgeist. These call on the youth to develop different qualities in different historical periods. As Erik Erikson explains in *Youngman Luther*, the corruption of the church in Martin Luther's time, the need for reform, instilled in young Luther's fearlessness, clarity, eloquence and perseverance of heroic proportions. He was inspired to revolt against the fanatic and pestilent society. Besides the influence of parents and home, society and zeitgeist play a major role in shaping the identity of an individual. In a less critical age, Luther might have remained an undifferentiated and undistinguished priest. It is the spirit and the need of the times that produced him. Thus, Luther's identity is the identity of the times, the contemporaneity. But it is not only the spirit of the times, but also the biological trait within the character, the inner drive and motivation which equally contribute to one's identity. The zeitgeist only acts as a catalyst to activate the latent instinctive traits within the character of an individual.

Our desire for a separate cultural identity is the offspring of our being alienated from the concept of unity in diversity. It becomes a problem for the nation-state to accommodate diverse cultural factions clamouring for unique identities: "The processes of foreign cultural penetration are already posing a serious threat to our national cultural identity."[1]

History shows that artificial means of creating an identity either through religion or through ideology are not sustainable. Striving for a separate cultural identity is to become culturally homogeneous, which is not geographically feasible. The cultural crises in Punjab, Kashmir, Assam and Tamil Nadu are basically and intrinsically a reflection of the search for cultural identity on the part of an alienated cultural fragment, and the need to be recognized as a separate cultural entity.

In the high mobility world of today, no geographical area is capable of staying culturally homogeneous and retaining its identity intact. Total cultural alienation from the neighbouring countries is practically impossible. Cross-cultural contact is bound to occur, either at the conscious or at the unconscious level. The culture-national identity nexus is intimately linked to the interior landscape and ethos of the country which moulds and colours our literature.

Erik H. Erikson uses the term "negative identity" for the state of an individual in which the "I" is suppressed, rendering him unable to participate in specialization. "I" is not impeded. It is expelled by his superior ego, i.e., his glorified self-image, his imaginative identity. As a result, he cannot arrive at true self-definition, and fails to decipher his real identity. Negative identity is a state in which the individual acts not in accordance with the dictates of his "core-self" or "inner conscience" but as per the promptings of the "other self" and "outer conscience," which is an ideational imposition from the external world of dreams and detours. In this state, there is total disgust and discord with the inner life, and hence the alienation of the self. Man defines himself in relation to the external world. He reckons his identity in others.

True, the change in the identity of an individual is on account of his psychic responses and emotional encounters, not "ethical responses"[2] as B.J. Paris suggests. The struggle between the two selves—the real and the idealized—engenders grave psycho-emotional imbalance when the real self is subdued and overpowered by destructive forces, which bring about psychotic alienation and the loss of real identity. R.D. Laing discusses at some length the phenomenon of psychotic alienation and the loss of contact with reality when a person can have mystical or magical experiences. "When the 'self' becomes more and more a participant in fantasy relationships; less and less a direct participant in real relationships; in doing so it loses its own reality."[3] Erikson maintains that identity is expressed in the core of the individual as well as that of the communal culture: "A mature psycho-social identity presupposes a community of people whose traditional values become significant to the growing person."[4]

An alien is bound to encounter cross-cultural contacts which may put him in a bewildering and frustrating situation. This bewilderment is the result of what Toffler calls "cultural shock." Assimilation and absorption in an alien culture "causes breakdown in communication, a misreading of reality, an inability to cope."[5] For instance, Sarah in *Voices in the City* is confounded by the transformation brought about by her cross-cultural marriage. She can neither assimilate her husband's culture, nor adopt herself to her own society. Normally, within one's own community, one has a unified and integrated self. The socio-cultural values give one a specific identity. Under certain pressures, the personality may split and disintegrate, giving way to different selves, with a different identity. Van den Berge prefers to call it "soclosis"[6] rather than "neurosis" when socio-historical mutations affect the psychology of an individual. This forging of a new identity on account of acculturisation may be called "socio-psychosis," since both social and psychic factors are involved in the emergence of the identity. Sarah's dual alienation is not the result of social transformation. It is the inevitable outcome of a cross-cultural catalysis. Cultural estrangement in Sarah is due to her socio-psychic alienation. The conflict between the actual self and the imagined or glorified self, the real self and the pride system, breeds depersonalization and disorientation, which in turn brings about the alienation of the self and an identity crisis. For instance, Maya in *Cry, the Peacock* feels many a time that she is not human, only a dream: "Maya—my very name means nothing, is nothing but an illusion."[7] From nothingness, she turns into a caged monkey. This symbolizes the loss of identity. In *The Waves*, Rhoda describes her precarious moments of near-madness in terms of lost identity: "I came to the puddle. I could not cross it. Identity failed me. We are nothing, I said, and fell."[8] Therefore, when the "inner self" loses the "self-world" affinity, disorientation occurs.

Identity is the projection of the self. Self-image moulds and transforms self-identity. One's identity is rooted in the culture in which one lives, and hence alienation from the culture leads to the loss of one's socio-cultural identity. The urge to identify with the present stimulates one in the quest for identity, which operates at public and private levels. The individual's alienation from the society is the manifestation of his quest for the assertion of his identity. Things otherwise taken for granted appear bewilderingly paradoxical when we seek a rationale behind them. It is this urge to discover a rationale in the transitivity of the objects around us that leads the alienated self in its quest for identity.

The characteristic features of a person fall into two broad categories: physical and psychological. Each of these features is subject to change. Personal identity judgments are made on the basis of these characteristics. Bodily continuity of memory serves as the justification for making identity judgements about persons. These continuities are our justification for ascribing identity to persons. However, any attempt to define personal identity in terms of these continuities may be an act of futility. Bodily continuity is often interpreted as spatio-temporal continuity. Personal identity is something ultimate and unanalyzable. This statement comes from the idea that our ordinary concept of a person is something whose unity is in itself unequivocal. Perceptible continuities, such as bodily continuity, are the only means to apprehend personal identity, which is more than these continuities—physical or psychic. The imaginary identity we ascribe to persons as well as to things is only a "fictitious" one. The identity with which we are concerned is the re-identification and persistence of things through time and change. It is spatio-temporal continuity. The nature and knowledge of our self-identity is reflected in all our sincere memory-statements. Self-identity is self-knowledge. The true nature of personal identity lies in self-identity, not in another identity. Identity in general is taken to be "a relation between a thing which is known to exist at one time, and a thing which is known to have existed in another time."[9]

The identity of a person may be established on evidences. John Locke describes personal identity as the "sameness of a rational being." A rational being can consider itself in different times and places, and can know of its identity through time, only by means of that consciousness which is inseparable from thinking and rooted to it. A person knows his identity by means of what Locke calls "consciousness," and it is this consciousness that constitutes personal identity. Analysis of personal identity in terms of memory, or what Locke called the continuity of consciousness, is but one of the criteria of establishing personal identity. Locke remained a memory theorist in his account of personal identity. Hume, on the other hand, after having reasoned that everything that lasts beyond a moment is only a "bundle or recollection" of rapidly changing perceptions, concluded that the identity we ascribe to persons (and things) is only a fictitious one.

Our impressions of objects are different at different moments; so no object of one moment can be the object of another moment. Hence identity cannot be static. It is dynamic and transient. This explains the logic of the transitivity of identity. Since every idea is derived from some impression, so must be the identity of the object, of which the idea is an idea. Butler, like Locke, gave consciousness or memory the prime importance in his account of personal identity. He was rather justly of the opinion that consciousness or memory of our past actions and experiences gives us the very sense of our identity through time, and assures us of our identity.

It is erroneous and fallacious, however, to deduce anything about the identity of things from the nature of the impressions, from which the ideas of the objects are derived. For instance, the impression which one has about one's writing table may not be continuous; it may be interpreted by some other impressions and ideas. But does it make one's writing table discontinuous and numerically different at different moments? Since memory gives us the sense of our identity, bodily considerations tend to be ignored, and often seem to be unessential. But this is an oversimplification. For when one considers whether he is the same person who did such-and-such things yesterday, he is not only concerned with his memory and inner perception. He also refers to his doing such-and-such, and this has an essential reference to his body, which, therefore, has a role to play. Further, there may be possible situations when one may doubt who one is and in such a case one has to rely on what others say about us—one's other identity. But what others say depends, pre-eminently, on their judgments about one's bodily continuity—and this is just what is missing in Hume's account of personal identity. Self-identity must go side by side with another identity. Had there been no possibility of there being other person, the question of one's own identity wouldn't arise. Personal identity is something intrinsic and can be known only by one's being conscious of it, or by intuiting one's identity with a past self. In our consciousness, our identity is unfailingly met with. The real self can only be an object of thought, not of knowledge. It follows therefore that the "real" nature of our identity is intractable and inscrutable. William James does not believe in the existence of a single self. What we call our "self" was construed by him as a series of momentary or fleeting selves, each one of which transmits all its consciousness to its successor self. That all "adopts" this consciousness as its own, and in its turn transmits its own consciousness together with what it had adopted from its earlier self. And so on.

Memory continuity cannot be a sufficient condition of personal identity, since bodily continuity is a necessary state of the latter. Every person can have non-criterial knowledge of his own identity, whereas his knowledge of the identity of other things has to be grounded on criteria. The Cartesians believed that persons are essentially minds or non-physical entities. What a person says will surely depend on what he remembers, since by supposition there is no bodily continuity here. This, in other words, defines personal identity in terms of memory. It is not true that what matters in personal identity is only "psychological continuity," while bodily continuity is totally and unjustly ignored. Indeed, bodily continuity plays a more significant role in knowing and making judgments about one's identity. To quote Mohapatra: "bodily continuity is a necessary condition of personal identity."[10] Bodily continuity is not a necessary condition of personal identity, if we don't mean the continuity of the brain. A man who has had brain transplantation is bound to behave differently from what he was before the operation. Since the brain of Mr. X, transplanted in the body of Mr. Y, will result either in Mr. Y's death or his becoming Mr. XY. Hence, "bodily continuity is but one of the factors and not the necessary condition of personal identity."[11]

Man's identity, observes Soren Kierkegaard, is threatened by the metaphysical systems in which his nature is irrevocably fixed. Kierkegaard discovers the real identity of man in his "inner self" which is the "true self." To him subjectivity is truth and reality; hence it is this inner self, which constitutes the real identity of man. Identity is the projection of the subjective self of a person; it depends on how he pictures himself, and his endeavours for the acquisition and formation of this self-image through a quest for identity.

References

1. P.C. Joshi, *Culture, Communication and Social Change* (New Delhi: Vikas, 1990), p. 12.

2. B.J. Paris, *A Psychological Approach to Fiction* (Bloomington: Indiana University Press, 1974), p. 24.
3. R.D. Laing, *The Divided Self* (1960; rpt. Harmondsworth: Penguin, 1973), p. 141.
4. Erik H. Erikson, "The Concept of Identity in Race Relations," *Daedalus* (Winter, 1966), p. 145.
5. Alvin Toffler, *Future Shock* (London: The Bodley Head, 1970), p. 13.
6. J.H. Van den Berge, "The Changing Nature of Man," *Introduction to a Historical Psychology* (New York: W.W. Norton, 1961), p. 30.
7. Anita Desai, *Cry, the Peacock* (New Delhi: Orient, 1980), p. 172.
8. Virginia Woolf, *The Waves* (1931; rpt. London: Hogarth, 1963), p. 46.
9. Shoemaker, *Self-Knowledge and Self-Identity* (Cornell, 1963), p. 33.
10. P.K. Mohapatra, *Concepts and Problems, Essays on Man, Mind and Metaphysics* (Cuttack: Santosh, 1988), p. 14.
11. Bernard Williams, "Personal Identity and Individuation," *Problems of the Self* (Cambridge University Press, 1973), p. 18.

Quest for Identity: A Study of Anita Desai's *Bye-Bye, Blackbird*

In *Bye-Bye, Blackbird*, the theme of alienation is explored from a different perspective and dimension. The novel is about the condition of Indian immigrants in England, their social, cultural and racial displacement. It explores the love-hate relationship of the immigrants towards their adopted land, their sense of alienation, their several attempts to adjust and integrate themselves to an alien society and their final realization with the discovery that total assimilation to a foreign culture is an impossibility. Anita Desai is concerned here with the socio-psychic experiences of the Indian immigrants in England.

Desai depicts the anabolic and katabolic impact of the metropolis on the individual and his subsequent alienation from the locale. The conversation between Adit and Dev at the outset of the novel sets the tone. Adit says: "No puja to the rising sun on the banks of the Thames, That is bad, Sen."[1]

Dev, too, voices his disgust at the metropolis of London which he contemptuously calls a jungle city. In *Voices in the City*, the city never alienates; the individual self gets itself alienated from the megalopolis of Calcutta. Compared with Adit and Sarah, Dev does not feel uncomfortable in London, since he had met with such a locale in the pages of Dickens and Lamb, Addison and Boswell and Dryden. The English suburbs inspire a sense of awe and wonder. The snarling attitude of the whites against the coloured immigrants derisively called "wogs" (15) breeds in Dev rancour and nausea. The novel traces Dev's psychic odyssey before he comes to terms with this new home. The conflict of the migratory blackbird is rendered in fictional terms through the character of Dev. His existential quest is a search for identity, a quest to belong. Each phase of his efforts at reconciliation involves a psychic situation arising out of cross-cultural actions and interactions. Dev's isolated self in the English milieu passes through a series of confrontations which lead to the disintegration of his identity. His weird experiences in a foreign land give him a culture shock. The conflict in him is between the images of the city in the conscious and in the unconscious. His agony comes from his failure to correlate the familiar picture of the city in the conscious with the unfamiliar images of the city in the unconscious. He dimly recounts the images he had encountered in his reading of the English books. The hiatus between the anticipated and the instantly received disturbs him. Self-awareness of the lost vision makes him nostalgic. Cross-cultural contacts do not give way to racial conflict or tension, though they alienate him from the milieu. He develops Anglophobic tendencies towards the locale. His is an ill-accommodated life of isolation. Along with the other coloured immigrants, he is scornfully addressed as "Macaulay's bastards." (138) Racial segregation serves as a prelude to alienation. Both in private and public life, Dev is confronted with identity crisis. Even a peddler refuses to tell him the price of a Russian icon, considering him too poor an Indian to buy it. The anguish of racial tensions shatters his zeal for life: "I would not live in a country where I was insulted and unwanted." (18) Besides the human environment, the geographical condition cuts him adrift like Sindi Oberoi in Joshi's *The Foreigner*. Sindi's is an alienation of the soul but Dev's is an alienation of geography. He says to Adit: "You must be masochists to live in this climate. . . . Masochists. What a climate, what a stinking climate?" (61)

For an immigrant like Dev or Adit, cultural confrontation sets in with the destructuring or restructuring of the self. The two heterogeneous sensibilities, one alien and the other native, are conditioned by the intrinsic value systems of their culture. The contrast between the value systems of the Orient and the Occident is so acute that for an immigrant, the first encounter is cultural resistance symbolically manifested through the alienation of the self. Adit says to Dev: "You must admit that is the trouble with the Orientals—we don't really believe in watches and clocks. We are romantics. We want time to fit in with our mood.

. . . How is the Englishman to understand that? He's been a clock watcher since the day he was born." (183) Severed from his natural ties and caught in the crossfire of love and hate; attraction and repulsion, Dev is hurt by the apathy of the people in the high streets of London:

> If I lived on a road like this in Calcutta, I would be aware—as aware as can be—of everyone around me. But not here. Here everyone is a stranger and lives in hiding. They live silently and invisibly. It could happen nowhere in India. (64)

The callousness of the people around alienates him from the social milieu and drives him to the state of a passive spectator. It paralyzes his ability to act and builds up "the tension in togetherness."[2] Dev is "a waste product thrown off like a trash on the face of the system."[3] His self disintegrates "consequent upon the division of function in the social systems of the Western world" (*Ibid.*) In the tube, he feels "like Alice falling, falling down the rabbit hole, like a Kafka stranger wandering through the dark labyrinth of a prison." (66)

The sights and sounds of England generate a morbid dread in Dev. Inside Clapham tube station, he feels claustrophobic. The milieu gives rises to a feeling of hollowness. His vision is blurred. The harrowing sight of the blackbirds amidst these eerie sensations finds a reflection in their faces that have become withdrawn and wane, and in their voices that are chilled and choked. They do not belong to these viscid voices and vampish visions. They do not participate in the bewitching gaiety of the city. They are outsiders. The silence of the streets of London appears to Dev horrifyingly disgusting. A foreigner in England, he reacts vehemently against English snobbery. The problem of alienation is felt both within and without. Dev sarcastically calls Adit, "Bootlicking toady, spineless imperialist lover." (21) The sense of dehumanization is so conspicuously felt by the Asiatics that they begin to doubt the very existence of the commonwealth. If the commonwealth really existed, then why does not everyone use the same lavatory? The genuineness of their commonwealth identity becomes questionable and ridiculous, a travesty and mockery. They are dubbed as hordes of black invaders who defile the emerald isle of the whites. Painfully, they feel the agony of abandonment and irascible moments of individual torment. The nostalgia of separateness incessantly haunts them.

Dev's response to the city of London is not emotional and subjective like that of Monisha and Nirode. He is a detached and mute observer, who feels offended by the silence and void of the city. Everything in the city seems dead and numb to him. To him, they are nothing but a barren stretch of wasteland. The milieu becomes the character of the despair-stricken and hypersensitive souls. Despite its dense population, the city seems silent and cold. The 'mighty heart' lies still. Throughout, Dev's reactions are unemotional and illogical. A flabbergasted alien, a stunned spectator, a shocked outsider and an anguished sightseer, Dev moves away from the centrality of experience, only to reckon at length that wherever he shifts, the centre of his being is always within the circumference of the same circle, i.e. England. Divisive traits within him split his self-identity. He tries to assimilate the acquired culture into his life but fails to catch up with the dilemma of alienation, unlike Srinivas in Markandaya's *The Nowhere Man*. Incertitude rules his life. Pulled apart by the claims of East and West, he simply zigzags. A swaggering cloud without rain, he fails to attain a tragic dimension. After a week with Sarah, he is seized by moods of melancholy. He is an urban self, with a flexible and fluid identity. His affinity with Ms. Pickering shows in him the fusion of East and West. Thus, his alienation is only peripheral, since deep within him lives the Indian ethos. He is often entangled and enmeshed in the web of his own ideas. The split in his identity is due to his vacillating nature. He grows quickly attached to Sarah, to her carefully preserved chilly and reticent territory. Laurel Lane remains to Dev a place of shut doors and curtained windows. In Calcutta he was aware of an audience but here everyone is an alien, a stranger who lives an indoor life. It would happen nowhere in India. Dev is a bewildered alien to the summer gaiety of English life. He is an outraged outsider. The tumult and confusion within him plagues him momentarily. He is baffled by the English way of life. He begins to see signs of imperialist insolence in the bland and mild manners of the British. He goes schizophrenic. Dev like Adit and like all other immigrants is the product of the novelist's own schizophrenic experience. Talking of the plight of the immigrants Anita Desai confesses: "Schizophrenia amused me while I was with them and continued to tease me when I returned to India. . . . I wrote it in an effort to understand the split psychology, the double loyalties of the immigrants."[4]

For an immigrant like Dev or Adit, cultural confrontation sets in with their social disorientation. Adit grows neurotic and schizophrenic with his disorientation from the social milieu. In his illness, he sees upon the wall "a barrow piled with such fruit as can only be seen in an Indian market." (139-40) But I.N. Kher associates this schizophrenia with "Dev and Adit's creative strategies to regain their freedom of choice and action, keeping their identities from erosion, in spite of their alien environment" and he "finds it highly useful in the context of Desai's own schizophrenic imagination."[5]

Leading wholly English lives, the immigrants in England were "Indians to the tips of their fingers. . . . Yet emotionally they were more Indian than the Indians at home. . . . Hardly any of them were able to sever their roots, not even those who tried hard. Indeed the roots seemed to have been strengthened by transplantation."[6] This is an instance of creative alienation.

Dev and Adit mirror two polarized responses to the locale. Adit is scientific in his outlook, whereas Dev is subjective, irrational, and dubious. Adit lives in the moment and for the moment, carefree and jolly; he hardly ponders over life. He passively yields to the newness and eeriness of London with a propensity for adjustment, whereas Dev feels ill-at-ease. His quest for sensation of life remains unrequited and unsatiated. He wanders on London streets in quest of his newfound identity and undergoes a psychic ordeal before he reckons his true self. Spiritual anguish and incertitude cause emotional instability. Dev's polarized responses to England are characteristic of the psychic traits of an ex-colonial, who suffers from a Caliban complex. The metropolis of London makes him aware of his other identity, his roots. It tells him that he is an expatriate in his own chosen world, which he mistakenly deems to be his. He goes through the entire gamut of love-hate relationship that exists between the colonialist and the colonized. Adit, similarly, becomes aware of his other self after his visit to the in-laws. Dev is alienated because he is disowned and rejected by the locale, but Sarah is alienated because she is unable to accommodate and adjust with the locale, although the locale accepts her. She remains an alien in her own domain.

The transformation in the identity of Dev is mystical, slow and gradual. An Anglophobe at the outset, he changes into an anglophile at the end of the story. Thus there seems to be a mystic dialectic between the individual and the locale, responsible for the manifestation of the individual's identity. This renders the character of Dev all the more romantic and stupefying. All along, Dev has been a champion of freedom and enterprise and not of discipline and restriction. He has a desire to start afresh. Direly in need of a job, he inquisitively responds to the advertisements but the result turns out to be elusive. As a result he lives amidst vague prospects, amidst panic and confusion, dismay and disbelief. Here is Dev's existential quest for identity:

> I am here, he intoned, as an ambassador. . . . I am here, he proselytized, to interpret my country to them, to conquest England as they once conquered India, to show them, to show them. . . . All I want is . . . well, yes, a good time. Not to return to India, not to marry and breed, go to office again but . . . to know a little freedom to indulge in a little adventure, to know, to know. (139-40)

Thus it is quite apparent, that Dev's quest for identity is stimulated by his desire to know, to know the English and to show them that Indians are a people with a distinct identity of their own, they are a free people, free in their own way. Strikingly, Adit's attachment for England is skin-deep:

> O England's green and grisly land,
> I love you as only a babu can. (146)

Dev's quest for identity in this 'green and grisly land' is ventilated by Adit: "You look like a shepherd in search of his lost flock." (171) Truly, Dev is in search of his lost flock, his Indian identity.

Despite his acquaintance with the literature of England, Dev is not entitled to the national identity of the country. Even belonging to the commonwealth also does not endow one with a common commonwealth identity. Belonging to the commonwealth, one remains away from the centrality of experience. Dev fails to notice this and claims the identity of an alien soil, something beyond the reach of his oriental upbringing and rearing. His Indian self becomes a hindrance in his quest. But Sarah universalizes Dev's predicament by saying that the English, too, face the same situation in their own soil. They too, lead an alienated and rootless life in their own land: "Oh, that is true of English people as well, Dev. The English feel restrained and deprived and discontented too." (123) The scenes that Dev sees in the countryside are not alien to his nature but are a part of it. In them, he recognizes the pattern and identity of his own nature. Something had happened to Dev. He no longer feels entrapped and ensnared by this 'grisly' land. He is no longer subjugated by the imperialistic designs of England, and the signs of imperialist innocence which prevailed at the initial stage of his life in England now gradually seemed to vanish. With the fading away of this attitude, Dev becomes quite certain of his emotional security in the English soil and decides to stay back. For the first time in his life in this foreign land, he feels an ecstasy, a joy that becomes so inextricably infused and impregnated in his being that there occurs an abrupt transformation in his identity. He bids adieu to his former Indian self and merges with the occidental self of the Britons. In reconciling himself to the English milieu, he discards and renounces the blackbird in him. His staggering and struggling Indian identity had to compromise with the English milieu. The blackbird is, at length, transformed into a white bird.

Dev seems not only culturally and psychologically conditioned by the west but he is 'possessed' by it. He is able to withstand the effects of double alienation and comes to a compromise. Gleefully owned and accepted by the expatriate soil, Adit could not compromise, and hence was disowned and rejected. Dev is ultimately assimilated and absorbed into an alien culture, his national identity completely dissolved in his newly acquired Anglo-Saxon identity. The difference and incertitude of his former self disappear with the departure of Adit from England. He regains his long-cherished desire for emotional stability and for the affirmation and actualization of his professional identity. His desire for a foothold on the England soil now ripens into a reality. The blackbird in him dies a partial death. He bids "Bye-Bye" to the internal blackbird, i.e. his Indian self, to the external blackbird, i.e. Adit, his companion, and to his oriental chums leaving England for India. Hence the refrain:

> Make my bed and light the light, I will arrive late tonight. Blackbird, bye-bye. (283)

Sarah opts out for an isolated life. She hesitates to talk about her Indian husband. The whole life of Sarah is given to the spurious task of role-playing. And "when she was not playing them, she was nobody. Her face was a mask, her body only a costume." (38) The real Sarah is lost somewhere between the two worlds:

> She wondered with great sadness if she would ever be allowed to step off the stage, leave the theatre and enter the real world. . . . Whether English or Indian, she did not care, she wanted only its sincerity, its truth. (38)

She is also wary of contact. Her alienation is not an instinctive need but a circumstantial necessity but to Kalpana Wanderekar, it is "self-imposed."[7]

Sarah has cut herself off from the mainstream of English life by marrying an immigrant Indian. She is a typical Anita Desai character, complex, hypersensitive and intelligent who can claim kinship with the introverted heroines of her two earlier novels *Cry, the Peacock* and *Voices in the City*. Doubtful, if Sarah has any identity at all, if she could enter the world of reality. She dreaded everything Indian, even Indian sweets. Sarah Sen is symbolic of double identity; Sarah, with an English affiliation and Sen, with an Indian identity. This is on account of her belonging to two incompatible worlds which cause a split in her self and breed anxiety in her:

> In the centre she sat feeling the waves rock her and the fear and questioning began: who is she? . . . Both these creatures were frauds, each had a large shadowed element of charade about it. . . . Her face was only a mask, her body only a costume. (39)

Sarah serves as a symbol of the tryst of two cultures—East and West. She has a cross-cultural identity. On the whole, the feeling of alienation in Sarah for India is transient and temporal. Hence her identity crisis wanes in the long run, and she begins to accommodate herself to the locale with ease and eagerness. "I feel I know India well, already," (90) Sarah ventured, turning for comfort and consolation to old Mr. Miller: "I feel, if I went I would not find it strange at all." (90) Anita Desai draws the dismantled, disgruntled and disrupted life of Sarah through the symbol of the symphony. She fails to compose the symphony she hears into a definite pattern, a harmony. The disintegration and dissonance of the symphony symbolizes the splitting up of her own life. To her closed eyes, darkness moved in a tumult of black clouds, shapes that would never settle.

Racial and cultural encounters breed anguish and estrangement. Sarah experiences an intoxicating wave of sporadic schizophrenia which was, to Adit, the outcome of her having been an Indian in a past incarnation and which sometimes allowed her to feel herself into an Indian mood while still able to observe herself undergoing this curious transformation with her normal Saxon detachment. (157)

She notices her father transformed into a log submerged. With her usual Anglo-Saxon composure and serenity, she adjusts to the new stillness in him or even to the lack of communication. She withstands the pangs of parental alienation. In her dealings with Adit, Sarah displays the traits of subordination and stoic forbearance but not masochistic passion. She accommodates her husband's Indian Identity, in the teeth of occasional clashes. Theirs is a symbiotic relationship that transcends their fragmentation of personality, their lost integrity and freedom. Their symbiotic nature of relatedness satisfies their craving for closeness and companionship. It brings about a transformation of her identity. Her stoicism is natural and instinctive. Well aware of the fact that her insubordinate and unpleasant behaviour might lead to conjugal misgivings and misapprehensions, she willingly submits to her husband's will. She silently and uncomplainingly bears her nausea that continues to torment her:

> So she had clutched the mouthpiece of the Head's telephone and mumbled, "Yes, yes, all right" and swallowed a few aspirins to still her headache. The nausea remained. (228)

Though she decides to give birth to her baby in India, she is afraid of the riddling identity of India.

> She placed her hands about it and wondered if she was doing right in going to India herself, to give birth to a child in a land made for the old, the dying, the unattached but hardly for infants, for the young, the growing. Old stories came to life against her will. . . . The warning of heat, sunstroke, disease, epidemics. . . . And they would be strangers, she and the baby. Awed, she cried, half laughing. Emma, you ought to be the one to go. I. . . . I do not believe, I have the courage, really. (240)

Sarah is an existentialist eager to affirm and discover her identity, eager to know, to strike roots:

> Who was she? . . . Mrs. Sen who had been married in a red and gold Benaras brocade sari one morning, bronzed day in September, or Mrs. Sen, the Head's Secretary. . . . Where was Sarah? Staring out of the window at the chimney pots and the clouds, she wondered if Sarah had any existence at all. (38)

Unlike many other English girls, Sarah has qualities of Indian housewife. With her humble, serene, submissive and obedient nature, she will have no problems in adjusting herself to the social topography of India. The old Sikh matriarch says:

> But when I look at you, when I see you going out in the morning and coming home, always so quiet with your head bent, not looking at anyone, then I think you are one of your own. You will have no trouble when you go to India. You will see it is your own country. (249)

At a point Sarah admits that she "won't feel alien on the Indian soil. I think when I go to India, I will not find it so strange after all. I am sure I shall feel quite at home very soon." (250) The Indian and the Anglo-Saxon blend into a single entity—Sarah.

Sarah becomes nameless. She sheds her name, her lineage, and her identity. She wishes to become what she is essentially not. She is alienated from Adit. She is alienated from Dev and in her frustration she feels "cut and slashed into living bleeding pieces . . . that enviable, cool, clear, quite state of apartness." (43) Meenakshi Mukherjee holds: "Sarah undergoes the suffering of daily duality as a result of her having to inhabit two incompatible worlds."[8]

Adit discovers that he did not fit in with the pattern Sarah had made of her life in which family counted very little. It never occurred to him that his marriage with Sarah could bring about this severance. The schizophrenic identity of India represented by the individual identity of her husband Adit, fails to suit her temperament. Hence, she is alienated from him, alienated only as housewife and not as a woman, Adit's alienation, on the other hand, is temperamental: "I am different. I love them. I love England. I admire England, I can appreciate her history and her poetry as much as any Englishman." (185)

Adit has "a dreadful vision of himself in the white shirt and shuffling slippers of a lunatic's garb at an asylum, an outsider not only by virtue of his colour but an imagination run amuck." (219) Adit's character reflects the awful plight of an alienated individual intensely longing for his roots. Erich Fromm observes: "It is surprising to find in the average a deep longing for the security and rootedness which the relationship to his mother once gave him? It is not to be expected that he cannot give up this intense longing unless he finds other ways of being rooted? In the most extreme form, we find the craving to return to the mother's womb. A person completely obsessed by this desire may be the picture of schizophrenia."[9]

In fact, Adit's longing for rootedness materializes with the discovery of his real self in discarding the mask of the alien and in throwing away the garb of a pukka sahib. From the unread and the artificial he moves on to the real and the natural:

> All our records and lamb curries and sing-songs, it's all so unreal. Whatever it is, it will be Indian, it will be my natural condition, my true circumstances. (234)

Adit does not live in the milieu but simply drifts through it. The milieu operates through him and brings about a drastic change in him, be it the idyllic surroundings of the Roscommon James in Hampshire, the High Streets of London, the Clapham tube or the Indo-Pak War of 1965, all these have a psychological effect on him. They make him schizophrenic and drive him to a state of frenzy:

> I've done with England now. Sarah, I'm going back. . . . To India—Home. . . . I can't live here any more. Our lives here—they've been so unreal. . . . I've got to go home and start living a real life. (232-34)

But, schizophrenia improves the life style of these blackbirds, makes them shock-proof and deepens their understanding of the fundamental problems of life, and of how to exist in an alien society and yet maintain one's individuality rather than suffering from a lack of society and a lack of belonging.

Adit's incommunication and silence contrast with Dev's instinctive urge for self-identification. Basically an urbanite, an admirer of the sooty and steamy smells of the overcrowded bus, he does not react with ecstasy so eerily generated in the more shielded and regimented Dev. Hence the estrangement between the two. He pays a visit to the London pubs, one by one, and feels that each is haunted by the dim and dark sensation of not belonging. Each remained alienated in his own way. In the footstep, he discovers the sound of a shameful escape. Voices and laughter ringing out in the glittering white caves of the tube stations seem mystically sinister and conspiratorial. He feels like an immigrant who can never accept his new home and continues to walk the streets as a stranger. He assumed a super-imposed, superficial identity. His own education, his 'feel' for British history and poetry is falling away from him. He looks forward to his departure for India, his home: "I am saving for my next visit home." (208) It was not only the occasional slights and affronts directed against him as an alien, a foreigner and a non-belonger that had, at length, proved too much for him, but the placidity, the munificence and the ease of England. The sights of the anniversaries and celebrations in England remind Adit of the Indian festivals. Though physically isolated, psychically he is quite at home with the splendour and gaiety of his motherland:

> Oh God, why does everything have to come to this that we are Indians and you are English and we are living in your country and, therefore, we have all got to behave in a special way, different from normal people. (213)

Alienation of blackbirds is, thus, an alienation of the soul. The reiterative use of the pronouns 'We' and 'You' stresses their inner crisis. Adit craves for his rock-solid mental and emotional being. He has a ghastly vision of himself in the white shirt and shuffling slippers of a lunatic's attire at an asylum, an outsider not only by virtue of his colour and race but by an imagination, a cramped one, run amuck. His inherent antipathy for the English creates in him the feeling of alienation, which gives rise to emotional estrangement and despair:

> Entering a store, he felt he could not bear to see one more pale, expressionless British face. If one more were to approach him, he would hit it, hit it. He put his shaking hands inside his pockets and left furtively. (219)

Adit's nostalgia and longing are briefly delineated in his melancholic urge for anything that is Indian. The monotonous steering of the traffic filled him with a sense of predictability and incensed him with a longing to see at least one bullock cart stray into the fray and make an alteration in the nimble tempo of the London traffic.

Adit's quest for identity is stimulated by his individual motivations and attitudes; his whims and caprices. Hence the quest is not a disinterested censure. It is disillusioned, nostalgic and humorous. His nostalgia mitigates his culture shock in an alien soil. His moods keep changing, depending on the identity of Sarah.

Sarah's identity has a direct impact on Adit's psychic states. The transformation of identity, thus, becomes a reciprocative and symbiotic phenomenon. Sarah feels that Adit's romantic involvement is waning, he is becoming disinterested in people and things, he is getting increasingly alienated from the milieu. But where on earth is he to discover his identity? Possibly in India, the place of his nativity. Hence his decision to leave England for home. He has a sickening and a paralyzing concern with himself and his homeland, He explains to Sarah: "No—England! England. I've done with England now, Sarah, I'm going back. . . . To India? . . . To India. . . . Home." (271)

Thus the blackbird is abruptly transformed into a homing bird, nostalgically longing for his homeland. He is glad that his son will be born in India and will take after the Indian identity of his father. But he doubts if the baby will be Indian, both body and soul. Won't the temperamental discord between him and Sarah have any impact on the psycho-physical constitution of the baby? Such problems perturb him. Contrarily, Sarah, his English wife, wants to fit her baby and herself into the pattern of her husband's life.

Adit perceives in Sarah her Anglo-Saxon identity and her oriental gentleness and submissiveness. Her oriental appearance and identity was only a masquerade. Intrinsically, she was an Anglo-Saxon. Deeply worried about the expenses to be incurred and the problems to be faced in raising the child, he seems to show no signs of tenderness and sympathy for Sarah's "condition." His pleasant thoughts about fatherhood are bedimmed. Sarah is shocked to find him very pale and cold, somewhat lacking in interest and sympathy in her, She is struck with despair at her husband's callousness, at a time when she needed his company the most. This may be due to Adit's failure to understand feminine sensibility. He fears Sarah may not agree to accompany him to India. She is probably opting out of his life. It is this inability to understand the feminine psyche that results in Adit's alienation from Sarah. Adit's affinity with her is an etiolated and possessive one which reminds us of Nora Helmer in Ibsen's *A Doll's House*. Sarah feels cut off: "Don't call me

Sally!" she cried, turning on him and he quailed at the anger and coldness of her face: "Don't you treat me as though I am not an individual with my own life to lead, but just . . . just some appendage to them, with nothing but duties and responsibilities instead . . . instead of rights." (247) Both Sarah and Adit were "tossed about by the flood like flotsam and then became a part of it, the black flood." (256)

Adit is disillusioned with England. The England he loves so much in Part I and Part II of the novel is looked down upon in Part III. Having settled in England for quite some years, Adit is still a misfit. He comes to regard himself as "a stranger, a non-belonger" (210) in England:

> His sleep-crumpled face looked incongruous with this brilliant outfit and was rather like a paper bag mask on top of a gorgeously dressed and opulently stuffed scarecrow. (8)

He wanders in London in a morbid search for belonging, to strike roots; but London muddles him with her myriad manifestations. The urban milieu breeds in him the feel of 'thrownness' or 'abandonment.' Promilla Kapur observes: "In the impersonal and de-individualised atmosphere of the big urban centres, one is liable to feel alienated as well as neglected and almost starved for genuine love and affection."[10] Hence like other Desai protagonists, Adit falls a prey to the onslaughts of an alienated existence:

> He simply could not recognize this work-a-day, weary London as his once golden Mecca. He took to trampling it after office hours in a kind of morbid search . . . he went to all the pubs he had ever known, one by one, and in each was haunted out by the black sensation of not belonging. (205-6)

It is this Anglophobic attitude of Adit that prompts him to shout irritatingly at his English wife, Sarah. It also leads to their psychic incommunication and void. Adit is determined to leave for India and be in India:

> Whatever it is, it will be Indian, it will be my natural condition, my true circumstance. I must go and face all that now. . . . Sarah, you know I have loved England more than you, I have often felt myself

> half English, but it was only a pretence, Sally. Now it has to be the real thing. I must go. You will come? (232)

The departure of Adit is instinctive, motivated by a mythical longing on the part of his alienated self for a tryst with his homeland. It is a psychic urge and an inner compulsion. Dogged by a sense of belonging, he wants his family to inherit an Indian and not an English identity. He wants his baby reared in India and not on this alien soil which is a land for the decrepit, old and decaying persons and not for the young and the infant.

These alienated beings dwell in lyrics of landscape, nuances of nostalgia, marooned and vitriolic moments of individual torment and tension. The nostalgia of isolation repels them and the ecstasy of togetherness attracts them, but they fail to choose between the two. Their identity wobbles between these two choices—whether to languish in isolation or laze in union. Their existential dilemma is rooted in the psyche.

The metaphor of the blackbird symbolically includes all humanity trapped in a world, where choices are almost impossible to make and where incertitude rules life. The alienated self of the three characters—Adit, Dev and Sarah—is quagmired in self-made images which distort their identity. Distortions, both comic and tragic, are caused by an anguished and prejudiced perception of reality. Anita Desai vividly recreates the London scene in order to show the interaction between the lone individual and the locale.

In her interview with Jasbir Jain, Anita Desai says: "Exile has never been my theme."[11] Hence, in this novel, she is concerned with the problem of alienation and adjustment, of how people cope with society without losing their sense of identity, and not with exile and expatriation. I.N. Kher observes: "She seems to suggest that the immigrants should try to cope with their alienation and cultural displacement through various strategies of replacement and repossession; they should make genuine attempts to integrate with the society of their adoption. They should try to blend but not to be assimilated or absorbed." (8)

Here, as in *Cry, the Peacock* and *Voices in the City*, we do find images of prey and predator, escape and sex through thrush, lark, vulture, owl, jackal and, peacock, which are but projections of the abandoned self. The bird imagery points to the bird-like identity of the individuals who are ever ready to take wings. Their escape is a socio-psychic release from the enslavement and etiolation of their beleaguered self. "An extended quibble, not a cry of the heart"[12] like *Cry, the Peacock, Bye-Bye, Blackbird* epitomises the incarceration of the self and its longing for emancipation.

References

1. Anita Desai, *Bye-Bye, Blackbird* (New Delhi: Orient Paperbacks, 1985), p. 8.
2. Hari Mohan Prasad, "Tension in Togetherness: An Explication of Biculturalism in Indo-English Fiction," *Chandrabhaga*, IV, No. 4, Winter, 1980, p. 73.
3. R.P. Blackmur, *The Lion and the Honeycomb: Essays in Solicitude and Critique* (London: Methuen, 1956), p. 61.
4. Anita Desai, "The Book I Enjoyed Writing Most," *Contemporary Indian Literature*, XII, 4 (1973), p. 24.
5. I.N. Kher, "The Immigrant Experience In Anita Desai's *Bye-Bye, Blackbird*," *The Journal of Indian Writing in English*, 22 (l), Jan. 1994, p. 9.
6. "The Book I Enjoyed Writing Most," p. 23.
7. Kalpana Wandrekar, "The Ailing Aliens: Anita Desai's *Bye-Bye, Blackbird*, A Symptomatic Study of Schizophrenia," *Image of India in the Indian Novel in English 1960-1985*, ed. Pandey and Rao (Bombay: Orient Longman, 1993), p. 42.
8. Meenakshi Mukherjee, "The Theme of Displacement in Anita Desai and Kamala Markandaya," *World Literature Written in English*, XVII (1), April 1978, p. 48.
9. Erich Fromm, *The Sane Society* (London: Routledge and Kegan Paul, 1956), p. 10.
10. Promilla Kapur, *Love, Marriage and Sex* (New Delhi: Vikas, 1973), p. 244.
11. Jasbir Jain, "Desai Interviewed," *Rajasthan University Studies in English*, Vol. XII (1979), p. 69.
12. Hari Mohan Prasad, "Sound or Sense: A Study of Anita Desai's *Bye-Bye, Blackbird*," *Journal of Indian Writing in English*, Vol. IX, No. 1, Jan. 1981, p. 66.

Hugo, the Nowhere Man: A Study of Anita Desai's *Baumgartner's Bombay*

Hugo, the protagonist of *Baumgartner's Bombay*, is a wounded self, an outsider, a wandering Jew all his life. His indomitable ambition to carve out a niche for himself in the face of an alien and hostile milieu singles him out from the other protagonists of Desai. From the upholstered luxury of his infancy to the pavements of Calcutta, from the fragrance of jasmine to the repelling odour of urine, Anita Desai has very vividly captured the brevity and pathos of his rootlessness. From the torturing and stunning scenes of his childhood in pre-war Berlin, through his spell of business in Calcutta and Bombay, he simply does not belong. He is an outsider. He remains a firanghi, a foreigner, wherever he goes. Through Hugo, Anita Desai plumbs the unexplored abyss of the estranged self.

"Accepting but not accepted."[1] That is the lot of Hugo Baumgartner. He is a prototype outsider, an alien in his own land:

> In Germany he had been dark, his darkness had marked him the Jew, der Jude. In India he was fair, and that marked him the firanghi. In both lands, the unacceptable. (20)

Not that he is alienated from the human world alone. In the words of Desai:

> Perhaps even where his cats were concerned, he was that . . . man, not feline, not theirs . . . it was a long time since he had felt, so acutely aware of his outlandishness. (20)

Hugo Baumgartner belongs to the 'insulted and injured,' the 'nobodies' of society. We often find him buried himself in an underworld, the hoary world of the subconscious. And yet he finds a strange delight in despair. An outsider, he is aware of realities to which we are blind. Yet he is dogged by the feeling of lonely impotence in the teeth of an implacably alien milieu. Like the other Desai protagonists, Hugo, in the extremity of his solitude, bears the burden of his troubles alone. The existential predicament of the Desai protagonist borders on the recognition of the fact that death makes the world and life absurd.

Hugo's sense of exile is not the sensation of his youth. It was a part of his infancy:

> Hugo collapsed into the dark ditch of his shame. What was the shame? The sense that he did not belong to the picture-book world of the fir tree, the gifts and the celebration? But no one had said that. Was it just that he sensed he did not belong to the radiant, the triumphant of the world. A strange sensation, surely, for a child. He could not understand it himself, or explain it. It baffled him, and frightened him even. (36)

The arrival of the boat which will take Hugo to the Orient triggers off a chain of bitter feelings of estrangement, apprehension and despair:

> Hugo felt a lurch of fear; he had to accept it . . . the prospect of at least seven days in this strange city, not only the first in which he had ever found himself alone but one so palpably foreign as to make him feel he was already transported to the East, it had so little relation to the Europe of the north. (58)

At San Marco, "the throngs in the chapels below, the incense, the candlewax, the flickers of light and colour in the furry dark, all oppressed him and seemed to repulse him till he was thrust out of the door into the piazza . . . sometimes the earnestness of the city disturbed him so much, he wondered if he would be able to face India." (60) No, he won't be able to face India, since his basic needs remain unfulfilled on this alien soil. His value-system is destroyed. His personality disintegrates. Alienation sets in.

The city life, be it Venice or San Marco, stifles him. However sweet and opulent the milieu, Hugo persistently experiences a feeling of nausea. He wants to escape. In the gluttonous surroundings of the piazza, "he felt himself to be inside a chocolate box, surfeited with sweetness and richness, and tore away to breathe freely." (60)

The East-West interface is a recurring motif in Indian English fiction. In *Bye-Bye, Blackbird*, Desai touches this only thinly. But *Baumgartner's Bombay* elaborately deals with the lone encounters of Hugo Baumgartner with the milieu of the locales. The interface becomes a part of his psychic odyssey through different locales and the changing milieu:

> Venice was the East, and it was Europe too; it was that magic boundary where the two met and blended, and for those seven days Hugo had been a part of their union. He realised it only now: that during his constant wandering, his ceaseless walking, he had been drawing closer and closer to this discovery of that bewitched point where they became one land of which he felt himself the natural citizen. . . . He had seen another world . . . it was the East, and he was both in it and travelling to it, at a distance and yet one with it. (63-64)

Thus Hugo has a natural, instinctive fascination for the East, the East that had started taking possession of his self before he embarked for India. The prospect of embarkation had already begun to Indianise him. The transformation of his identity had set in.

A bizarre, weird and eerie conglomeration of remembrances and reminiscences lends a poignant and trenchant touch to Baumgartner's distraught self. Beautifully observed, the novel deftly recovers a lost slice of history in its portrayal of a wounded survivour. Through the scraps of time past and time present, Desai captures the sepulchral and mossy labyrinths of Hugo's lacerated psyche, struggling for an emotional release from the past, in order to adjust with the present. The past is a haunting, harrowing presence in Hugo's psyche:

> alongside the train was always the shadow of the past, of elsewhere, of what had been and could never be abandoned. . . . An animal like a jackal in the day, a hyena in the night. In the darkness, it continued to chase the train, chase Baumgartner. (89)

The past is an inextricable presence, which Hugo has to intermittently encounter in his socio-psychic travails on the Indian soil. He is an enemy alien. The spatio-temporal progression of the story centres round his lone and renegade self. The infrequent shifts in the setting fit in with his psychic transformations.

Hugo suffers a double alienation: from his native Germany, and from India. Alienation from his native land is not only a matter of geographical and cultural isolation but also a problem of linguistic estrangement. Elaine Y.L. Ho opines: "German is Baumgartner's first language, the language of his identity and cultural filiation. In the course of the novel, this Germanness, or what remains of it, is placed in relation to various language systems—Hebrew and languages of India—which encode the values of the different cultures that Baumgartner encounters. The disharmonies that ensue are often rendered as miscommunication or an inability to communicate. Thus, Desai interweaves Baumgartner's German origins and his subsequent alienation from the cultures and societies he encounters."[2]

The roots of Hugo's colonial exile go deep into the formation of his identity. The German culture alienates him as well as provides him with a model for his estrangement and "in exile Baumgartner's cultural alienation takes corporeal form and forces him to re-examine consciously his Germanness."[3] Baumgartner fails to discern his own space of signification:

> He is of no system. His thoughts deteriorate at moments into the vantagepoint of the surreal for if he were real, then surely the scene, the setting was not. How could the two exist together in one land? The match was improbable beyond belief. (93)

Baumgartner's alienation from the locale and the milieu is not deliberately pre-planned or self-willed as is wont among the expatriates and aliens. It is the result of his failure at psychic communication and identification. The stink of cow-dung, the odour of cattle and men, of smoke from the village hearths, of cattle food and cattle urine, of dust, of pungent food cooking, of ragged clothes washed without soap and put out to dry, and the aroma of poverty—all formed a part of his alien sensibility. Even the sight of the village women approaching him made him tremble. This desire for communication and rapport at the visual plane is a unique quality with him, a trait seldom found among the other protagonists of Desai. This imparts a peculiar appeal and colour to his lonely and beleaguered plight. The women talk to one another with an absorption that excludes Baumgartner—a foreigner, a firanghi. They exclude him but he cannot exclude them.

The internment camp drowns his craving for companionship. The absurdities of his life both at home and here in this 'alien territory' make him submit to the sound and fury of life in a half-hearted way, learnt through years of helpless surrender to bullying, first in Germany, then in the camp. When others roar, "Hail Hitler!" he gratefully remains silent, for "silence was his natural condition." (117)

Even among the alien outsiders, there are marked signs of estrangement and isolation. The Jews remain aloof from the Nazis in the internment camp. Cast off by the morning assembly, they stand excluded from most camp duties. The Nazis among the Germans seem to be running the camp on behalf of or in collaboration with the British. They are willing to have the Jews do the menial work for them. But the Jews decline. To a Jew like Hugo, such an attitude of his Nazi contemporaries is not only disheartening but also intimidating, generating an emptiness and vacuum in him. Baumgartner greedily gathers all information that comes his way—the situation of Jews in Germany, their disappearance, the labour camps, Nazi propaganda, etc.—while he frantically builds "a defensive barrier against it." (118) It seemed as if his mind was trying to construct a wall against history, a wall behind which he could crouch and hide, desperately dreaming of a Germany of his childhood where his mother continued to live the life they had spent together. He lives, "ostrich-like, under the sands of this illusion, because although the letters written by the Jews were now taken in and posted . . . so they were assured . . . there was still no word in reply. . . . He asked once more for his mail to be forwarded but received nothing. What could this continuing silence from his mother mean? Had she been swept into the horrors of which the others in the barracks whispered and muttered in the dark?" (118) The terrible thoughts flood in, an invading army that his closed eyes cannot keep out, cannot stop.

Hugo is poised between timelessness and time, the Occident and the Orient, his own magic land of Utopia and India—the India of his dreams that remains ineluctably alien to him. His alienation from India springs chiefly out of his failure to establish a linguistic rapport with his milieu. His linguistic incapacity brings about the disintegration of his socio-psychic self. Both socially and psychically, he is an outsider to the Indian soil. He wanders in vain for "a signboard . . . in a familiar language" (53) and towards the fag end of his life he is still "uncertain as ever of which language to employ" (6) to accost a native watchman. He does not belong to any of India's linguistic communities. He is not with their weal and woe, their vicissitudes of interpersonal ties in the historiography of existence—from colonialism to post-colonialism, from subjugation to freedom. Elaine Y.L. Ho observes: "India is kept at bay; for a long time, it shows little interest in either penetrating or disallowing the 'boundary' Baumgartner draws for himself. Reticent among the riches of the languages that surround him, Baumgartner has re-negotiated his alienation from Europe as the condition of his survival as an alien in India." (101)

Hugo symbolises the European culture whose colonial past not only 'displaces' its own subjects but also spawns out the alienation between the Orient and the Occident. An alien in his own land. That is Hugo Baumgartner. A marooned and castaway self washed ashore Colaba by the fatal tide of his life, Baumgartner has been disowned and abandoned by his own country, Germany. A Jew and an outcast, he is rejected by the fair-haired Aryans of Hitler's regime. Cut off from the fond care of his childhood, Hugo steps into the terror and gloom of his adolescence with none to prop him up. His father's affluence as a dealer in quality furniture gradually wanes. Prompted by the Teuton who had taken over his father's home and business, he migrates to India and fetches up in Calcutta of the pre-war and pre-partition period, starts timber business and plunges headlong into the subterranean world of Calcutta with the booming and zooming night-clubs, bards and restaurants. Here, he chances upon Lotte, another homeless outsider like himself, who ekes out a doubtful and precarious living by singing and dancing in night-clubs.

Baumgartner's escape from Nazi Germany to India in search of a cushioned and protected life leaves him utterly dejected and frustrated. He slips from one inferno into another. His frantic quest for roots is indeed a journey from one state of void to another, from nowhere to nowhere. The Jews during the Great War were so much wolfed down that they had but little choice to make. Whether India or Germany, to them it was all the same. There they languished in the concentration camps and here they fumbled and nauseated in the internment camps. Hugo Baumgartner's Calcutta is not the Calcutta of *Voices in the City*. It is neither the 'City of Joy' of Lapierre nor the city of Anand's Hari. It is the black, ugly and dismal city of the 'hostile aliens' like Kipling's 'city of night.'

Alienation in *Baumgartner's Bombay* has no mythical element about it as we find in *Cry, the Peacock*. It is authentic on two counts. First, the story has, as its backdrop, a psychically captured historical setting: "her mother's experience of India from the late 1920s onwards and her memories of pre-war Germany she had talked a lot about, and the memories of her German friends, who had actually been in internment camps during the war."[4] Secondly, Hugo is modelled on an Austrian Jew Desai knew in Bombay, one who "used to walk around in back streets looking for scraps to feed his cats."[5] A friend of Desai handed in a bunch of letters in German left by the old man—the letters from the Nazi regime in Germany which were the muted mementos of the Nazi concentration camps, projecting the abject moral depravity of the times and the loss of values. Desai filled in the blank spaces in the letters with her inventive skill. Hugo shares the suffering and mortification of that Austrian Jew, 'a decrepit old man' of Bombay's slum, mockingly called 'Billi-wallah Pagal.' It is this awful plight of a real character on which he is modelled that lends a poignant touch to Hugo's alienation. The image of the city, with its dirt and squalor, its oppressiveness and violence serves as a foil to the protagonist's alienated self.

The problem of alienation in Desai's early novels from *Cry, the Peacock* to *Clear Light of Day* seems "rooted in that world of childhood, old Delhi of pre-Independence India which was very quiet and sober and regular"[6] but with *In Custody* and *Baumgartner's Bombay*, it gains a new artistic dimension. It grows into an estrangement of the adolescent in a rapidly changing spatio-temporal psychic continuum. The obsessions and fantasies of childhood no longer haunt the protagonists. They come as a fleeting impression of the past but not as a torturing obsession as in *Cry, the Peacock*, where they form an integral part of Maya. The sequestered world of the earlier novels now gives way to the socio-psychic entrapment of the self. The 'tranquil and cocooned' world of childhood crumbles down. The poetic outpourings of the lone self are now replaced by subtle and supple prose, by a penetrating observation of the milieu: "That was the evening when the breeze came up with the tide, and the sun fell headlong into the waves . . . and people strolled. . . . One was not conscious if one loitered too."[7]

Despite Hugo's confinement and immurement in the internment camp, he had learnt the art of weathering the vicissitudes of existence, he accepts the monotony of camp life. He is the perennial outsider whose life is marred and ruined by fissiparous and inscrutable forces. Religious strife breeds in him frenzy and excitement. In the Nazi Germany too, he had met with this religious strife and bigotry. He flees his past to meet his future, leaves Germany and comes to India. In Colaba, he encounters the aliens who, having abandoned their native land, lie scattered like pale autumnal leaves. Baumgartner consorts with neither, but, surrounded by the entire alien outsiders and the drug peddlers and liquor vendors, he earns his living as a business associate of Chimanlal. But nothing sticks to Hugo, not even the pack of cards which "fall away from him into an abyss." (216)

Baumgartner's history is the cumulative and collective experience of diaspora. History has dispelled Hugo as an outsider, a marginal man whose centre of existence is everywhere—it is the east and also in the west. It is nowhere. Hence, Baumgartner belongs neither to the west nor to the east. Neither on the margins nor at the centre but straddling the spaces of west and east, Baumgartner cannot feel at home. His marginality symbolises his historical and cultural entrapment. In the words of Elaine Ho, "only on a margin might a marginal feel at home," (100) but Hugo remains neither on the margins nor at the centre. He wobbles between the two.

Baumgartner is not with the mainstream. He had missed it:

> He felt his life blur, turn grey, like a curtain wrapping him in its dusty felt. If he became aware from time to time that the world beyond the curtain was growing steadily more crowded, more clamorous, and the lives of others more hectic, then he felt the only relief that he had never been a part of the mainstream. Always, somehow, he had escaped the mainstream. (211)

Baumgartner wants to escape his temporal existence. He seeks isolation from the crushing impact of time, and hence his search for company. The Calcutta of the black, back streets, the steaming rubbish tips, the scarred tenement, its hunger, its squalor, its desolation and, above all, its hopelessness become a part of his own experience of estrangement. And Bombay, which had been his life or rather the setting for his life for thirty years remains behind. He had never actually entered it, never quite captured it. It had been elusive. On his daily rounds of nearby cafes and restaurants in search of scraps, the kitchen staff snigger at him mockingly, "Pagal sahib, billiwallah Sahib." But the cats greet him exuberantly, regardless of his uncouth, untidy life.

Looking at the photographs the companions had pinned over their bunks, and which he had previously shunned, Hugo becomes morosely reflective: "he only glanced furtively as if looking through windows, fascinated by what he saw, but certain it was not for him to share." (129) Very stoically, he bears and forbears the scene remaining within his own ambit of alienation. He contemplates escape from the internment camp, but it leads him out of the frying pan into the fire. Alienation leads to emancipation, but emancipation from one world enslaves and imprisons him in another world—India. His is a case of double alienation. Yet Baumgartner does not view his confinement in the camp as alienation and imprisonment. He takes it as freedom and belongingness:

> Baumgartner and others in the Jewish quarter had good reason to feel thankful for the protection of the British-run camp, however sick with sorrow over the fate of their relations or of Germany, however restless and frustrated and bored by the lifeless monotony of the camp. At least it was a refuge, even if temporary. (132)

But this anguished fatigue that the internees along with Hugo felt gathers momentum as the news of the war spreads. He wonders if the long internment had not incapacitated him, made him unfit for the outer world:

> And what would they find outside? Germany destroyed . . . no possibility of returning, so that he would have to accept India as his permanent residence. He wonders at his ability to survive, so reduced he was to an abject state of helplessness. He begins to fear the time when he would no longer be in the company of Julius, of Schwarz, of the others in the camp with whom he had become so familiar. It was not that any of them regarded him as a friend, but with them, he could pretend he was not solitary. Outside he would be that—a man without a family or a country. (133)

Tense silence and strained emotion overshadow the urge for self-expression in Hugo. "Defeat was heaped on him, whether he desired it or not." (135) He finds his concern piqued in spite of himself. His forlornness urges him to befriend the destitute German youth he met en route to a restaurant. The desperate and desolate state of the boy moves Hugo to commiseration and sympathy. He brings him home but this hospitality proves his undoing, it results in bringing about a horrific, grotesque and spine-chilling end to the novel. It is the human factor in Hugo that makes him horrifyingly engaging:

> Unlike the youths who came from the west now, Baumgartner had been to none of the tourist spots, not even Benares, never been drawn to temples or ashrams, an alien world to him, something he had walked past quickly, not entered, not even glanced at. (148)

Hence the boy's allusion to the 'burning ghats of Benares' remains a mystery to him. He senses in it 'hostility and censure.'

Baumgartner never consciously "searched for Europeans in Bombay for company . . . he had ceased to crave the sound of his own language, the feel of it on his tongue." (150) His life at the internment camp had choked that desire. However, Lotte keeps him in touch with the mother tongue. Hugo's friendship with her is not because she belonged to Germany but because she belonged to 'Baumgartner's India,' the India of his voices and visions. Though Lotte's experience of India was different in many ways, yet they share enough. "But from other Europeans in Bombay he kept away, discreetly." (150) Hugo is not a die-hard rebel. He is not a deep-dyed alien, since he had human attachment with the other internees in the camp, and led a communal life to last a lifetime.

The German boy, Kurt, serves as a foil to Hugo's imprisoned self. Kurt moves everywhere in India, he is with everyone:

> In Benares, he had lived with the doms in the burning ghat. . . . The tantrics he had met in the ashram in Bihar where he had lived on a rock. . . . In Kathmandu he had loved a temple priest's boy. . . . In Calcutta he had lived with the lepers. . . . In Goa—he had lived on the beach. (156-59)

Unlike Hugo, Kurt is free wherever he goes:

> "In a prison also you have been?"
> "No prison for me—I am free wherever I go." (159)
> I go out—and come in, see? I am free, always. I can go out—and come in—then go out—how I want. (161)

But in spite of Kurt's movement everywhere, like Hugo, he is dogged by the feeling of 'sickness,' the feeling of 'estrangement':

> Sick in Goa? Sick in Benares. Sick in Kathmandu. Sick in Sarnath, sick, sick, everywhere. Oh, I am crank. (156)

Despite his sickness, Kurt never falls into splinters, he is never bruised:

> But you have no scars? No wounds? No. I am whole. I make myself whole again and again. (159)

But Hugo has scars—the scars of his irretrievable past as captured in the nursery rhymes (in German script). He shuttles between Calcutta and Bombay, not everywhere in India. He is a fragmented self—languishing in his feline world, not the human world of Kurt. Hugo's attachment with the human world is but mercurial.

Hugo is the 'nowhere man' in quest of a meaning and an identity in life. Lack of focus and centrality of experience, of needs and desires builds up the psychic tension in him. He plods through the city streets aimlessly, for he hates going back to his room. With the simmering of the communal cauldron in the city, his consternation and alienation get reactivated. The war unleashes his muted voice:

> The lunacy of performing acts one did not wish to perform, living lives one did not wish to live, becoming what one was not. Always another will opposed to one's own, always another fate, not the one of one's choice or even making. A great web in which each one was trapped, a nightmare from which one could not emerge. (173)

Hugo lingers between two worlds—Indian and German—belonging to neither and a stranger to both. An outsider, he travels from place to place, in search of socio-psychic and socio-economic stability. The episodic movements of this anti-hero are tragi-comic. During the course of his travel, he is confronted with a number of psycho-moral, religious and socio-political issues. Hugo seems to have an affinity with the picaro. He is not a social reject because his associations are chiefly societal. The episodic structure of the novel is symbolic of Hugo's fragmentary character. Hugo is not whole but his quest is for wholeness. The novel, to quote Stuart Miller, "merely records fragmented happening after fragmented happening."[8] Hugo's intrinsic and interiorized quest is an attempt at affirming his identity. But does Hugo's quest end in self-affirmation? No, it ends with a forlorn sense of anticipation in an atmosphere of apprehension. Apprehensions leading to self-annihilation—that is the lot of Hugo.

One is reminded of Ruby Miranda in *Combat of Shadows* by Manohar Malgonkar. Ruby's longings are not particularised but Hugo's are localised. Ruby's husband, Winton, has no strength to withstand alienation, but Hugo has it. He does not shy away from reality but boldly and stoically faces it. Like Krishnan in Rajan's *The Dark Dancer* he is not totally alienated. He has not cut himself off from his Teutonic heritage nor has he forgotten what he knew. Like Srinivas in Markandaya's *The Nowhere Man*, Hugo is a solitary self in an alien land. Cut off from his cultural moorings, he tries to get succour from an adopted one—Indian. But Hugo is an 'enemy alien,' in quest of a new identity, the nowhere man in search of a nowhere country.

References

1. Anita Desai, *Baumgartner's Bombay* (London: Penguin, 1989), p. 20.
2. Y.L. Elain Ho, "The Languages of Identity in Anita Desai's *Baumgartner's Bombay*," *World Literature Written in English*, 72.1 (1982), p. 97.
3. *Ibid.*, p. 99.
4. Andrew Robson, "Interview with Anita Desai," *The Saturday Statesman*, 12 August 1988, p. 8.
5. *Loc. cit.*
6. *Loc. cit.*
7. *Ibid.*, p. 9.
8. Stuart Miller, *The Picaresque Novel* (Cleveland: Press of Case Western Reserve University, 1967), p. 12.

Theme of Fragmentation: Salman Rushdie's *Midnight's Children*

Classified as a "picaresque novel," *Midnight's Children* documents the demented wanderings of a split self in quest of wholeness and an identity. It is a political elegy delineating the disappointed hopes of the self placed in a critical juncture of history. We may say it is a series of stories by people from no man's land. Saleem Sinai is India and India's history between 1947 and 1975 is literally written on Saleem's body. He carries India's history between dream and nightmare. This is delineated through the complexity and the stratification of several strands of reality which impart a fragmentary look to the novel. The several strata of the novel symbolise Saleem's gradual amputation and loss of freedom, sanity and individuality. *Midnight's Children* becomes a symbol of man's fundamental human conditions, that of the alienation of the self.

Saleem Sinai, the narrator-protagonist defines himself by identifying his lot with the fate of his country. Born at midnight on August 15, 1947, the date on which India emerged as an independent state, Saleem from birth has greatness prophesied for him because of this nexus. In the course of his story, he discovers that he is not the centre of India's history but only a small and an insignificant factor in larger forces of history. He gradually realises that history is not men's consciousness and that he does not form a single centre for society. A native alien and a hopeless and hapless victim of history, he leads a life of anguish and isolation. Since he cannot undo the historical injustices and establish his "rootedness," he takes recourse to fantasy and myth to discover his "imaginary roots" which lie here and everywhere, dispersed and scattered. Saleem seeks to resolve his agonising problems of identity by withdrawing himself into the realm of fantasy:

> After news of my grandfather's death and the arrival of Reverend Mother in Pakistan, I began to dream repeatedly of Kashmir; although I had never walked in Shalimar Bagh, I did so at night; I floated in Shikaras and climbed Sankara Acharya's hill as my grandfather had; I saw lotus roots and mountains like angry jaws. This, too, may seem an aspect of the detachment which came to afflict us all . . . a reminder of my family's separateness from both India and Pakistan.[1]

Saleem sees the isolated facts of history only as they relate to him as an individual, only a fragment of the societal self and not to society as a whole. George Lukacs in *History and Class-Consciousness* writes, "Only in this context which sees the isolated facts of social life as aspects of the historical process and integrates them in a totality, can knowledge of the facts hope to become knowledge of reality."[2] Rushdie himself writes in *Midnight's Children*:

> Reality is a question of perspective; the further you get from the past, the more concrete and plausible it seems—but as you approach the present, it inevitably seems more and more incredible . . . tiny details assume grotesque proportions [first]; [then] the illusion dissolves—or rather, it becomes clear that the illusion itself is reality. (197)

Saleem Sinai sustains so many simultaneous identities. He is by turns defiant, modest strident subtle, fatalistic, recalcitrant, fastidious, bawdy, flippant and solemn but seldom composed and never in tune with his inner self. Always divided from within, he leads a breathless and desultory life. Ashutosh Banerjee observes: "Now Saleem is maddening, keeping his interlocutrix Padma, on the tenterhooks, being dilatory in revealing his parentage. And again he is pouring a long narrative out all at once at one go in breathless haste in large paragraphs without any full stops."[3]

A breathless passage without the appropriate punctuational pauses indicates haste and confusion, psychic turmoil and estrangement of Saleem. "But imagine the confusion in my head! Where, behind the hideous face, above the tongue tasting of soap, hard by the perforated ear-drum, lurked a not very tidy mind, as full of bric-a-brac as nine year old's pockets." (202) Saleem has extraordinary powers of thought-reading in order to make his omniscient accounts of a dozen different lives as well as the life of the nation credible as coming from a single individual, Saleem the narrator protagonist himself, whose concentre is a part of the societal centre dispersed to many individuals in a collective.

Saleem's life is a perforated sheet and he feels a hole in the centre of his body. Everything slips and trickles through it. Everything leaks into everything else in *Midnight's Children* and more things have to be portrayed "because a human being, inside himself, is anything but a whole, anything but homogeneous; all kinds of everywhichthing are jumbled up inside him, and he is one person one minute and another the next." (236-37)

Rushdie does not see a human being as "a unified whole" but as a fragment of his spatio-temporal existence. Like Saleem, his is a deliberately distanced voice—ironical, funny and disillusioned. Saleem is a part of history reduced to this partitioned state by the Indo-Pak War of 1965. He and his family are reduced to fragments and almost ruined by this war: "Sheets of flame rose from a Rawalpindi bungalow perforated sheets at whose centre hung a mysterious dark hole . . . and one by one the war eliminated my drained hapless family from the earth." (342)

Saleem's family and its historical past have ceased to exist as tangible and perceptible objects. They have simply been reduced to figments of his memory, rather his fancy, by the devastating war. He never sees himself as a complete whole but as a splintered bit of his fractured self. He sees himself schizophrenically, in both the first and third person. Hence, the reality of the character as a "unified whole" and "a separate entity" is marred. Keeping in point of view the split self of the narrator protagonist, Rushdie's narrative technique defies clear outlines. The unities of time and place are not uniformly adhered to throughout the novel. The wavering and shaky nature of Saleem chimes with the unstable and sloppy narrative technique of the novel. Saleem adopts various narrative modes to convey experience. He is yet to attain adequacy and wholeness, stability and equipoise:

> There are so many stories to tell . . . such an excess on intertwined lives, events, miracles, places, rumours, so dense a commingling of the improbable and the mundane. (4)

Saleem, the self-conscious narrator, oscillates between the past and the present, the historical and the personal, the apocalyptic and the expansive. He has no stable identity but he assumes many identities. He is at the crease with Polly Umrigar at the Brabourne Stadium, he unravels in the seamy gossip in *Filmfare* about the dancer Vijayantimala, he is a Congress party worker, a Kerala peasant who votes for the Communists, a landlord in Uttar Pradesh ordering his peasants to set his surplus grain on fire and starve to death. But as a fragment also, he is complete. Rushdie's intricate narrative technique enables him to sustain the simultaneous identities he has to assume as a human being and a narrator—capturing within his self the euphoria, expectations, tensions and traumas of independence.

Throughout the novel, Saleem's inner life is a function of the historical forces affecting his state. He is, in his own mind, the latent, elusive centre of India's history. His parodying the history of India makes the entire narrative a historiographic metafication. From seeing himself as the centre of the state, he begins to look upon himself as an integral and an inalienable part of the state. His hold upon reality comes from a view that the reality of the state is fragmented and dispersed in the consciousness of all individuals and not in the consciousness of any one individual.

Midnight's Children belongs to the "look-back-in-anger" or "protest" type of fiction written by one who is alienated by option or compelled expatriation haunted by "an upsurge to look back even at the risk of being mutated into pillars of salt."[4]

Saleem is doomed to lead the life of a social outcast, an exile: "At every turn I am thwarted, a prophet in the wilderness, like Maslama; . . . No matter how I try, the desert is my lot." (471) Throughout his life, he remains "adrift in this haze of anticipation of a better life." (180) But till the end he remains consigned to the margins, "the peripheries of history." (470) Reduced to fragments by forces beyond his control, he is conscious of the loss of his historical centrality which is dispersed to many individuals. Without a clear sense of purpose, he develops uneasy symptoms of schizophrenia. Saleem's is a fragmented and frustrated quest for meaning in life:

> I became afraid that everything was wrong—that my much trumpeted existence might turn out to be utterly useless, void and without the shred of a purpose. (180)

His variegated experiences simultaneously make him "confused about being good." (239) Alienated, he admits: "I am so far gone, in my desperate need for meaning, that I am prepared to distort everything. . . . In my confusion I can't judge." (198) Split within, he becomes abysmally self-estranged. Insecurity and uncertainty make him confused about his stance in the scheme of things and he finds himself "elusive as rainbows, unpredictable as lightning, garrulous as Ganesh." (234) "An unfortunate fellow with a face like a cartoon," he is fatally "gripped by some deep malaise." (385) "A general fatigue so profound" makes Saleem "adrift, disoriented." (389) Even he forgets his own name. Flung to live, he feels that he is "cast as a ghost." (29) Look at the disintegration of his self in the face of a hostile milieu: "Please believe that I am falling apart . . . I mean quite simply that I have begun to crack all over like an old jug. . . . In short, I am literally disintegrating, slowly for the moment, although there are signs of an acceleration." (37)

Saleem's fragmentation of self occurs partly due to his abnormally morbid nature and partly due to his nurture and inheritance. The whole household was very often torn by the conflict between grandpaternal scepticism and grandmaternal credulity. Saleem's father was "unnerved, adrift, unmanned" (397) and his mother became the victim of the "Spirit of detached fatigue" (392) and, eventually "fell apart." (393) His sister Jamila was filled with "the pain of exile" and "the lovelessness of life." (472) Hence, he has the sensation of being "pulled up by his roots to be flung unceremoniously across the years, (and) fated to plunge memoryless into an adulthood whose every aspect grew daily more grotesque." (414) He meanders through his existential predicament "like a puppet with broken strings." (509)

He had "more mothers than most mothers have children" (243) and all his life he says, "consciously or unconsciously I have sought out fathers." (426) All this testifies to Saleem's lack of roots and the concomitant fragmentation of personality. R.S. Pathak rightly observes: "The motif of fragmentation is present throughout the novel. But in no case it is prominent as it is in the case of Saleem. He is fully aware of his problems and plights, misfortunes and discordances, so typical of a rootless person."[5] At the height of self-estrangement, Saleem looks at himself as only the broken bits and fragments of his former self:

> I am tearing myself apart; can't even agree with myself talking and arguing like a wild fellow, cracking up, memory going, yes, memory plunging into chasms and being swallowed by the dark only fragments remain, none of it makes sense any more. (503)

"Saleem Sinai," observes Kathleen Flanagan "sees himself as a part of society, not a detached mind-reader at its centre. The self of Saleem Sinai undergoes a metamorphosis from being a character whose consciousness as a child and young man determines his whole existence, to being a character whose social existence determines his vision of the world."[6] But socio-historical forces crush him down and his private self is reduced "to specks of voiceless dust." (552) Saleem now begins to see himself as a vulnerable part of society.

His struggle to tell his story and India's is an attempt to achieve self-consummation or rather to make whole his fragmentary private existence. William Walsh aptly holds that Rushdie's *Midnight's Children* is "the personification and realisation of Indian life."[7] But how far is this realisation possible? It is just a fractionated realisation, feeling India in fragments of memory. Rushdie remarks: "Our physical alienation from India almost inevitably means that we will not be capable of reclaiming precisely the thing that was lost; that we will in short, create fictions, not actual cities or villages, but invisible ones, imaginary homelands, Indias of the mind."[8] O.P. Mathur maintains: "Saleem Sinai who is the embodiment of a supreme moment of history, a crystallization of an evolving mood, a distillation of a vision nostalgic, critical and philosophical, is a camera eye, which is itself cracked and fragmented, with, as the novelist remarks, some of its fragments missing. But in spite of it or perhaps because of it, he is able to project what may be called a sort of prismatic vision of reality, partial, fissured and fragmented, but highly absorbing and deeply meaningful."[9]

Saleem's "literally disintegrating" and "fissured" body from which history pours out is a possible allusion to the underlying political fragmentation and fissiparous tendencies of Indian politics, past and present, which have contributed to the making of its history. In fact, fragmentation, the bane of Indian society and politics, runs through the theme and technique of the novel. Saleem's life covers the period from Independence to the lifting of the Emergency, but charming spots of bygone times are also visible through the "open sesame" of the perforated bedsheet. Rushdie has narrated, commented upon or referred to these events and their multifarious real or imaginary relationships with Saleem, his family and the "midnight's children." He has also portrayed the feel of those times through the fertile but rambling imagination and the fragmented but meaningful vision of an ironical narrator with a representatively multiple identity.

Saleem is linked to history by different modes of connection, through manifold relationships, both literal and metaphorical. He is its twin companion—its creator and its victim. Like the other midnight's children, he is the metaphor of Indian society and the "very essence of multiplicity" who is constantly haunted by the phantasm of a partitioned man, "a broken creature spilling pieces of itself into the street." (552)

There is something of incarceration in the personality and career of the picaresque hero Saleem Sinai but he is not away from society. He does not seem to lack an identity: it is only that multiple identities press upon him—a mirror of the fragmentation and multiplicity of Indian society and the confusion of social, religious, regional and parochial identities under which Indians suffer. Saleem's mind is the parliament of various viewpoints and hence a whole, unifying various fragments into the episodes of history. He is a paradigm of an alienated human soul,

"Sucked into the annihilating whirlpool of the multitudes, and unable to live or die in peace." (552) He is also a provoking metaphor for the contemporary fragmented Indian reality and a unified philosophical vision enveloping it: "to understand me, you'll have to swallow a world." (458) Saleem, the narrator-protagonist, is not a lucid reflector of history but a whimsical and capricious refractor of reality and thus the episodic and fragmentary nature of his self-revelation and self-projection which ironically helps us towards a better understanding of contemporary society and history. He is at the centre of things instead of a victim at the periphery and he realises his centripetal role in recreating history in the phantasm of his psyche when he rhetorically questions himself:

> Am I so far gone, in my desperate need for meaning, that I am prepared to distort everything—to re-write the whole history of my times purely in order to place myself in a central role? (166)

And verily Saleem distorts everything, subverts everything in his own lacerated self still cringing, to the centre desperately.

The desultory style of narration, leaping from one matter to another, constant shifts of perspective, frequent eruptions into the narrative of marginally related incidents, symbols and anecdotes and ubiquitous drift of the narrative into dream and nightmare etc, tend to blur the spatio-temporal continuum and symbolise the fragmentary existence of Saleem, the narrator protagonist who tells the story "in the way in which Indian people tell stories, which is very roundabout, full of digressions, and jokes, and asides, and parentheses and goes on forever, and exaggerates, and fantasises."[10]

Midnight's Children is an expression of the despair of Saleem Sinai, a broken self, living on the edges, in fragments. In his interview with Kumkum Sangari, Rushdie admits:

> Instead of being an insignificant dot in this multitude, Saleem Sinai actually contains the multitude. It is an aspect of him, rather than he an aspect of it. The sadness of the book is in the discovery that this is not so. When your picture of yourself, your self-image, breaks, you die. And that is what happens to Saleem.[11]

In fact, Saleem has no real self-image. He exists only on the metafictional canvas of historiography. Too romantic to be rational and too subjective to be polemical, he is a veritable postmodern hero that fits squarely into the mode of postmodernist fantasy in his ability of splitting into doubles and multiples. The theme of fragmentation runs throughout. Even it is perceptible in Saleem's personal appearance especially his grotesque face: "His large moon-face was too large: too perfectly round" (124) and the "rampant cucumber of the nose" and "temples like stunted horns" (124) indicate his lack of the unity of being, his disorderly and split existence. Fragmentation of identity in an alien world is pursued through motifs of compartmentalisation of the self pertaining to each generation of Saleem's family which relegates him to the margins of history.

References

1. Salman Rushdie, *Midnight's Children* (N.Y.: Avon, 1982), p. 195.
2. George Lukacs, *History and Class-Consciousness*, trans. Rodney Livingstone (1922; rpt. Cambridge: MIT Press, 1976), p. 8.
3. Ashutosh Banerjee, "Narrative Technique in *Midnight's Children*," *The Commonwealth Review*, Vol. 1, No. 21, 1990, pp. 24-25.
4. Dilip Fernandez, "Such Angst, Such Loneliness, Such Rootlessness," *Gentleman*, February 1984, p. 102.
5. R.S. Pathak, "Salman Rushdie's Treatment of Alienation," *Indian Fiction in English: Problems and Promises*, ed. R.S. Pathak (New Delhi: Northern Book Centre, 1990).
6. Kathleen Flanagan, "The Fragmented Self in Salman Rushdie's *Midnight's Children*," *Commonwealth Novel in English*, Vol. 5, No. 1, Spring 1992, p. 44.
7. William Walsh, "India and the Novel," *The New Pelican Guide to English Literature*, Vol. 8 (London: Penguin, 1983), p. 257.
8. Salman Rushdie, *The Indian Express*, March 11, 1984, p. 8.
9. O.P. Mathur, "A Metaphor of Reality: A Study of the Protagonist of *Midnight's Children*," *Image of India in the Indian Novel in English 1960-1985*, ed. Pandey and Rao (Bombay: Orient Longman, 1993), pp. 113-14.
10. Chinweizu, "Interview: Novelist Salman Rushdie," *South: The Third World Magazine*, Jan. 1993, p. 24.
11. Kumkum Sangari, "Interview with Salman Rushdie," *The Book Review*, Mar.-Apr. 1984, Vol. 3, No. 5, p. 247.

Problems of Identity: A Study of Bharati Mukherjee's *Desirable Daughters*

> We immigrants have fascinating tales to relate. Many of us have lived in newly independent or emerging countries . . . when we uproot ourselves from those countries and come here, either by choice or out of necessity, we suddenly must absorb two hundred years of American history and learn to adapt to American society. . . . I attempt to illustrate this in my novels and short stories. My aim is to expose Americans to the energetic voices of new settlers in this country.[1]

The issues of diaspora, globalisation, consumerism, transnationalism cultural hybridity, alienation and identity crisis have become the leit motif of most postcolonial literatures. The self, dislocated in space and time from its roots has a homing instinct—the desire to discover its "inbetweenness" in a transnational and trans-cultural space. Problems of identity figure more prominently in the novels of Salman Rushdie, V.S. Naipaul, Caryl Phillips, Bharati Mukherjee and Anita Desai. In these writers the quest for identity is not tagged to the self alone. It goes beyond the self to issues of culture and linguistics (as in Desai's *Baumgartner's Bombay* in relation to Hugo's Teutonic background). All these factors give rise to emergent trends and tendencies like hybrid cultural forms among the migrants. These migrant writings deal with issues like home, self and identity. Jopi Nyman lucidly observes: "Rather than searching for roots and authenticity, migrant writing constructs itself in the space of in-betweenness between different cultures, societies and homelands. In this process it reflects on both the old and the new, and questions existing political and cultural binaries."[2]

In *Desirable Daughters*, Bharati Mukherjee has delineated the individual self quagmired in the kaleidoscopic spatio-temporal reality of the American as well as the Indian society. The novel traces the life of the three Brahmin daughters, Tara,

Padma and Parvati, all agog to forge an identity of their own in very trying and complex socio-cultural situations. Tara, Padma and Parvati were born into a wealthy Brahmin Bengali family presided over by their fond father and a tradition-bound orthodox mother. The daughters are intelligent and artistic. They never feel bogged down or suffocated by a conventional society which has little regard for women. They rebel against this hackneyed and constraining socio-cultural set up and chart out their own course of action. Moving in different directions and different straining circumstances, each of them tries to carve out a unique identity of her own. But it is an identity in flux since all of them are ever on the go towards self-realisation and self-actualisation. Each of them tries to connect her past with the present, memory with desire. Each of them is on the move. Mukherjee portrays through these three moving and identity-shifting characters who have "partial affiliations, disinterested identities, tactical belongings,"[3] their sense of belongingness which is constantly re-invented and relocated, like the name of Tara—"Our Tara Lata" and "Tara Lata, the Tree-Bride" of Mishtigunj and anew the Tara Banerjee Cartwright of Mukherjee's other novel *Tiger's Daughter*. Unlike the Tara of *Tiger's Daughter*, "Our Lata" has deep affiliations with her ancestry, her culture. She wants to connect her own with the mythic Tara Lata, the "Tree Bride." This myth provides the base for Tara Lata's curiosity to establish her identity through interrogations of cross-cultural rapprochement and conflictual-cultural ties. The novel is not just an idyllic tale of the three desirable daughters and their diversitarian circumstances of upbringing but it is a complex transnational narrative commenting on the intricate and enigmatic process of growing up and of the feminist struggle of these three sisters to stick to their own protean self, their cultural moorings in times of crisis. Their fascinating childhood reminiscences are dovetailed with dramatic scenes from Indian history:

> In a palanquin borne by four servants sit a rich man's three daughters, the youngest dressed in her bridal sari, her little hands painted with red lac dye, her hair oiled and set. Childish voices chant a song, hands clap, gold bracelets tinkle. . . . A Bengali girl's happi-

> est night is about to become her lifetime imprisonment. It seems all the sorrow of history, all that is unjust in society and cruel in religion has settled on her. Even constructing it from the merest scraps of family memory fills me with rage and bitterness.[4]

D.K. Pabby, in his erudite paper presented at the MELUS Conference, says: "the book is a very mature narrative commenting on the complex process of growing up, retaining one's balance in times of crisis, struggle involved in making sense of one's ongoing journey of life, certain aspects of which may be shaped by forces and circumstances beyond one's control."[5]

The novel is not only a nostalgic romanticisation of the past but also a reconstruction and revalidation of Tara's identity. It is "her inverted story of mobility."[6] The events and locales that form a part of Tara's identity have been nostalgically delineated by Bharati Mukherjee. The spatio-temporal construction of Tara's identity is based on "fragments of place memories, on desires and experiences."[7] In describing the cross-cultural impact on Tara's identity partly Indian and partly Americanized, the novelist portrays her as a hybrid subject, a mimicry of the American socio-cultural ethos. She travels through a hybridized space where the novelist reconstructs the notion of "homeland" in the context of a rapidly transitional society in the era of hectic globalization and consumerism. Susheila Nasta rightly observes: "Diaspora does not create an unrequited desire for a lost homeland but also a 'homing desire,' a desire to re-invent and rewrite home as much as a desire to come to terms with an exile from it."[8]

The concept of home and migration is very much embedded in the narratology that Bharati Mukherjee presents in *Desirable Daughters*. It is the sense of migration which brings about a change to the identity of Padma, who has finally made New York her home, her land of choice. But her inalienable attachment to her home makes her the sustainer and preserver of Bengali tradition in America. The alien culture thus fails to subvert her traditional identity. On the other hand it only remaps and reconstructs her cultural identity. Hence migration plays a crucial role in restructuring individual identities and cultural attitudes and perceptions. Linda McDowell rightly opines: "movement involves the remapping of cultural identities." (210)

Bharati Mukherjee looks at India from the perspective of a Third World writer, an expatriate and an immigrant. India figures in the novel as a part of memory, as a third world place, as a fragment of nostalgia. Experiences, psychic or fictional, which are so commonplace like that of "Tara Lata, the Tree Bride" as to be of little or no importance to us, become extraordinarily significant to the expatriate novelist. The "Indian self of these novelists is receding and they try to restore or save it through their writings,"[9] a typically postcolonial situation. Writers like Bharati Mukherjee provide the west with "a picture of India such as Westerners themselves might not have dared to provide." (*Ibid.*, 137) India in this novel is not an identifiable presence. It is just a psychic reality. Though far away from India, Parvati is still conscious of her tradition. This is what she writes in her letter to Tara: "We Indians don't run to psychiatrists for every problem. Come to think of it, I don't know a single psychiatrist. . . . I hope you aren't doing bad things to yourself like taking Prozac and having cosmetic surgery. Please, please, don't become that Americanized." (104-5)

Parvati's consciousness of the Indian tradition and an Indian's socio-cultural identity is further manifested in the following lines which describe her Daddy's renunciation and detachment from the mundane world:

> Daddy is becoming more and more detached from the world, which I suppose is a good thing, at least it is something we are supposed to aspire to, but in his case I feel Daddy is fleeing this world, rather than seeking the next (106)

Again in the same letter to Tara, Parvati alludes to Aunt Bandana's love of the Bengali tradition and the laws of Manu. Aunt Bandana wants a suitable Bengali girl for her fourth son, a good Hindu Brahmin family settled in California. A good family indeed but not an Indian citizen. Aunt B's two main requirements are: "the girl be an American citizen or green card holder who can legally sponsor her husband's immigration to the United

States, and that she be a Brahmin." (107) Parvati says that Aunt B. "is of the old school." (107) She is of tradition. Referring to Manu, Parvati says, "I think it comes from the Laws of Manu . . . if you sow wrong kind of seed in the wrong kind of soil, you are bound to end up with an unhealthy sapling. That means no inter-caste alliances." (107) Even Tara, the protagonist imbues in her a sense of tradition which is manifested through her arranged marriage which has been organized: "There is a boy and we have found him suitable. Here is his picture. The marriage will be in three weeks." (23)

Parvati's identity crisis is not so acute as in the case of Tara. Parvati is a static type of identity with her emphasis on tradition and convention whereas for Tara, identity is dynamic, it is in flux, constantly changing. A divorce, her life-style is totally different from her other sisters. Dislocated as she is, she lives in San Francisco, still cherishing the American Dream possibilities and promises but to her utter dismay, she finds that life fails to deliver these promises. Hence her frustration and loneliness. The milieu dissatisfies and disappoints her. She feels in her a longing for the past:

> It is a happy landscape, I like to think, reaching from the shallow depression of Golden Gate Park and climbing to the communication towers atop Twin Peaks. The area is given to summer fogs that make conventional gardening impossible, but that remind me, not unhappily, of mountain resorts in India. I almost expect the chattering of monkeys, corn and peanuts smoking on open braziers, the tinkling of women's bangles and Buddhist prayer wheels. (24)

Tara is but partially assimilated into the alien soil of America. Her attachment to the American culture is only skin-deep and superficial. Jopi Nyman rightly calls this attachment an "ambiguous relationship with Americanness." (59) Bharati Mukherjee has aptly brought out Tara's marginality and her estrangement in the following lines:

> The moment I step outside the bookstore on to the crowded Haight Street, I lose the heady kinship with the world that I feel through my reading. Nobody pays attention to me other than to ask for

> spare change or press a handbill into my closed fist. I am not the only blue-jeaned woman with a Pashmina shawl around my shoulders and broken-down running shoes on my feet. I am not the only Indian on the block. All the same, I stand out, I'm convinced. I don't belong here, despite my political leanings; worse, I don't want to belong. (79)

Tara has a searing feeling of being cut off from her community and its life-style. She "stands out," she is in the milieu but not with the milieu. As a racialized subject, she encounters the racist and nationalist ideology segregating her, pushing her away from the centre of American experience. Hence she "stands out" from the rest. She emerges with a new identity:

> I felt as though I were lost inside a Salman Rushdie novel, a once-firm identity smashed by hammer blows, melted down and re-emerging as something wondrous, or grotesque. (195-96)

Bharati Mukherjee depicts a liquid society in her novels, i.e. a society in flux. It is a society of constant flow, the flow of migrants, the flow of machines, flow of criminals, flow of "exterritorial" power-structures, flow of people and commodities. Even we have the crossing of geographical boundaries when Tara in an assay to search her roots remembers her ancestral ties with Tara Lata, the "Tree-Bride" of Mishtigunj.

Bish is also an upholder of tradition. He prefers the values of an imagined past than those of contemporaneity. He wants a son of traditional outlook: "Bish could not tolerate a son who was not a perfect replica of himself; hardworking, respectful, brilliant, soberly, sociable. Effortlessly athletic." (154) But contrary to his aims and expectations, his son Rabi will not become a gentleman like him. This materialises when he acquires the stigma of a homosexual, something which shocks his parents.

Loneliness had made Tara a little wanton and wantonness had made her very lonely. In these five years she had changed beyond recognition, but Bish had not changed at all. By California standards he was still young, a "Bay Area Bachelor to Die For." (262) Bish adhered to the Bengali middle-class way of life. He was endeavouring to reconstruct tradition: "He lived and prospered by commonsense precepts that are ingrained in any middle-class Bengali boy. . . . Whatever he had liked at twenty, and still liked at forty-two, now had tenure in his life." (263)

Tara, on the other hand, was trying to reconstruct her identity through her diasporic experience. She was attempting to redefine the importance of her cultures through space and time. This is reflected in her assay to discover some ancestral link with Tara-Lata, the "Tree-Bride" of Mishtigunj and the vicissitudes of her life in America. Sense of home plays a significant role in Tara's construction of her identity: "we have to stop living in a place that's changed on us while we've been away. I don't want to be a perfectly preserved bug trapped in amber, Didi. I can't deal with modern India, it's changed too much and too fast, and I don't want to live in a half-India kept on life-support." (184)

Tara's reconstruction of identity is rooted in her nostalgic and romantic recollection of her past. It is based on the flux of her thoughts about the past coming to her mind in the present but in fragments, and not whole. It is a spatio-temporal reconstruction of her identity. Jopi Nyman has made a fine and penetrating analysis of Tara's character: "In discussing the significance of the past and in showing how much of Tara's identity, however Americanized it is, is based on her memories of India, and her grandmother's stories of the past, the novel reconstructs Tara as hybrid subject. Like her namesake Tara Lata of Mishtigunj, the Tree-Bride, she learns to resist colonization and the fixing of identities." (65)

Tara belongs to both tradition and modernity. Her identity is highly assimilative. She can adopt and accommodate herself both to her traditional Indian way of life and to her newly adopted American ethos. But she does not stick to the value systems of either of these ways of life. She moves on both the planes—the Indian and the American. She vacillates between two lives: "maybe I really was between two lives." (251) Yet to strike roots, yet to belong to any of these lives, she exemplifies the "existential dilemma" of diaspora and the problems an immigrant who has a fluid identity associated with mobility and plurality rather than stasis and singularity.

In *Desirable Daughters*, Bharati Mukherjee has struck a balance between the past and the present through a deft blending of tradition and modernity. This she achieves through the character of Tara who has outwardly severed her links with tradition but still remains tied to her native country. She is influenced by ancient customs and traditions, but is also very much rooted to the modern zeitgeist. She is searingly conscious of her existential predicament which is mirrored in the epigraph: "No one behind, no one ahead the path the ancients cleared has closed. And the other path everyone's path, . . . goes nowhere, I am alone and find my way." Tara is thus the alienated self, languishing in the angst and ennui of the diasporic experience, yet to carve out a niche for herself. She is the "nowhere woman" oscillating between the nostalgic fascinations of a traditional past and the romantic and adventurous allurements of the present. Like the other diasporic characters of Bharati Mukherjee, she "stands in the shaky ground where East meets West and the sound of cultures clashing could shatter glass." (*Los Angeles Times*)

References

1. Bharati Mukherjee, Interview, *The Times of India*, October 1, 1989, p. 1.
2. Jopi Nyman, "Transnational Travel in Bharati Mukherjee's *Desirable Daughters*," *The Atlantic Literary Review*, Vol. 3, No. 4, Oct.-Dec. 2002, p. 53.
3. Roger Bromley, *Narratives for a New Belonging: Diasporic Cultural Fictions* (Edinburgh: Edinburgh Univ. Press, 2000), p. 27.
4. Bharati Mukherjee, *Desirable Daughters: A Novel* (New York: Hyperion, 2002), p. 4.
5. D.K. Pabby, "Portrayal of the Diasporic Experience in Bharati Mukherjee's *Desirable Daughters*," Paper presented at the MELUS Conference, 4-5 April 2003, Punjab Univ., Chandigarh.
6. Nyman, p. 65.
7. Linda McDowell, *Gender, Identity and Place: Understanding Feminist Geographies* (Oxford: Polity, 1999), p. 220.
8. Makarand Paranjape, "Indo-Anglian as Anglo-Indian: Ideology, Politics, and Cross-Cultural Representation," *New Quest*, May-June 1995, p. 136.

The Crisis of Identity: Naipaul's *A House for Mr. Biswas*

A collaborative creation between a son and his father's life and writings, *A House for Mr. Biswas* (1961) depicts communities being moulded and transferred by larger socio-cultural forces. From East Indian villages to an urban ambience of the Port of Spain, it documents the transition of a colony from a rural to an urban, industrialized society. The life of its protagonist Mohun Biswas, is the story of the Indian immigrant's dilemma. It is the tale of an exile's desire to strike roots and attain an authentic selfhood. Mr. Biswas's life is a perpetual struggle between desires and obligations, inner motivations and circumstantial necessities. Besides focusing on the personal life of the protagonist, the novel also tells the ethnic and social history of a community, its acculturation to an alien society and acquisition of a social identity. Naipaul takes the reader into the dimly lit corridors of Mohun's inner world. "The laughter broke but Mr. Biswas could take no part in it . . . the rain encouraged him to stay, silent and unlistening on a tall stool."[1]

The novel maintains a subtle balance between the sympathetic inner views and the disinterested outer perspective of the narrator protagonist. The life of Mr. Biswas is the life of Naipaul himself. The experiences of exile work to devalue the society that the author has deserted. In a way, the novel is about the author's apprehensions of his Trinidadian life. Naipaul writes that *A House for Mr. Biswas* was his "father's book . . . written out of his journalism and stories, out of . . . knowledge he had got from the way of looking, Mac Gowan (former managing editor at the *Trinidad Guardian*) had trained him in. It was written out of his writing."[2] But this does not make the novel a biography. Mohun Biswas and Vidiadhar Seeperasad Naipaul are not the same person. The novel is but a fictional rendering of a son's forging into art, his father's life and writings in order to assert his ancestral identity. Mr. Biswas emerges out of the author's alienational experience within exile. Like Naipaul, he is an outsider eager to strike roots, to belong. Living in 'exile' from the society, his ambitions go unrealised. Alienated, he falls into the arduous process of acculturisation and socialisation. *A House for Mr. Biswas* delineates the formation of an individual's socio-cultural identity.

Mohun Biswas and his family drift from country to town, from Hindi to English, and from sprawling joint family system to a nuclear family. Hence, the novel traces Mr. Biswas's search for order and identity amidst socio-cultural change. Mr. Biswas's identity crisis springs from his agonising historical experience of slavery and his psychic encounter with the people who constitute a forlorn culture. His is the fate of the despairing and the excruciating lot who "carry about them the mark, in their attitudes, sensibilities and convictions, of the slave, the unnecessary man."[3] While other writers of fiction depict ordered and established societies, Naipaul writes about a society that is chaotic and centreless, a society of customs, rituals and superstitions that drive the individual away from his roots. Mohun is branded unlucky by the horoscope, a catalyst, which drives him away from the Indian world. He becomes the lonely expatriate seeking a new social role in a world of cross-cultural connections and encounters.

In Part One of the novel, we get a picture of the circumstances of Mr. Biswas and the conflict between his desires and the lacerating milieus. His infancy is as agonising as it is painful. His body is left unwashed, becoming soiled and muddy. Malnutrition stunts his growth, giving him a shallow chest, feeble limbs and a "rising belly." (22) His pastoral infancy is in tune with the rural setting of the novel. The novel presents an unromantic portrait of the colonial West Indies set against the story of a painfully split self and its quest for wholeness. Mohun Biswas changes for a child whose consciousness, or ability to read minds and hear voices that determine his existence, to a man who discovers that it is not his mind that controls the events of his life, but instead the fragmented events of his life that shape his mind, that make him realise that he is just somebody. Aware of his ambivalent position, he tells his son: "I am just somebody. Nobody at all. I am just a man you know." (279)

The East Indian villages that emerged through the migration of indentured labourers in the nineteenth and twentieth centuries forms the socio-historical context against which Mohun's life is gauged. Eric Williams focuses on the economic impulse behind the migration of the labourers to the Caribbean in *From Columbus to Castro: The History of the Caribbean* (1984).[4] With the abolition of the slave trade in 1807 planters turned to East India seeking labour on the sugarcane estates. A large number of East Indians immigrated to the Caribbean as indentured workers between 1838 and 1924. They first came to Trinidad. Mohun's grandfather was one such indentured labourer on a Trinidad sugar estate. So also his father, though slightly better off than his grandfather. Thus, Mohun and his brothers inherit the social identity of an indentured worker. While his brothers are sent to work on sugar estate, he looks after his uncle's shop.

For the most part of his life, Mohun relies on his uncle Bhandat and later on the Tulsi family for food and shelter. But Bhandat Store holds no attraction for him. After leaving it, he works as a painter of signs at the Tulsi Store in Arwacas. There he meets Shama, Tulsi's daughter, whom he marries in course of time. The newly wed couple lives at Hanuman House with the other Tulsi sons and daughters and their families.

The unwanted and unnecessary man, Mohun becomes an alien insider in the Tulsi family and its establishment. The Hanuman House symbolises the traditional and conventional Hindu world abounding in all sorts of ritualistic vagaries and superstitious hypocrisies. It is an abode of sham and pretension, an abandoned white fortress:

> Among the tumbledown timber-and-corrugated-iron building in the High streets at Arwacas, Hanuman House stood like an alien white fortress. The concrete walls looked as thick as they were, and when the narrow doors of the Tulsi Store on the ground floor were closed the House became bulky, impregnable and blank. The sidewalls

> were windowless and on the upper two floors the windows were mere slits in the facade. The balustrade which hedged the flat roof was crowned with a concrete statue of the benevolent monkey-God Hanuman. From the ground the whitewashed features could scarcely be distinguished and were, if anything, slightly sinister, for dust had settled on projections and the effect was that of face lit up from below. (80-81)

To Mohun, the Hanuman House was a world "more real . . . and less exposed" (188) where he was treated with "indifference rather than hostility." (188) "When everyone worked with energy and joy, . . . he remained aloof." (188) Mohun Biswas becomes so much nauseated in the House that he grows languid and at times suffers from neurotic inertia: "Food and tobacco were tasteless. He was always tired, and always restless. He went often to Hanuman House; as soon as he was there he wanted to leave. . . . When he closed the door of his room for the night, it was like an imprisonment." (227-28) Within the Hanuman House and even outside it, Mohun Biswas is a stranger: "Everything beyond its gate was foreign and unimportant." (188)

Mr. Biswas had all regards for the Tulsis. He looked at them with devout reverence. He wanted to belong to their world but "he could not imagine the Tulsi anywhere else except at Arwacas. Separate from their house, and lands, they would be separate from the labourers, tenants and friends who respected them for their piety and the memory of Pundit Tulsi." (390) It is not that Mr. Biswas cannot relate himself to the world of the Tulsis because of their stand-offish attitude but it is because Mr. Biswas himself becomes wooden to the Tulsi household: "Back in Port of Spain they noticed Mr. Biswas' stillness, his silence, his withdrawal. He did not complain about the noise; he discouraged, but gently, all efforts to engage him in conversation; he went alone for long night walks." (481)

Mr. Biswas' literal gift for writing draws him into the trap—marriage into Tulsi ménage—from which for the rest of his life he attempts, more or less in vain, to escape. In fact, it is his marriage into the Tulsi family that determines the shape of much of his future life. His literal gift is his sole means of evading the abject and grinding penury which was his father's lot. Mr. Biswas takes a correspondence course from London on "How to write articles?" His articles mirror his longing self, all agog to build a house of his own. Mohun's crisis of identity manifests itself in self-assertion and self-affirmation—the yearning to carve out a personality of his own, to own a house. His life is the story of the Trinidadian Indian community, decadent and moribund. Against this disintegrating backdrop, the Tulsi household goes to rack and ruins. But Mr. Biswas continues to maintain an uncanny consistency in his struggle to possess a house, which forms the focus of the novel. The Hanuman House serves as an integrating and unifying symbol in the novel. Mr. Biswas' stories with their recurrent fantasies of escape from the marriage trap has genuine link with its relevance to the building of a house. The house represents not only a recognisable location and identity for the displaced second generation colonial out of sympathy with his Indian roots and unable to identify with his new surroundings. It also stands for the acceptance of the roles of husband, father and breadwinner which both circumstances and temperament invite Mr. Biswas to resist for so long. It is only when that resistance is abandoned that Mr. Biswas succeeds in attaining a home which survives him and can become a point of growth for the new generation of Savi and Anand. For Mr. Biswas writing represents the channel for the realisation of his self, for the fulfillment of his quest. Throughout, we find Mr. Biswas desperately searching for his identity in an agonising milieu.

The Tulsi establishment governed by the shrewd coloniser Mrs. Tulsi and her bullying slave master Seth creates an oppressive ambience for Mr. Biswas. Both Mr. Tulsi and Seth are blind to the positive aspects of Hindu culture as well as to individual urges and aims. The Tulsis are hypocritically materialised. They are philistines who shut their eyes to the creative things of life. Biswas abhors such an attitude and begins to develop in him a deep-seated hatred for the Tulsis. The "pointless and degrading" (131) campaign against the Tulsis leads him nowhere. At the Hanuman House, he receives only "aggrieved and aggressive stares" (131) which are irritatingly disgusting. Stranded in such a milieu, "Mr. Biswas grew very still, and listened to his own breathing. . . . He could make out the rafters and the loose straws that hung straight down, threatening to fall into his eyes." (149) To accept the rules of the Hanuman House would be to stoop to the state of slave and a servant. Hence, he hesitates and pauses before he acquiesces to the dogged convention of the House. He has his identity and he must assert it. He struggles hard to release himself from the clutches of a stifling and suffocating world, symbolized by the Hanuman House. In his defiance and rebellion against the overwhelming odds of a traditionally haunted house, Mr. Biswas suffers from deep psychic tension for he cannot openly defy the authority of the Tulsis. His whole endeavour is to seek, and assert his identity but he is intermittently bogged down by the pretended posture and the superimposingly domineering role of the Tulsi household. The dehumanising effects of such domination serve as a metaphor for subjugating power-structures. Mohun suffers from the pull exerted by the inner urge to relate himself to the Hanuman House and his archetypal longing to have a house of his own. He suffers because of a lack of self-integration, which reveals as a failure and an inability to attain whole identity. His quest for identity is an indication of his unease and his need for assurance. He is unable to find a viable strategy to cope with the destabilising sense of the lack of an adequate identity. Frustrated, he shies away from the notion of giving up sign-painting. He says to Tulsi's son-in-law: "Give up sign painting? And my independence? No, boy. My motto is: Paddle your own canoe." (107) Sign-painting for Mr. Biswas is a means of preserving his identity.

Mohun Biswas has several fluctuations in his life, necessitated by changes of job and residence. The basic necessities, to a large extent, mould the life of Mr. Biswas. His need for identity and self-dignity and the constant pressures on him and his family reverse his intentions and undermine his vision of an El Dorado. From the dejected and disappointed role of a truck driver to the job at the Tulsi family as a business manager, Mohun simply does not belong. The marginal man living in a metahistorical world, he is ever at the mercy of the Tulsis for his and his family's sustenance. Between the Tulsis and him, there is no proper form of relatedness and hence his alienation from them. Mohun's is a mode of experience in which he experiences himself as an alien. Whatever work he undertakes he feels estranged from it. He seems to be drawn away from the centrality of his experience by some inscrutable centrifugal force. As a Brahmin he does not get a becoming treatment from the Tulsis. Instead he is pushed to a low rung in the Tulsi family hierarchy because he is the "son of a labourer" and because he is a financial liability and burden to the family enterprise. The hierarchy of the inhabitants of the Hanuman House mirrors the stereotyped and hackneyed caste attitudes of the East Indian community where Mohun Biswas is a "have-not," an outsider. His designation as a labourer, his landlessness and joblessness make him 'a nobody,' the nowhere man. Mohun develops an "idealised image" of himself, so different from big "self-image" that there exists a profound "gap between his idealized image and his real self."[5] The Tulsis' image of Biswas conflicts with his self-image of a person with a high and sublime ideal, a dignified person-to-be whose real life of accomplishments and enterprises is yet to begin. The Tulsis are exasperated at Biswas' declining to work either in their store or in the sugarcane estate. Biswas on the other hand is hurt by the Tulsis' utter apathy to his Brahmin status and their reluctance to treat him as an educated, civilised person.

To Biswas, the Tulsi household is an object of dislike and hostility. He abhors the Tulsis and delights in imaginatively upsetting the family hierarchy. Hence, he sarcastically mocks at the family members by re-naming them. Thus, Mrs. Tulsi becomes the "old cow," the "old hen," the "old queen"; Seth, the elder brother-in-law and business manager, the "Big Boss"; Tulsi's pampered sons, Oswad and Vidiadhar, the "Young god." Look at a flabbergasted houseless wanderer like Mohun who on the one hand wants to be treated as a Brahmin and on the other hand wants to destroy the class and caste system. Dependent on the Tulsis for his bread and butter at the expense of his own self-mortification, he becomes ridiculously irritating to the Tulsis.

His mockery of the Tulsis leads to his expulsion from the Hanuman House. Seth says, "You refuse to help in the store, you refuse to help on the estate. All right! But then to turn around and insult us." (109)

Biswas' conflict with the Tulsis symbolises the thematic conflict of the novel between desire and necessity. Mohun lives in a world of fantasy and dream. He dreams to be somebody in the Tulsi household but his desires and expectations only lead to his utter humiliation at the hands of the Tulsis. His double life—a life of what he is and a life of what he would like to be—reality and illusion—reminds one of the "romancers" of *Miguel Street* (1959). Biswas tries to escape from the harrowing world of the Tulsis by taking recourse to the romances of Hall Caine Marie Corelli and Samuel Smiles whose exotic tales nourish his fantasy and make him "despair of finding romance in his own dull green land." (78) These telling romantic tales provide a contrast to the dull and dreary milieu at Hanuman House where "there can be no romance" (93) and no hope of a new life and a new identity. Out of necessity he comes to the Tulsi household but he exists as an exile of sorts. He lacks genuine involvement in the Tulsi household and hence his estrangement. His association with the Tulsi goes primarily into appearance. He does not truly belong to the Tulsi enterprise. "Real life was to begin . . . soon, and elsewhere" (147) is what Mohun believes. His search for a profession and his dream of a house of his own symbolise his desire for a sense of identity and belonging. He never really owns his own house and he never feels at home in his work or in any group within Trinidad society. He is self-alienated. He loathes to work as an agricultural labourer as his ancestors had to do.

He does everything in his power to escape his inherited class identity—an indentured labourer. His dream of becoming "someone" recedes. Unreality overshadows his desire to be a "somebody" in the Tulsi household. His attitude towards the Green Vale workers mirrors his shame at his own class designation and his dependency on the Tulsis. Biswas longs to escape from the degradation of the agricultural labourer, who belonged to the lowest rung of the socio-economic ladder. Throughout his life he remains sensitive to his class and caste designation which is closely linked to his dream of a house of his own but look at the harsh and painful reality of his crowded and shabby room:

> In Tara's house he became once more only a labourer's child—father's occupation: labourer was the only entry in the birth certificate—living with a penniless mother in one room of a mud hut. And throughout life his position was like that. As one of the Tulsi's sons-in-law and as a journalist he found himself among people with money and sometimes with graces; with them his manner was unforcedly easy and he could summon up luxurious instincts; but always, at the end, he returned to his crowded, shabby room. (49)

The "crowded, shabby room" to which Biswas returns symbolises his class designation, dependency and rootlessness.

As a reporter-journalist, Biswas not only acquires a professional identity, but also finds an outlet for his creativity. Through writing, he takes hold of his world, seeing and defining it in his own eccentric way. As a feature-story writer, he imaginatively plays out dark possibilities of his own life. He writes articles about "night-soil remover, mosquito killer, undertaker, birth certificate searcher, and lunatic-asylum warden etc." This romantic fascination for writing leads to his purchase of a typewriter, enrolment in a London Ideal School of Journalism Correspondence Course, and the beginning of a short story, "Escape." His typewriter and his short story "Escape" signify his partially realised dream of another identity and life. The leitmotif of the stories written by Biswas, as the narrator elaborates was "the hero, trapped into marriage, burdened with a family, his youth gone, meets a young girl. . . . Beyond the meeting the stories never went." (344-45) The young girl symbolises the wish fulfillment transparent in these stories. The girl is Biswas' fantasy life. She exists outside history and forms but a fragment of his metahistorical imagination.

In Biswas' life, houses are the meeting grounds for the clash between dreams and reality. The very idea of having a house of his own functions as a container of desires. As a boy, he abandons his home after his father's drowning and taking away of the family's property. His dream of a house of his own is, among other things, a longing for the lost father and lost security of his infancy. Save for a brief period of residency in houses he builds in Green Vale and Shorthills and in the houses he buys on Sikkim Street, Biswas lives his life in others' houses which signify his other identity. A life of humiliation, migrancy, and not-belonging is the context of the planning and construction of Biswas' house at Green Vale. He does not have enough money to build the kind of house he envisions. The result is that the house turns into an embarrassment and a target, when in Mr. Biswas' absence, disgruntled workers burn it down.

Like the Indians of Trinidad, as shown in Naipaul's novels, Mohun Biswas belongs to a decadent culture. Broken away from his historical and cultural roots, he lives in a world of cultural confusion. He makes strenuous efforts to earn money and have a house of his own but all in vain. Mohun's is a picaroon society, a society of limitations, of a paucity of traditions and institutions where the individual carries the burden of making meaning and making his way through life. It is a society on the margins of other's power and prosperity. It is for this reason its people may feel, as Biswas often does, an unreality and futility about their lives. It is a society of individuals in search of whatever identity they can make for themselves. In Biswas' career we reckon aspects of the individual's struggle to acquire a professional identity in a colonial society with aspects of the picaroon world but his identity as a professional is always insecure and fragile. It has not been conferred by an institution or a professional society, and therefore can disappear just as suddenly as it appeared. Throughout his working life, Mohun constantly fears being "sacked" because he feels at times that he is masquerading as a journalist writer. His idle typewriter and his unfinished short story partly symbolise his insecurity.

He is not what he seems to be. In his sense of inverted reality, we see an effect of his enslaved ethnic community and his colonial society. He believes that his "real life" is always about to begin and that reality lies somewhere far beyond Trinidad. His dark humour and brooding unhappiness lend him the distanced "exotopic" perspective on an exile. His dreams and desires to be somebody beguile him and isolate him from others. His inner and outer worlds have physical separateness, they do not coexist. His is a Creole culture. Mr. Biswas declines to submit to the traditional practices and many times in the novel he makes a solitary stand against others. In this he resembles a Desai protagonist who "faces single-handed, the ferocious assaults of existence"[6]

Mohun Biswas symbolizes the expatriate experience of a minority culture adapting to a cosmopolitan society and the shifting scenario of socio-moral values. The quest for identity amidst social transition is what Naipaul sets out to explore in the novel. As in the other works of the author, here too, change is a complex motif carrying two ambivalent and contradictory representations and evaluations. Naipaul views change as positive since it is through change that Mohun breaks out of his inherited identity as the son of a labourer and the suffocating hierarchy of the traditionalist Tulsi family. Through socio-economic changes, Mr. Biswas steps out of his caste identity and tenuously joins the middle class. Thus, change gives an identity to his fleeting self by emancipating him from the stifled authoritarian caste order symbolised by the Tulsi family and pushes the Agricultural East Indian Community into the centre of Trinidad society. Like an exile, Mr. Biswas is a stranger to himself, a fragmented self, almost nomadic: "As a boy he had moved from one house of strangers to another and since his marriage he felt he had lived nowhere." (8) An observer from the margins, he is in search of his centre which is 'here and anywhere.' Being alienated from society, he is a passive spectator who only 'sees' but never 'feels.' Sandwiched between an old identity in a traditional community and a new identity in a post-industrial society, Mr. Biswas becomes an exile trapped in the cultural collisions of his epoch. He lives without a stable social identity. Empty and fragmented, he simply drifts in the cross-cultural current of a transitional society. He lives because "life has to be lived." (192)

Mr. Biswas' search for identity is not natural and instinctive but is inspired by forces of ritual, myth and custom. His struggle to attain an identity is not that of a man constitutionally recalcitrant and rebellious. Detestable yet dignified, weak but independent, Mohun Biswas is an ordinary man with extraordinary interests and visions. Naipaul has made a virtue of Biswas' rootlessness by making it a positive and constructive concept, which finds its objective correlative in the image of the house which ironically becomes in this novel, a symbol of cage, a trap. Like Rudyard Kipling's Kim, Mohun Biswas has lost his own country and has not acquired any other and hence his search for identity.

References

1. V.S. Naipaul, *A House for Mr. Biswas* (New Delhi: Penguin, 1992), p. 560.
2. V.S. Naipaul, *Finding the Centre: Two Narratives* (New York: Alfred A. Knopf, 1984; Vintage, 1986), p. 60.
3. William Walsh, *A Manifold Voice* (London, 1970), p. 71.
4. Karen Horney, *Our Inner Conflict* (New York: W.W. Norton, 1945), p. 111.
5. Eric Williams, *From Columbus to Castro: The History of the Caribbean (1492-1969)* (New York: Vintage, 1984).
6. "Desai interviewed," *The Times of India*, April 21, 1979, p. 9.

V.S. Naipaul's *The Middle Passage*: Centre and Marginality

A writer on the margins Vidiadhar Suraj Perasad Naipaul, the native Trinidadian, is a part of, yet not a part of, the English milieu. He is both included and excluded from it by birth and growth; inheritance and history. Timothy F. Weiss rightly observes: "The whiff of Jasmine and the separation between word and flower focus imagistically the dislocations within the experience of identity of Vidiadhar Suraj Perasad Naipaul, a colonial Trinidadian of Asian origin writing about the Caribbean and West Indies for metropolitan English readers."[1] The gap between the flower and the word symbolised the "immense distance between islands separated by the Atlantic and between his colonial identity and his aspirations to become a metropolitan writer."[2] Naipaul's colonial experience and understanding is symbolised by the distance between jasmine, the fascinating word and jasmine the cold and uninteresting vegetation. "Like the other colonials, Naipaul was marginalised through the ideology and myths of Englishness, and through this and other began to learn to see as an exile."[3]

As an exile enmeshed in the cultural collisions of his epoch, Naipaul does not escape their alienating effects. His dislocation from his roots enables him to treat his own alienation as an instance of his quest for identity of colonial and postcolonial peoples. Like a veritable exile, he pursues the middle passage by living 'in-between' and through this sharing of both origins and ends, he discovers his centre. His marginality is a division between self and others among whom he has lived or continues to live. It is his exile which signifies a dislocation from the centre and a manner of perception from the margins of other worlds. The exile executes, what Bakhtin calls an "exotopy"[4] a vision from the outside or 'the outsideness' in which one finds oneself from outside, i.e. from the margins. His exotopy conveys the basic idea that one can better know the centre from the margins. Naipaul too believes that in order to find the centre, one must look from the margins, for the margins can be "an unprecedented source of creative energy."[5]

Naipaul is a person on the margins by inheritance and choice. He is a child shuffled from house to house, as the son of an iconoclastic journalist, as an East Indian in a primarily black West Indian society, as a colonial in the English metropolis (where he has lived, in his own words, as a "refugee," as someone "peripheral" and in "Limbo").[6]

To Naipaul, the history of the islands can never be satisfactorily told and as such "history is built around achievement and creation; and nothing was created in the West Indies." (29) *The Middle Passage* treats the enduring effects of Caribbean societies' histories of imperial depredation and depletion and colonial marginality:

> The Caribbean has been described as Europe's other sea, the Mediterranean of the New World. It was a Mediterranean which summoned up every dark instinct without the complementary impulses towards nobility and beauty of older lands, a Mediterranean where civilization turned satanic, perverting those it attracted. And if one considers this sea, which the tourist enlivens in his fantastic uniform, as a wasteful consumer of men through more than three centuries—the aboriginal population of some millions wiped out; the insatiable plantations; 300,000 slaves taken to Surinam, which today has a Negro population of 90,000; the interminable wars; 40,000 British soldiers dead between 1794 and 1796 alone, and another 40,000 discharged as unfit—it would seem that simply to have survived in the West Indies is to have triumphed. (169)

The Middle Passage is about clients and consumers who have consumed human beings by turning them to slaves and indentured workers—Amerindians, African slaves, Asian indentured labourers and European colonists, soldiers and missionaries.

Divided into six chapters, the book portrays five colonial West Indian and Caribbean societies: Trinidad, British Guiana (Guyana), Surinam (Suriname), Martinique and Jamaica. In each chapter,[7] the socio-cultural, socio-psychic and socio-economic ills of these colonial societies in relation to their colonial history and its concomitant problems in the late 1950s and early 1960s, have been graphically presented. The novel alludes primarily to the freighting of slaves between Africa and the America and to the voyages of Columbus and other explorers, conquistadors, and colonists from old world to new; from the centre to the periphery. Most of these slaves constituted mainly the West Indian immigrants who were barred from social intercourse by the colour of their skin. Racial tensions both in the colonies and in the metropolis are lasting effects of the empire. Racial attitudes and gradations can be traced back to hundreds of years in West Indian history: "The Creole slaves . . . looked upon the newly imported Africans with scorn, and sustained in their turn that of the Mulattos, whose complexions were browner; all were kept at a distance from the intercourse of the whites." (27) Such is the marginality of their existence, always at a distance from the centre. They were only a feature of enslavement. The Trinidadians are still slaves in that they are chiefly clients and consumers in a distant colony; like Britons of the Roman Empire. They are decentred by the Euro-American civilisation, are dependent on foreign economies and are attached to foreign modes of cultural identity. Equally pitiable is their incarcerated attachment to values projected by the American and British media. Remoulding itself in the image of "the Hollywood B-man," the West Indian has stooped to the status of the "mimic man." Its modernity is the "extreme susceptibility of people unsure of themselves," without a centre of their own, without a lifestyle. Like other colonials, Trinidadians have been forced to sell cheaply and buy dearly, to accept and to imitate. As a colonial people on the margins of empires, Trinidadians have learned to live in ignorance of their own history and in a fantasy of the world beyond the island: "We could never be convinced of the value of reading the history of [Trinidad] which was, as everyone said, only a dot on the map of the world. Our interest was all in the world outside. . . . Our past was buried and no one cared to dig it up." (43)

In Chapter 3, "British Guiana," Naipaul sees in Guyana signs of the country's three-hundred year slave era, that created a people who want only "to be left alone." (118) For the West Indian, his colonial culture leads to the split in his identity and also to his isolation from the milieu. Naipaul argues that West Indian colonies are plagued by a sense of marginality. The colonial metropolitan relationship has rendered the colonies unknown to themselves and ignored or unseen by others; thus, colonial Trindadians, although perhaps fascinated by the world far beyond and knowing something of the history of the metropolis, do not know their own island's history: "Our interest was all in the world outside, the remoter the better; Australia was more important than Venezuela, which we could see on a clear day. . . . The England of 1914 was the England of yesterday; the Trinidad of 1914 belonged to the dark ages." (43)

Colonials believe that they have an identity only in relation to the metropolitan country, and thus they think of themselves as marginal and insignificant. The sickness that Naipaul seeks to diagnose in these colonial societies derives from colonialism and imperialism: slavery, the plantation system, the immigration of indentured workers, and treatment of the Caribbean and West Indies only as a resource to be exploited have created an unstable and shaky amalgam of peoples uncertain of their roots and doubtful of their identity. Their centre of existence seems to be 'nowhere and everywhere' and hence they move on the periphery only uncertain of the means and ways to develop their societies. Naipaul calls West Indies a "Client culture" and a "Client economy." (5) Citing the noted English historian James Anthony Froude, Naipaul says: "The West Indies were valued only for the wealth which they yielded, and society there has never assumed any particularly, noble aspect." (9) In other words the West Indians lacked particularity since their centre of existence was dispersed here and there and they were only marginal beings generalised into a common centrality of experience.

Imperialism and marginality fostered West Indian imitation of Europe and North America. Naipaul dwells on the deleterious effects of the Western Media, especially cinema. Colonial Trinidadians mimic the attitudes and the behaviour presented in the films: "In the immigrant colonial society, with no standards of its own, subjected for years to the second-rate in newspapers, radio and cinema, minds are rigidly closed; and Trinidadians of all races and classes are remaking themselves in the image of the Hollywood B-man." (61)

Naipaul is certainly caricaturing a culture to comprehend his own exile and his own marginality of existence. Citing Aime Cesaire, James Clifford contends that mimicry can also turn into syncretism, a construction of a new identity: "The Caribbean history from which Cesaire derives, an inventive and tactical 'negritude' is a history of degradation, mimicry, violence, and blocked possibilities. [Yet] it is also rebellious, syncretistic, and creative. This kind of ambiguity keeps the planet's local futures uncertain and open. There is no master narrative that can reconcile the tragic and comic plots of global cultural history.[8] Thus, it is clear that mimicry and imitation of another culture leads to a dislocation from the margins to the centre of another circle.

Besides documenting the dirt and squalor of the colonial people, *The Middle Passage* also records the failure of the colonial Trinidadians and West Indians to discover their roots, to find a viable centre for their existence: "There is an important difference between the self-other relationship in European colonial discourse and in Naipaul's discourse on the West Indies and the Caribbean. In the former, the European self reduces the colonial other to an object, an entity devoid of an "I"; because colonial subjectivity has been denied, there can only be a hollow colonial mimicry of the European self. In the latter discourse, the author as exile who returns temporarily to the Caribbean is torn between conflicting aspects of his own identity; the colonial subject cannot be made to disappear because, in a sense, Naipaul is himself the subject of his own travels and critique. . . . Unable to deny the colonial self, he wrestles with his malaise."[9]

It portrays an anguished quest for an understanding of the fragmented self. In this book, Naipaul diagnoses the problems of the marginal man—uncertainty of identity, feelings of inferiority, scorn for one's own culture and society. His diagnosis is a colonial exile's languished enquiry, registering a search for a better grasp, of the society and milieu that he has deserted. It echoes European colonial discourse and at the same time does away with the Western stereotyped images of the Caribbean as a tropical paradise. The book sets in motion a new liberating urge and potentiality since with the collapse of the colonial's dislocation of centrality of experience, it makes visible the peripheries wherein the exile moves. Hence, with the collapse of the centre, the peripheries are not obliterated, rather made more manifest. Thus, the book, besides being an autobiography of the author himself, is an exile's break with the centre and a perception from the margins of other worlds where things are never seen whole but only broken and twisted against themselves.

References

1. Timothy F. Weiss, *On the Margins: The Art of Exile in V.S. Naipaul* (Amherst: University of Massachusetts Press, 1992), p. 3.
2. V.S. Naipaul, *The Middle Passage: Impressions of Five Societies—British, French and Dutch—in the West Indies and South America* (London, 1962; New York: Vintage, 1981), p. 29.
3. Weiss, p. 4.
4. The word 'exotopy' is Tzvetan Todorov's coinage to match M.M. Bakhtin's coinage of a term that signifies "outsideness." See Tzvetan Todorov, *Mikhail Bakhtin: The Dialogic Principle*, trans. Wlad Godzich (Minneapolis: University of Minnesota Press, 1984), p. 99.
5. Bill Ashcroft, Gareth Griffiths, and Helen Tiffin, *The Empire Writes Back: Theory and Practice of Post-Colonial Literature* (London and New York: Routledge, 1989), p. 12.
6. "Jasmine," *The Overcrowded Barracoon* (NY: Vintage, 1984).
7. In an interview with Ian Hamilton, Naipaul remarks: "London is my metropolitan centre; it is my commercial centre; and yet I know that it is a kind of limbo and that I am a refugee in the sense that I am always peripheral." See "Without a Place: Interview, Ian Hamilton," *Critical Perspectives on V.S. Naipaul*, ed. R.D. Hamner (Washington, D.C: Three Continents Press, 1977), p. 41.
8. James Clifford, *The Predicament of Culture: Twentieth Century Ethnography, Literature and Art* (Cambridge: Harvard University Press, 1988), p. 15.
9. Weiss, p. 76

Self and Society: A Study of Bhabani Bhattacharya's *So Many Hungers!*

The fictional world of Bhabani Bhattacharya posits an engaging picture of the human being torn between two worlds—the self and the society. The fettered self struggling for emancipation from the stranglehold of a chaotic society appears to be a dominant trait in Bhabani Bhattacharya's novels. The individual struggles for self-liberation but is silenced by the buffets of societal values, falters and then puts up a faltering fight, but never yields, never gives in to the forces of evil. The struggle of the self for liberation culminates in a compromise, in an affirmation and an assertion of the right to live. This note of faith in societal values, and in man's hope for survival despite all the bludgeoning of fate, lends grandeur and magnanimity to the Bhattacharya protagonist. The nobility of the individual in spite of all sufferings imparts an epic dimension to the self, be he Rahoul or Kajoli. Suffering and hunger ennobles and strengthens it. Rahoul says: "In the agonies of war the soul would be cleansed."[1]

The Bhattacharya protagonist lives and thrives enduringly and ethically. Pain and hunger cannot brutalise him. Nor can it degrade and debase him: "Live. We do not fear to live dangerously." (40) Thus, the individual self doesn't escape from life, but escapes into it. It wrestles with the worn-out societal values and endeavours to transcend its mundane limitations through self-sacrifice. The only thing that stands out in Bhattacharya's novels is the magnanimity of the self in putting up a heroic fight against a hostile milieu. The 'self' in the novel is a conscious sensibility struggling for socio-psychic emancipation from a physico-moral world. It is an "algebraic symbol, jostled into an expression of the plight of humanity in Calcutta, in Bengal, in India."[2] Bhattacharya doesn't make the conflict metaphysical, rather the conflict is socio-spiritual. Moreover the social world in the novel is a time-space construction of rational and moral values. The paper attempts a study of the nature of the conflict between self and society and it intends to show that the conflict, at the end, becomes an assertion of the goodness of the self.

Bhabani Bhattacharya in one of his interviews admits that *So Many Hungers!* is an offspring of his emotionally disturbed self in the hunger-stricken society:

> Then the great famine swept down upon Bengal. The emotional stirrings I felt (more than two million men, women and children died of slow starvation amid a manmade scarcity) were a sheer compulsion to creativity. The result was the novel *So Many Hungers!*[3]

Deeply committed to a social purpose, Bhattacharya ridicules art for art's sake. He believes that "a novel must have a social purpose"[4] and that art should "preach but unobtrusively, by the vivid interpretation of life."[5] Catalysts of social change, his novels live out the predicament of the contemporary human situation. A socio-political novel, *So Many Hungers!* portrays the unflinching faith of the individuals in human values even in the teeth of all miseries and privations. Suffering does not snatch them away from values which they cherish high. The grandfather says to Rahoul: "I have scores of daughters and sons in Baruni. I am proud of my people—they are good people. Centuries of hardship and strain have not destroyed their faith in human values." (24) Kajoli too has a sense of tradition and respect for its values even in this mechanical age when man has a craze for the modern fashions and ways of life. A well-bred peasant girl, "she has a legacy of manners as old as India. How could she give up her manners and proprieties to suit your new-fangled city ideas?" (28)

The different thematic patterns of the novel are held together neither by the socio-political forces at war with one another nor the intense poetic appeal of Rahoul or Kajoli but by the individual predicament of the hungry self on the one hand and the socio-historical forces on the other. The two fundamental strands of the Indian society—the materialistic and the Westernised modern society of the urban folk and the traditional and unsophisticated society of the rural folk—are at conflict within the self of the individual generating the dilemma of existence. Whether to stick to this or to that, to do this or that, is the problem. But the characters are not bedevilled and befogged in the face of such social odds. Rather they emerge out of such a dilemma triumphantly. In spite of all her sufferings and self-mortifications, Kajoli doesn't shun traditional values. She sells her body out of dire necessity but not her soul, not her socio-historical self nurtured in the traditional social values of faith and hope. As has been pointed out earlier, she has "a legacy of manners as old as India." (28)

So Many Hungers! is a tour de force of self-realisation and self-assertion. The characters like Rahoul and Kajoli justify the latent potentiality of their spirit by self-transcendence. "There was a streak of light" in Rahoul's "inward gloom." (183) It was not all dark with him. He had an unflinching faith in life, its invincibility and eternity. The picture that Bhattacharya presents in the novel is ghastly and grim. Its heart-rending sights of human misery and suffering move us to tears but at the same time convey to us the assertion of life amidst hunger, the flickering of light in the ashes. Look at the awful plight of the fishermen at the monstrous hands of the boat-wreckers who are deputed by "the Gorement" (55) which takes their boats and gives them money. The reluctant fisher-folk keep on crying "My boat! My boat!" but the boat-wreckers pay no heed and snatch away their boats to make a fine bonfire. But all is not lost. Still there is hope, still the light burns: "the end of one tale was the beginning of another. For, like a quenchless heritage of hate, the bonfire of boats was present and ever-alive in each fistful of ash." (58) Rahoul believes that the death of millions of human beings will but usher in a new world order:

> The elation that made his heart swell! Two exciting things had happened to him this autumn day. The Prime Minister of Britain had declared war on the Swastika. Manju had given birth to a baby girl. Either event was a profound experience that made his emo-

> tions vibrate, as though he had achieved some personal fulfilment. In the blood-bath of war much else would be drowned besides the Swastika. A million youths would not die in vain. (10)

Bhabani Bhattacharya makes use of symbols to project the theme of self-affirmation and self-elation. In Chapter 2, "the bright new day" symbolises the dawn of "the new epoch round the corner." (11) It fills Rahoul with new hopes. "In his blood he felt the voice of India throb." (12) Hindu taboos which deprive the self of its autonomy, its longing for realisation of the ends are "fast dying off" revealing an "inner purpose," (12) a positive and an affirmative vision of life, the spiritual desire for the purification of the self through suffering. Amidst all misery and pain, Rahoul's grandfather Devata becomes a beacon of hope, inspiration and guidance to the villagers: "Do not rush to sell your grain. Think it over." (63) He is worried about the village economy going to pieces in the hands of the Government agents and private entrepreneurs. S.K. Desai observes that the characters "are often frankly presented as symbols, types or representatives of certain classes or social forces."[6] But they are not merely symbols of social forces but emblems of the societal self in conflict with the spiritual urges of the individual. More than an individual, they symbolise Indian nationalism, all agog to liberate the nation from the hands of the British rulers.

Bhattacharya depicts the nobility and fearlessness of the individual in the face of the ferocious assaults of existence. Be it Kanu, Kajoli, Onu or the mother—everyone is a crusader, "soldiers all." (76) His characters hardly shed tears amidst pain and suffering. Though they lead a tortured life, they endure it with a smile. The arrest of Devata and Kajoli's father doesn't deter the members of their family from the usual tenor of their life. Unshelled and desperate, they never break down but feel themselves enlivened like an undaunted soldier in the battlefield. Through the character of Dadu, the novelist emphasises the self's abiding faith in life and its commitment to a higher life: "Do not betray yourselves. The supreme test has come. Be strong. Be true. Be deathless." (77) A life of eternity that transcends the circumscriptions of our death-bound mundane self is what Bhattacharya pleads for. A life of higher values, which is above greed and temptation will indubitably lead to the transcendence of the self. The novelist expostulates this through the character of Kajoli and Onu, who move on the higher plane of existence, one that is ideally noble. They do not sell their rice to the hoarders and black-marketeers, which they could have done to get more money. The storeman offers Kajoli a blue ribbon for the hair and to Onu a white rubber ball but he fails to get round them that way. They are above such temptations and greed. Instead, they sell it to the poor and the needy. Kajoli says: "She would sell rice to the homeless folk, and to none else." (80) Onu faces the famine heroically and inspires the village folk to do so. He has inexhaustible courage to move on through hunger and penury: "Every little branch at the top I can reach with my hand." (116) Thus, Onu is not cowed down by dread and despair. He triumphs over it. He has to feed a famished family. The general feeling of helplessness and hopelessness definitely breeds tension within the characters but such an internal conflict is dispelled with the self's idealistic and ethical urge to do good to the suffering and the starving. Despite its being famished, it rises above the petty and trivial mundane desires and renders selfless service to the hunger-stricken mass. Kajoli's mother for instance does not sell the cow, Mangala, since she regards her as a mother symbol who has provided nourishment to her family. On meeting a desperate, starving young woman with no milk in her breast for her dying baby, she consoles her forlorn heart by providing her all possible hope and inspiration. She advises her to go to Calcutta where she can eke out a living for herself and her family:

> Why, girl, you can go to Calcutta city; you never thought of that!—You will be looked after. You will find work, big wages! Nothing to worry about—nothing. (123)

This is not all. The starving old mother, an embodiment of selfless dedication, pity and inspiration, is prepared to give her dear Mangala to the emaciated woman. She wants to save her life as well as her cadaverous and anaemic infant struggling with life and death. She reconciles with the teeming millions, and is ready to forgo her most precious possessions for the cause of humanity. Her socio-ethical sense prevails. It propels her to the altar of sacrifice: "Take my cow. Sell her. Go to the wonder city and be saved." (123)

Thus, Bhattacharya evinces an affirmative vision of life issuing out of one's socio-moral and socio-ethical sense of values. In *So Many Hungers!*, it is this sense that prevails over one's utter feeling of desolation and desperation, culminating at times in self-abnegation or self-effacement. Nihilism has seldom any place in the fictional world of Bhattacharya since his characters live on hope and live for hope. Their dark and dismal life has a silver lining too: "In the hour of midnight the lone mother stood on the pavement of a strange city and saw bright silver streaking the edges of a massive pitch-black cloud." (152) The novelist has symbolically suggested the spiritual consolation and solace that human beings derive from the world of nature. The grief-stricken self harrowing in misery and despair gets solace from the natural objects. Thus, Kajoli's mother is comforted and soothed by the sight of a swarm of fire-flies:

> The mother gazed, and her heart was comforted by the tender beauty, and it was as though the tiny points of light were a sign, a message from the Image of Light. On to the city of a million lights! The city of humanity. The city of civilized living. (139)

Even the twittering of the song-birds "casting their joyous cry over the fields" (139) rejuvenates the down-hearted self of Kajoli. The big jackfruit tree near which the deceased lie in utter isolation and neglect symbolises the continuity and the perpetuation of life amidst death. Life that transcends death is what the novelist seems to convey. The mother, even in her despondency and dejection, feels a sense of hope and joy:

> and even in her wretchedness in the presence of the mutilated corpse the mother felt her heart grow faint with joy. The jackfruit would sustain the lives of her children and herself for two or three days. (141)

Society is not all bad. There are good elements in it who do not hesitate to come to the rescue of the famished and the desperate.

The soldier who commits rape upon Kajoli and the military doctor who takes utmost care of her are symbols of the societal self. They are gifted with the fundamental human values. The soldier has an ethical conscience. He feels deeply for his wrong-doing and repents for it. He curses himself for the crime he has perpetrated to this famished pregnant girl. But he feels a bit relieved and relaxed when he is able to save her by placing her in the hands of a military doctor. Thus, virtue compromises with vice and the individual self reconciles with the societal self. The character delivers itself from gross mundane values and rises above to evince its intrinsic nobility and goodness, its strength and endurance. Kajoli's mother believes:

> she and her son would surely find a roof for their heads—they would work hard and earn their keep, for they were no beggars, she and her son—the people had great kindness in their hearts, like the young khaki-clad military doctor. There would be food. One would go to school. (152)

It is evident from this that the self in a hostile and adverse milieu as depicted by Bhattacharya does not lose heart but gets more inspiration to live. It is not dogged down by the awful scenes of death and desolation. It transcends all these to assert its right to live—and to live with dignity and self-respect. The novelist observes:

> Out of the flame of travail that had consumed one woman a glow quickened in another, an understanding, a humanizing tenderness, so that the creatures of misery were no longer a race apart, soulless and dead-men and women all. (168)

The accursed self in Bhattacharya exhibits tremendous patience and stoic forbearance. The self undergoes all mortifications and abasement to help the famished and the destitute. The body is sacrificed for the sake of ideals but the spirit is not tarnished. The destitute girl is a case in point. She bares her body for money which she distributes among the suffering and the starving ones. Though she undergoes self-abasement, she never blackens her spirit which remains pure and chaste. "That was the streak of light to illuminate the gloom of his heart," (19) is what

Rahoul thinks of her. Besides there are others too, who come out to help the needy. An aged destitute villager holds out his card of free food to Rahoul. The ration card provides food to the starving ones.

Throughout the novel we come across instances of misery, poverty and starvation deaths but these negative elements are relegated to background when we consider the flickering of hope and assertion of the self. Does Kajoli's selling away of her body amounts to self-abasement and self-degradation? No. She does it to keep her mother and her younger brother alive. She is an incarnation of self-sacrifice. Her self-effacement leads to self-ennoblement. In the self-immolation of the famished people, we beckon the very affirmation of life and the negation of a brute and near-canine existence. They prefer dying to being humiliated and debased by an insouciant social conscience. They are men still undefeated, "fighters all . . . undefeated all. No jail-house could ever break their spirit." (196) Rahoul's character testifies to the nobility of the self. A self-possessed and dedicated self, he was least bothered about the individual. His concern was the society, the life of other people:

> What happened to him as an individual did not matter. It only mattered what happened to his people. He was indifferent, too, towards his captors, and his mind was without hate, without anger, in a nirvana of passionlessness. (204)

The conflict of the self throughout the novel has not been with the materialistic forces of evil and vice but with the social forces of exploitation and degradation. The self doesn't submit to these forces but fights it out, even at the risk of its immolation and annihilation, thus establishing its nobility and grandeur. It transcends all man-made barriers and hurdles, all human values to rise to the spiritual plane of martyrdom, martyred for the cause of their fellow brothers and for humanity at large. Besides portraying man's inhumanity to man and the tragic predicament of mankind upon the universe, *So Many Hungers!* posits an affirmative view of life in the very assertion of the self in a hostile milieu: "The more they tighten the chains the more the chains loosen!" (205)

Indeed, these chains can do not harm to the indomitable and invincible spirit of the heroic self that can create order out of chaos that can transmute suffering into blessing. Bhattacharya justifies the very *raison d'être* of existence which is not merely to live but to live courageously and spiritually. He has affirmed the very sanctity of human self and its epic dimension, which cannot be obliterated and crushed by evil forces or a hostile milieu. Unswayed by the sufferings of life, the individual self continues to live calmly and strongly and it looks beyond these bitter privations to a world of spiritual consolation and bliss. Bhattacharya ends the novel with a positive note. The stifled passions of the lacerated self triumphs over the sufferings of humanity: "There was no defeat in the voices, but a secret, excited triumphs . . . freedom could not drop from the skies, nor be asked from lands beyond the seas; but there, in the vast swamp of suffering and struggle, would it bloom, growing out of the seeds of the spirit." (205)

References

1. Bhabani Bhattacharya, *So Many Hungers!* (New Delhi: Orient Paperbacks, 1978), p. 9.
2. K.R. Srinivasa Iyengar, *Indian Writing in English* (Bombay: Asia, 1973), p. 412.
3. Bhattacharya interviewed, *Contemporary Novelists in the English Language* (New York: St. Martin's Press, 1972), p. 71.
4. Sudhakar Joshi, "An Evening with Bhabani," *The Sunday Standard*, April 27, 1969.
5. Bhabani Bhattacharya, "Literature and Social Reality," *The Aryan Path*, Vol. XXVI, No. 9 (Sept. 1955), p. 39.
6. S.K. Desai, "Bhabani Bhattacharya: The Writer Who Rides a Tiger," *The Perspectives on Indian Fiction in English*, ed. M.K. Naik (New Delhi: Abhinav, 1985), p. 124.

The Alienated Protagonists in Bhabani Bhattacharya's *So Many Hungers!* and *Music for Mohini*: A Comparative Study

In all his novels, Bhabani Bhattacharya deals with the theme of suffering and estrangement. His novels are the novels of ideas. Lila Ray writes: "As we read his writings, we hear the dialogue between men and ideas he lives by."[1] His novels portray different types of alienated characters—characters who seems to be at war with both the self and the society.

In *So Many Hungers!*, Kajoli, the chief female character, suffers the pangs of disintegration of her sprightly and innocent self on account of the catastrophic famine. She has a brief spell of happiness after she is married to Kishore but this happiness is but an occasional episode in the general drama of pain. It is ephemeral. As conditions deteriorate in the village, Kishore decides to go to Calcutta where he hopes to get employment in a mill. But fortune proves otherwise. There, he is shot by a soldier and dies. His sad fate remains unknown to the family right up to the end of the novel.

Kajoli is now in the family way. There is no rice to eat in the house. The husband and wife sell whatever can be sold. The condition worsens to such a degree that they find it impossible to live in the village and like thousands of other families, Kajoli sets out on a long and hazardous trek to Calcutta. Isolated from her husband and excluded from the society, Kajoli suffers the anguish of a torturous state of loneliness. Her socio-economic poverty alienates her from both her husband and the society. The famine of Bengal drives her to this miserable plight. But poverty fails to bog her down, to stultify her endeavouring and sanguine self. She persists in her lone and solitary struggle against the ferocious assaults of existence.

On her way to Calcutta, Kajoli has a painfully tragic experience. She meets an Indian soldier and begs him for food. Food she gets but only after surrendering herself to the animalistic and rapacious desires of the soldier. Temptation comes to Kajoli as to countless other destitute women like her. A woman who sells betel leaves and also runs a brothel offers her eighty rupees for a life of harlotry. At first she spurns the offer, but the escalating misery and suffering of her life makes her accept the woman's offer so that she can eke out a living for her mother and Onu. After days of anxious brooding and vacillation, she decides to plunge into the flesh-trade. Hence her sudden and abrupt departure with the betel-woman one early morning.

Alienated from her 'self,' Kajoli suffers from the conflict between situational compulsions and moral considerations. She never intends to live a sinful life but her utter poverty urges her to sacrifice her virginity and stoop to moral turpitude. Consequently it leads to the loss of her identity. Desperate and despair-stricken, she becomes frustrated and has negative emotions of great pain and privation. She turns psychopathic and suffers from rootlessness and meaninglessness. But all is not lost. On her way to the house of ill-fame, she hears the news of her dear Devata going to become the leader of the Satyagrahis. This information transforms the tenor and tempo of her life.

Kajoli's alienation from herself is the offspring of her needs and necessities. It is a phenotypical manifestation of her inner drives and desires. Her mundane self transforms societal values into something ugly and profane. Unable to adapt herself to the transient social milieu and the wretched plight in which her family is enmeshed, she becomes an easy prey to the rapacity of circumstances. Through her character, Bhabani Bhattacharya portrays the dehumanization of man in a mechanical society, where an individual remains alienated form the human aspect of his identity. Kajoli's struggle is not with the materialistic forces of evil and vice but with the social forces of exploitation and degradation. Her self does not submit wholeheartedly to these forces but fights it out, even at the risk of its own self-effacement.

The transformation in the identity of Kajoli is due to her awareness of the fact that strength of character and truth to life are enduring human values. She says: "Be strong, be true, be deathless."[2] This brings to her mind an inner realization of the self. Sorrows and sufferings have not destroyed her spirit which remains unconquered and invincible. She still identifies herself with the positive and assertive aspects of her self.

Bhattacharya's second novel *Music for Mohini* delineates the theme of incertitude, alienation and communication in married life. Here the loneliness of a housewife is rendered on a more general plane. It is the alienation of a woman, a wife, a mother—an alienation conditioned by society as well as family. Kajoli's anguish in *So Many Hungers!* is existential and psychic, but Mohini's anguish in this novel is domestic and mundane. There are lacerated and tense moments in her life giving it an existential dimension. Here, Bhattacharya dramatizes the conflict between two temperaments and two diametrically opposed attitudes. One is reminded of Maya and Gautama, the ill-assorted couple of Anita Desai's *Cry, the Peacock*. The protagonist of *Music for Mohini*, like Maya in *Cry, the Peacock*, is a sensitive, young, newly married girl, who is isolated from her husband and family because of her inability, rather, her reluctance to accept the traditions of her husband's family and their societal norms and values. Unable to accommodate and adjust herself with her in-laws, she withdraws from this milieu into her own sequestered and cocooned shell. Mohini symbolizes the strife and struggle of a sensitive individual in an indifferent social milieu.

A modern sophisticated girl, Mohini is suave and urbane. She is an upcoming radio-artist. She likes all good things of life and looks at the world around her in terms of aesthetic values. Her heart is full of love for her husband and she wants to be admired and loved by him in turn. But what does she get? Only disappointment. Disappointments breeding estrangement. Sharma maintains: "The marriage between Jaydev and Mohini symbolizes the union of asceticism and aestheticism. Jaydev is an embodiment of ascetic qualities; while Mohini is an incarnation of the aesthetic and emotional side of human life."[3]

Her modern attitudes are detested by her mother-in-law who is in a way the ruthless past re-incarnated. She is all for the family tradition whereas Mohini is against such a stifling and compartmentalizing way of life. For her, tradition is a straightjacket. She is jaded with such a hackneyed and stereotyped way of life. In reality mother represents the Big House which is "much more than a residence . . . a way of living, a stern discipline and iron tradition."[4] Jaydev had made Mohini aware of the fact that she will have to adjust herself to a great extent to the traditional life pattern of the Big House. Thus Mohini feels lonely and lovelorn. At first Mohini finds life at the Big House almost unbearable. Her mother-in-law is stern and exacting and puts a number of restraints upon her. Mohini's wearing a gay-coloured saree as she becomes a new bride irritates her. She likes Mohini all covered by a white cotton sheet instead of a "mill-made saree." She tells her that modern songs are trash. They make no sense and that Mohini should sing religious songs only. She does not like her climbing a tree perch as it is a very unbecoming thing for the young mistress of the Big House. She scoffs at Mohini's putting on the glass and lac bangles. Thus the Big House makes heavy demands on its young mistress—demands that she "finds unreasonable" and demands that "will have to be met with patience and a spirit of give and take." (78) There is no end to prohibitions and restraints on Mohini, which finally brings about the disintegration of her marital and conjugal identity. Subdued by these "straitjackets," Mohini falls into a tortuous state of loneliness and isolation. Yet she shows great fortitude and stoic forbearance. She has patience to bear the brunt of her hapless lot.

In course of time, Mohini tries to adjust herself to the old ways and modes of life in a rural society and in this process of acculturation, her identity also changes:

> The young mistress of the Big House took deeper colour from her life everyday. Slowly she fitted herself to the rural design. Her sprightliness, her quick girlish laugh, she easily subdued. The mother was a ruthless teacher. (130)

Music for Mohini is a novel of tensions—tensions between mind and body—the cravings of the flesh and the demands of the spirit. It is a tension between the mind of the husband and the body of the wife, a tension between East and West, village and town, tradition and modernity, the daughter-in-law and the mother-in-law. Marital discord between husband and wife forms the thematic focus of the novel. Mohini and her husband, Jaydev, play their part, but at no time in their life, do they trust at a common point. Srinivasa Iyengar observes: "It is the difference in the intellectual level of husband and wife and the consequences of this gulf forms the integral part of the theme of the novel, *Music for Mohini*."[5]

Music for Mohini presents a microcosmic picture of convention-ridden society. It shows that below the smooth and unruffled tenor of human life, there is a simmering of discontent and a recalcitrant and disgruntled voice. Jaydev tells Mohini that it is their duty to defy conventional and superstitious beliefs: "We're fighting ignorance and superstition, aren't we? We are fighting the false clay foot gods. They've had their day and now they must quit." (203) Even at a crucial juncture of her life, when her mother-in-law commands her to bow to superstition, she fancies she hears the voice of her father urging defiance:

> Do not bow down to such insult. You are the new India. The old orthodox ways have been our yoke, have enslaved us. Let us be free. (204)

As has been pointed out earlier, the loneliness and forlornness of Mohini is on account of the temperamental incompatibility between the husband and the wife. Brought up in two entirely different milieus, they are poles apart from each other. Jaydev is a visionary and an idealist. He expects his wife to be different from an ordinary young woman with basic physical needs and requirements. He sees her as "Gargi" or "Maitreyi." "No household dredge nor decorative being but an intellectual striding beside man in a tireless quest for knowledge." (71)

Jaydev wants Mohini to be with him in everything he does. Himself a scholar of eminence, he is disappointed to learn that there is no scholarship in his wife. Moreover a grave mistake that Jaydev makes is to discern between spiritual love and physical love and to treat them as two separate ideals. This is against the codes of real or true love since real love cannot be attained unless the physical and spiritual aspects of love are in tune with each other and unless they exist in the same being as two harmonious entities.

Mohini, on the other hand, stands for life. She rebels against the coldness and artificiality of the pattern sought to be imposed on her. But as time rolls on she arrives at the epiphanic realization that she has to learn and grow, she has to modify her stand and make all concessions and adjustments if she is to play the role of a wife and the mistress of an illustrious house—the Big House. She has her duties to her husband—chiefly that of helping him in a pragmatic way in furthering his programmes of social work. Hence, she makes a conspicuous and significant beginning by conducting classes for women of the village imparting them some elementary general education. Husband and wife now seem to ascend to a common pedestal. They develop a common interest in selfless public work. This sharing of interests brings them closer to each other and puts an end to reticence and reserve" on one side and "suspicion and mistrust" on the other. Gradually we find that an impulsive girl like Mohini is transformed into an understanding and competent housewife. Thus, the protagonist moves from alienation to identification.

References

1. Lila Ray, "Bhabani Bhattacharya, A Profile," *Indian Literature*, Vol. XI, No. 2, April-July 1968, p. 112.
2. Bhabhani Bhattacharya, *So Many Hungers!* (Bombay: Jaico, 1964), p. 28.
3. K.K. Sharma, *Bhabani Bhattacharya, His Vision and Themes* (New Delhi: Abhinav, 1989), p. 103.
4. Bhabhani Bhattacharya, *Music for Mohini* (Bombay: Jaico, 1964), p. 78.
5. K.R. Srinivasa Iyengar, *Indian Writing in English* (Bombay: Asia, 1962), p. 52.

Sindi Oberoi: Arun Joshi's Alienated Hero

Arun Joshi's novels portray the traumas and tensions, probing and pinning of the contemporary man through an exploration of the lacerated psyche of the characters. They register the existential dilemmas and predicaments of the incarcerated self and limn out the harried experiences of the protagonists in a philosophically stifling and morally stultifying world. Isolated from the self as well as the society, Joshi's characters are forlorn and lovelorn. They are so obsessively and neurotically involved in the mundane affairs of life that they fail to choose and decide the tenor of their life. Experiencing the "disgusting absurdity" and "void" of existence, they discover meaning and value through self-probing and self-exploration. Joshi makes an exploratory exposition of the self through perceptions of the past and through the alienational experiences of the present. Alienation of the self in Joshi often leads to the quest for identity.

Joshi does not write a novel according to a set of theories. Rather, he grapples with the psychic moments and situations in human life. A great artist of psychological insight, he delves deep into the human psyche to unveil the hidden and mute motives and impulses behind the individual's mental odyssey. "My novels," says Joshi, "are essentially attempts towards a better understanding of the world and myself. If I didn't write, I imagine I would use some other medium to carry on my exploration."[1] His novels anatomize the self and centripetalize its involvement in the alienation from socio-psychic forces. The paper intends to study Sindi's alienation.

The Foreigner, Arun Joshi's first novel, written in the form of remembrance of things past, probes the existential predicament of Sindi Oberoi, the nowhere man. O.P. Bhatnagar observes: "A strange feeling of aloneness and aloofness . . . permeates the entire narrative and provides the necessary texture and structure to the novel."[2] In her review of the novel, Meenakshi Mukherjee describes Sindi as "a perennial outsider."[3]

Sindi is portrayed as isolated from the world. Alienated, he falls a prey to inaction and indecision. At the outset, he is shown maintaining a shockingly apathetic attitude to the death of Babu Rao Khemka:

> They uncovered his face and I turned in spite of myself.
> "Will you please look at the body, Mr. Oberoi?"
> "No," I said quickly, "Don't bother."[4]

Babu's death has a paralyzing effect on his mind. It makes him desperately confused: "It was rush hour and the Boston crowd milled around me. I stood on the pavement and tried to think. Nothing came to my mind except the rumble of engines and the screeching of tyres." (6)

Having lost his parents, at the age of four, Sindi is brought up by his uncle settled in Kenya. He gets his school education in Kenya, higher education in Engineering in England, and finally lands up a job in the United States. But wherever he is, he is an alien. His having been brought up in a multicultural milieu gives him a sense of detachment, which he seems to relish throughout his life. He does not belong anywhere. Completely rootless, he is alienated culturally as well as spiritually. Even in Delhi, he feels an outsider: "I was considered quite a misfit. My foreign background stood against me." (15) Sindi has a temperament for remaining aloof from the mainstream of life and hence occasionally he "ran into a lone beauty hidden away in this crowd of obesity." (16)

Hysterically stalked by Babu's ghost, he desperately watches his past overtake him. He wished the veil that masked the gloom of his existence would forever remain drawn. Having a deep-seated abhorrence for faces since they disown him and generate in him feelings of attachment and involvement, he feels lonely at the sight of the distorted faces in a cheap mirror behind a bar. Even the crowded room does not give him any sense of belongingness: "I drank and watched the crowd bob up and down in the huge mirror behind the bar. All those faces distorted in the cheap mirror made me feel even more like an alien." (23) Cut off from the human world, Sindi frantically desires human communication: "I wished I could talk to somebody." (25) But could he? No. Born an Indian, "he had been spat upon." (29) He is a castaway all agog to carve out a niche for himself. June Blyth very lucidly ventilates the outlandish nature of Sindi: "There is something strange about you, you know. Something distant. . . . I have a feeling you'd be a foreigner anywhere." (33)

Sindi is isolated from the human world. In religion too, he faces the same music: "Anyway I can't really be called a Hindu. My mother was English and my father, I am told, a sceptic." (33) His responses to life are coloured by his childhood deprivation of love from his parents. Being brought up in a loveless world, he harbours in him a deep sense of insecurity and unreality. Things seem to have an ephemeral existence for him as he tells June: "Nothing ever seems real to me, leave alone permanent. Nothing seems very important." (113) His insecure and sequestered life grudges him to love others as well as be loved by others. He admits: "I was not the kind of man one could love: I had learnt that long ago." (38) His lackadaisical attitude to life urges him to deny the reality and permanence of existence. It is this attitude which spawns in him a fear of involvement: "I don't want to get involved. I repeated to myself. Everywhere I turned I saw involvement." (170) He is so much scared of attachment and involvement that he is even afraid to make love. The words of his uncle still linger in his mind: "To love is to invite others to break your heart." (78)

Unlike Babu, Sindi's forlorn self endeavours to assess its involvement in the estrangement from the family and society: "I worked in New York for a few weeks, just enough to finish the project I had started. As it had happened after Babu's death the laboratory provided me a sanctuary where I could forget my conflicts, at least at the conscious level. But in the inner recesses of my mind the trial went on. Each day the judges met and examined the witnesses. My parents, my uncle, my lovers, Babu and June, their parents, and finally myself, one by one all were called by the invisible judges and asked to give their evidence. Under normal conditions this would have been painful but after the shock of June's death it came as a great therapeutic process. I felt as if some indefatigable surgeon was cleansing up my soul with the sharp edge of his scalpel." (195)

Arun Joshi's exploration of the lone self of Sindi is indeed a great therapeutic process. Besides, Joshi lays bare the different planes of consciousness through which Sindi passes. A sense of guilt overawes him after the death of Babu. He has an unconscious and inscrutable fear that he has caused Babu's death. Thus he imagines of being tried in a court. This psychic awareness coming to his disconsolate self makes him dejected. But the memory of Babu's death keeps on "growing and probing . . . ripping dry scars open and dipping into old wounds," (48) making him more and more estranged. Sindi was so sensitive to words and phrases, that they sent him "racing back through the skeleton of dead years." (47) Totally withdrawn he becomes an alien insider. He is in the society but not with the society: "I had no social life to speak of." (45) He has no ambition to move up. Indecision rules his life. His pointless and shaky self-wobbling between involvement and detachment makes him drift like a flotsam in the main of life. He does not love but toys with the charms of love just to have a smack of it. Though physically attached, emotionally and spiritually he remains alienated. As he tells June about his relationship with Kathy:

> "Did you love her?"
> "No I had only wanted to possess her." (67)

And again he didn't love her because he "didn't want to get involved." (70) With June also Sindi is only physically attached. He lustily hankers for her body: "I wanted to possess her as I had never wanted to possess anyone before." (71) Sindi's plight reminds one of Torvald Helmer in *A Doll's House* who too wanted to possess Nora just as he possessed the furniture in the house. Love here is isolated from its elixir. It is this possessive love of Sindi that renders his life insecure, bringing in its wake existential anguish and agony. But passionate moments of ecstatic lust, almost bacchanalian, reveal to us that the cause of Sindi's estrangement lay within him. It was of his own making and all his preaching of detachment and non-involvement is but the 'apotheosis of foppery and folly.' He is unable to harmonize and reconcile his sayings with his doings. Look at the 'Mr. Hyde' aspect of Sindi: "I slipped my hand under her dress . . . she lay down in my arms again, her body shivered with passion. Desire rose within me like water behind a broken dam. I nearly cried with the burden of my lust." (81) The imagery of the 'broken dam' is an apt indication of the estranged plight of Sindi. Like the sweeping water of the broken dam, his desires within him, his lust for carnal pleasures bring his ruin.

Sindi has the desire to be a saint but he believes that "it is difficult to be a saint." (81) He is a splintered mirror who broods over the ions of his detachment, their gains and losses. And it eventually results in his being mocked like a detestable buffoon: "the losses mocked me like an abominable joker." (81) Sindi's foreignness makes him morosely passive. He gives in to the 'call' from within. Throughout the novel, we find him passing through variegated moods and attitudes. The memory of Kathy does not allow him to develop a harmonious relationship with June who frets for him. What he gives her is but a part of her lovelorn self. Her presence escalates his sense of guilt and aggravates his despair. He feels insanity creeping into his being: "What made matters worse was the fact that nearly everytime we met, June told me that she loved me. This only aggravated the burden of my guilt." (85) He is afraid of marriage and all familial ties: "I was only aware of a dull fear. I was afraid of possessing anybody and I was afraid of being possessed, any marriage meant both." (106) It is this attitude that prevents him from being spiritually attached to June. Rootless, he feels lost. Feeling of lostness sags his life. A ruffled and distraught Sindi drags drowsily through the sapless ordeal of existence. Finding his life a burden, he contemplates suicide. His hopping from one land to another as an escape from the heavy taxation of life lands him nowhere. In a Scotland village, he enlarges on his problems with a Catholic priest but the priest fails to provide him any solution. The very hollowness and vanity of his existence dawns upon him at the age of twenty-five. He ruminates over the nausea of his own life: "And yet all shores are alien when you don't belong anywhere. Twenty-fifth Christmas on this planet, twenty five years largely wasted in search of wrong things in wrong places. Twenty five years gone in search of peace, and what did I have to show for achievement: a ten stone body that had to be fed four times a day, twenty eight times a week. This was the sum of a life time striving." (92)

Sindi is unable to carve out a niche for himself. He remains an outsider everywhere. He belongs to no land: "I wondered in what way, if any, did I belong to the world that roared beneath my apartment window. Somebody had begotten me without a purpose and so far I had lived without a purpose, unless you could call the search for peace a purpose. . . . Perhaps I felt like that because I was a foreigner in America. But then what difference would it have made if I had lived in Kenya or India or any other place for that matter? It seemed to me that I would still be a foreigner. My foreignness lay within me and I could not leave myself behind wherever I went." (61)

Sindi's estranged plight symbolizes the suffering of the modern man, his malaise and incarceration. A man of no land and no culture, Sindi leads a near bohemian life without any sense of morality, without any sense of purpose. He limps and drags through life in quest of meaning. Imprisoned and immured within his self, his assays to flee the absurdity and conundrum of existence in search of meaning and reality end in futility. He realizes the error in conceiving such escapades: "Like many of my breed, I believed erroneously that I could escape from a part of myself by hopping from one land to another." (176)

Sindi sees an ogre in the invariable structures of both American and Indian cultures. Hence to encounter this katabolic element in both the civilizations, he adopts a callous attitude. His isolation turns to madness, a madness which he accepts as a reality. While in bed with June, he finds communication vanishing fast; he has no language for her to understand him since 'the eternal joker' snickered within him to mock at the game of omission of life's essential offering—human love:

> Marriage wouldn't help, June. We are alone, both you and I. That is the problem. And our aloneness must be resolved within. . . . The Statue of Liberty promises you this optimism. But in my world many things are inevitable and what's more, most of them are sad and painful. I can't come to your world. I have no escape, June. I just have no escape. (126)

But Sindi's sense of desperation is strange and unusual. Though he is not in a position to make a tryst with the world of June, to fuse with it, yet he "couldn't stop thinking of June." (129) Such is the intensity of his attachment to June that he can't bear separation from her. It drives him insane: "The strain grew so great that I almost lost ability to think logically for any length of time, often I suspected I was going mad." (129) He had permitted himself "to become a battlefield where the child and the adult warred unceasingly." (129) June is never an alien to him, never a stranger to his world but a part of it. Her departure dumbfounds him: "For a while it left me completely dazed. . . . For me it was just one long coma. It was as if somebody had given me a big dose of anesthesia, it left me completely numb. I had known all along that June would go away someday but I didn't realise she had already become a part of me. Our separation had been like an unforeseen abortion." (141) Finally, the death of June breaks his attachment to himself and makes him self-alienated. Sindi represents the stifled and choked voice of human agony and despair, not any individual malaise. He witnesses the pangs of insanity beneath both the occidental and oriental civilizations stemming from a cloistered sensibility of despair.

In reality, Sindi was in love with June but he gave himself the air "to remain detached under the circumstances." (126) Hence he avoids getting married to her. It is his "high" talk of "detachment and non-involvement" that alienates June from him. We reckon a sense of contradiction and dichotomy in the character of Sindi who on the one hand talks of the lofty ideals of the *Gita* like detachment but on the other hand develops intimate relationships with many girls and even has sex with them. This discrepancy between what he is and what he desires to be makes him a veritable joker and his estrangement humorous and amusing. At times, he feels like laughing to himself. Born and brought up in Kenya by his uncle he was not an African. His parents didn't belong to Africa. He was neither an Englishman because his father was an Indian. But was he American? America was "too sterilized," "too clean and optimistic and empty." (89) He had not seen India till he was twenty-six. His coming to India was decided by the flip of a coin: "He took out a dime and flipped it high into the air. 'Heads for Nigeria,' he said. The coin showed tails, New Delhi."

In fact Sindi's escape from one country to another is just a change of scene, the theatre remaining the same. Babu's death had drained away the elixir of life from Sindi, "most of what he had cherished in life was taken away." (175) He feels within him an "aching void." Deserted and anguished, he broods over Babu's death:

> Babu had kicked out all my beliefs and disproved all my theories. I felt like a desert or like a vast field of naked oaks in winter time. I felt more alone and naked in the world than I had ever felt before. . . . The feeling of nakedness in the hands of existence grew with every passing day and a strong urge possessed me to once again roam the streets of the world. I didn't know where I would go or what the future held for me, but one thing was certain: my search had to continue. . . . I only wanted a place where I could experiment with myself. (175)

Hence Sindi's quest for identity is an exploration and experimentation with the palpitating rhythm of life. Sindi's alienation turns him cynical: "I was cynical and exhausted, grown old before my time, weary with my own loneliness." (152) Uprooted, Sindi becomes aimless and without a fixed purpose in life, he grows unreasonable and surly: "Look at me, I have no roots. I have no system of morality. . . . I have no reason to be one thing rather than another. . . . I don't even have a reason to live." (136) His cynicism and angst make him utterly indifferent to what he studied and the profession he pursued. In Boston he takes his doctorate degree in mechanical engineering but he least cares for the profession: "I cared two pins for all the mechanical engineers in the world." (14)

Sindi has a number of ideas but he fails to act upto them. Hence his alienation from the self. His desire to remain free and uninvolved is but an illusion. He has a number of affairs—with Anna, Kathy, June and others. He is only "fancy free." Fully aware of the depth of his intimacy with June, he becomes nervous: "How long could I stay free! . . . Our hands would soon give place to our bodies and then the worst will come; our souls will get involved. It was only a matter of time." (70)

Commenting on the detachment of Sindi, K. Radha aptly observes: "The story of Sindi's relationship with June is a story of the gradual breaking down of the barriers of detachment and non-involvement that had built up all his life. He was quite conscious of what was happening and he tried valiantly to resist it, but in vain."[5] With the passing away of June, all his objectivity and plea for detachment break down. Ultimately he has the searing realization, a revelation that true detachment "consisted of right action and not an escape from it." (92) The cynical Sindi doesn't remain detached in the real sense of the term. He has his epiphanic moments too. It is Muthu, a low paid employee in Khemka's office, who makes an earnest plea to Sindi to take charge of Khemka's business and save the hapless lot of people like him from starvation. Muthu convinces him that "Sometimes detachment lies in actually getting involved." (225) Sindi takes on the charge of the office and effects several changes and sets the ball rolling. The business gets a boost with his disinterested service: "The fruit of it was really not my concern." (228) Thus the cynical Sindi becomes a man of action truly involved in the affairs of life. The rootless Sindi finds a direction and purpose in the 'sick hurry and divided aims' of life. No more hopping for Sindi. On the personal and private side too, he gets involved with Sheila, Babu's sister without any sexual motive as he had with the girls like Kathy and June whom he had met earlier in his life.

Sindi is not alienated from the society; he is outside it. He is more a stranger to himself than to the society. Shuttling between attachment and detachment, love and hate, participation and withdrawal, he drifts in the flux of time. Throughout, we find him indulging in an interminable and ransacking dialogue with his self to resolve the existential tangles and ties of life which attain consummation in his final decision to take over the charge of Mr. Khemka's office and even his tender love for Sheila Khemka. He is not a "perennial outsider," as Meenakshi Mukherjee points out. He is strangely alienated. He finally settles down in India for he truly belongs to it. From a life of alienation in America and England, he moves to a life of identification in India.

Unlike Srinivas in Kamala Markandaya's *The Nowhere Man*, he moves from self-alienation to self-identification, from uninvolvement to involvement. Srinivas bears his estrangement and isolation with stoic forbearance but Sindi becomes neurotically impatient and ventilates his isolationism as a defence mechanism. He is humorously isolated. His detachment is amusingly ambivalent. His philosophical outbursts about renunciation are a masquerade, a veneer to hide his inner compulsions and motivations. His alienation is of the soul, not of geography. It lay within him and propelled him from crisis to crisis. He is not alienated like Monsieur Meursault in Camus's *The Outsider*. Meursault's isolation is inextricably woven into the fabric of his being. His is a case of total isolation. He remains an outsider to all that happens to him whereas Sindi's is an instance of fractioned and fragmentary isolation since he is not completely cut off from his surroundings. He is psychically present in the happenings around him though physically distanced. All said, Sindi Oberoi is consciously alienated and his alienation is metaphysically confounding in the context of the fluidity of his intercultural background.

References

1. Reply to M.R. Dua, dated September 3, 1971.
2. O.P. Bhatnagar, "Arun Joshi's *The Foreigner*. A Critique of East and West," *Journal of Indian Writing in English*, 1 and 2 (July 1973), pp. 13-14.
3. *Quest*, 60 (Jan.-March 1969), p. 101.
4. Arun Joshi, *The Foreigner* (New Delhi: Hind, 1968), p. 5.
5. K. Radha, "From Detachment to Involvement: The Case of Sindi Oberoi," *The Fictional World of Arun Joshi*, ed. R.K. Dhawan (New Delhi: Classical, 1986), p. 180.

The Problem of Alienation and the Quest for Identity in Arun Joshi's Novels

The fictional world of Arun Joshi postulates the clash between alienated self and the socio-cultural forces. The protagonists of his novels are subjected to extreme social, cultural and psychological pressures. The inter-generational tensions engendered with the changing ethos make increasing demands on the individual and contribute in creating a void which is nothing but a chaotic feeling of rootlessness in life, incessantly haunting their psyche and corroding every sphere of their life. This awareness of rootlessness and consequential anxiety is the keynote of Joshi's existential vision of the plight of modern men. The protagonists discover the meaning and value of life probing through the dark mossy labyrinths of the soul. This search for identity is the leitmotif of Arun Joshi's novels.

Joshi's protagonists are confused men who find themselves participating in a wild rat race with no clear goal in mind. The economic drudgery, social pressures, the dissolution of old faiths and dogmas and uncertain loyalties mercilessly crumple their life and wound their psyche. So they adopt a cynical attitude towards life and the established social norms and values.

They rebel against the socio-cultural pressures and pursue their quest for identity. Through self-probing and self-exploration, through perceptions of the past and alienating experiences of the present they discover the higher values of life.

Alienation in Joshi's novels stems from a clash between the socio-cultural and psychological forces. The urge for alienation arises out of social maladjustment and emotional insecurity. Incertitude leads to the quest for identity which is a psychic revolt on the part of the alienated self. This "quest motif" operates more on the socio-psychic plane than on the metaphysical plane. The quest attains spiritual dimensions at certain levels. "My novels," says Joshi, "are essentially attempts towards a better understanding of the world and of myself."[1] Joshi was influenced by Albert Camus and other existentialist writers: "I did read Camus and Sartre, I liked *The Plague* and read *The Outsider*. I might have been influenced by them."[2]

In *The Foreigner*, Arun Joshi presents Sindi Oberoi as a confused man, a product of diverse cultures. His mixed parental blood and upbringing in an alien country instills in him a sense of rootlessness. Devoid of a spiritual and cultural anchorage, and being brought up in a loveless world, he harbours in him a deep sense of insecurity and unreality. Against this cultural background Sindi cultivates a sense of detachment to overpower the sad experiences of life. He is a self-deceiver, detached with a sense of delusion.

He even avoids marriage because he is afraid of all familial ties: "I was afraid of possessing anybody and I was afraid of being possessed and marriage meant both."[3] His parentage and early life made him the nowhere man.

Sindi's alienation is of the soul and not of geography. He comes to India in search of his ancestral roots. But he fails to carve out a niche for himself. He finds himself as good as a foreigner in India as in America: "My foreignness lay within me and I would not leave myself behind wherever I went." (61) Rootless and alienated, Sindi becomes quite cynical and detached. Gradually he realises that detachment does not mean an escape or isolation but it means devotional sacrifice and involvement. Sindi asserts his identity by fixing his goal in life and settling down to a domestic life in India with Sheela. Hari Mohan Prasad observes "From Boston to Delhi has been a journey from alienation to arrival, from selfishness to sacrifice, from an anomie responsible to himself, to a member of mankind, from being to becoming."[4] From 'detachment to involvement' constitutes the odyssey of Sindi's search for identity.

The search for identity in *The Strange Case of Billy Biswas* assumes a spiritual dimension. It is born out of the socio-cultural clashes to which Billy is subjected. Although Billy belongs to a highly placed bourgeois society with good ancestral background, he feels stifled. He is alienated from the higher middle class society in which he is nursed and nurtured. He suffers from acute social alienation and he cannot identify himself with the society to which he belongs. He often wondered: "Who was I? Where had I come from? Where was I going."[5]

The artificiality and pretensions of the bourgeois society are repulsive to him. In a psychic revolt against the existing social norms, he intends to discard his family. He feels a strong force, urkraft . . . a primitive force," (101) a deep attraction towards primitivism and the unpretentious life style of nomads. This force compels him to leave his family and seek refuge in the Satpura hills. The natural beauty of Bilasia charms him and he feels a deep satisfaction after his physical union with her. The primitive life style suits him but his search for the higher values of life does not end. "Billy is a refugee from civilization." (140) He says: "Layer upon layer was peeled off me until nothing but my primitive self was left trembling." (121) Such a feeling irks him. He could not rest. His search for identity is more than a psychological process. It is a spiritual quest. Billy says to Romesh: "Becoming a primitive was only a first step, a means to an end. Of course I realised it only after I ran away. I realised that I was seeking something else." (189) This search for the higher values of life becomes the crux of Billy's life but is cut short by his tragic end.

In *The Apprentice*, Joshi portrays Ratan Rathore as a young man from an impoverished middle class family. He has to find his own way and pay his own price in this world. With his mind full of idealism and patriotic fervour, Ratan steps into the arena of job hunting only to be disappointed again and again. To Ratan, it was money that "brought respect and brought security. Money made friends, money succeeded where all else failed. There were many laws . . . but money was law into itself."[6] He mortgages his integrity and idealism for money and a position in society. As he acquires wealth and power, his personality disintegrates and his conscience reels and groans under the weight of his sins. His dying conscience pricks him but he does not give in. The tussle between idealism and morality on the one hand and the craze for money and career on the other creates a void in his psyche. He wants to extricate his identity from the heap of corruption but fails. The ghastly death of his friend, the Brigadier, shakes him out of his moral inertia. He confesses to Himmat Singh: "There are many sorrows in the world but there is nothing in this world to match the sorrow of a wasted life." (140) In this novel Joshi portrays the most acute kind of self-alienation.

Ratan wants to free himself from the shackles of a valueless urban civilization. Hence, his search for his identity in doing humble and humiliating jobs like shining the shoes at the temple door. His is the spiritual quest for a clean and healthy mind. His repentance and his penance help him to realise his self-identity in this disintegrating world.

Joshi's *The Last Labyrinth* probes into the turbulent inner world of an industrialist Som Bhaskar whose Indian cultural background and foreign education are at perpetual war with each other. A close scrutiny of his personality reveals insecurity and hollowness which propel him from one goal to another. He is relentlessly driven by undefined hungers—hunger for money, hunger for fame, hunger for Anuradha's body and a hunger for some spiritual sublimity.

He tells Anuradha: "I'll tell you what is wrong . . . I am dislocated. My mind is out of focus. There is something sitting right in front of me and I cannot see it."[7] This something is his other identity, his philistine self. All his life Som has sung the strident song, "I want, I want." (11) This search for the higher values of life involves many probings into the haunted labyrinth of the psyche. Unaware of the nature of his wants, he hankers after Aftab's shares. The spiritual influence of Gargi is like balm to his wounded soul but he refuses to accept her spiritual guidance. Som's dilemma is the predicament of the modern man. Born out of the diverse cultural influences his problems disturb him. The Western world of science and rationalism, the Indian world of faith and transcendentalism contribute to his already confused mind. He is completely alienated from his self and gropes about in his search for identity. His mind is like a labyrinth where there are mazes. At length, he realises the futility of his running after wealth. Anuradha's disappearance leaves him psychologically and emotionally wounded. In sheer desperation, he cries out:

> Anuradha, if there is a God and if you have met him and if He is willing to listen then Anuradha, my soul, tell Him, tell this God to have mercy upon me. Tell Him I am of so many fears, so much doubting. (223)

The novel. according to K.R. Srinivasa Iyengar, is a delineation of the pestilent-stricken modern world where people have lost their sense of identity. It is "a paradigm of the contemporary diseased world where discontents grow their own pestilential vapours, and self-doomed humanity—lacking faith, lacking grace—is tragically resigned to being suffocated by them in the 'Last Labyrinth.'"[8]

Joshi's last novel, *The City and the River*, treats the predicament of his characters in a hostile milieu. The crisis of the individual is replaced by the socio-political crisis of the city which represents the whole community. It is the symbol of the collective identity of the mass. The words of the professor reveal a feeling of hopelessness: "God gave me life that I might serve this earth: I have squandered it on a bauble."[9] In a relentless search for their identities, they withdraw from human ambience to natural environs of peace and tranquillity but here too they find no repose and equanimity. They are nowhere men in quest of a somewhere place. They grope about in a blind alley. Confronted by the self and problems of existence, they fall into the labyrinthine flux of life and become searingly aware of the inevitability of death, its tragic finality and existential certainty. Hence, their search for identity, for authentic selfhood, in the teeth of debilitating and disintegrating socio-political forces, is doomed to end in fiasco. They compromise but not with life and creativity, but with death and destructivity.

The novels of Arun Joshi successfully reveal the subtleties and complexities of modern life. They have excelled in exemplifying the existential dilemma of the self in the society. As Edmund Fuller observes: "In our age man suffers not only from persecution, famine and ruin but from an inner problem . . . a conviction of isolation, randomness and meaninglessness in his way of existence."[10] In Joshi, this meaninglessness leads to the search for identity, "a perpetual quest for reality."[11] Joshi's protagonists explore that mysterious underworld which is the human soul. His novels delineate the spiritual agony of his lonely questers. To Joshi, life's meaning lies not "in the glossy surfaces of pretensions but in the dark mossy labyrinths of the soul."[12]

Sindi Oberoi, observes O.P. Bhatnagar, has "a strange feeling of aloneness and aloofness."[13] But Meenakshi Mukherjee views Sindi as "a perennial outsider."[14] In the long run, Sindi realises that his foreignness lay within him and was an integral part of him. His obsession with the notion of detachment makes him shirk his responsibility. Like Camus's Meursault, he is always bored with the world and like Neil of Philip Roth's *Good Bye, Columbus*, he does not want to shoulder even ordinary responsibilities. In a revolt against the societal pre-conceived values and traditions, he adopts an attitude of non-attachment. In *The Strange Case of Billy Biswas*, the protagonist Billy rebels against the sham bourgeois society and its artificial way of living.

He is attracted towards the ancient and primitive forces of pristine sublimity. In a revolt against the modern life and its hollow meaninglessness he takes refuge in the arms of Bilasia amidst the tribal people. Ratan in *The Apprentice* gets swallowed in the dirty, murky waters of corruption despite his better self. His patriotic feelings get crumpled under the burden of joblessness, poverty and hunger. But when realisation dawns on him, he takes to shoe-shinning to redeem his past misdeeds. Although Ratan is steeped in corruption, he lashes out against corruption in his writings in journals and newspapers. These confessional expressions are the revolts of his overburdened soul. *The Last Labyrinth* explores the turbulent inner world of a wealthy young Indian, Som Bhaskar. The diverse influences of his mother's spirituality and father's rational scientific theories confuse his mind. His soul always cries out for something of which he is himself unaware. He clamours after wealth and lust without finding any peace of mind. The search for spiritual bliss and a true identity becomes the goal of his life. All the angst-ridden protagonists of Joshi are relentlessly in search of an identity unblemished by the filth of the modern corruption and its degenerating forces. They flounder through the labyrinthine lanes of their inner psyche to reach some sort of illumination. Madhusudan Prasad observes that Joshi's novels "are singularised by certain existentialist problems and the resultant anger, agony, psychic quest and the like."[15]

Commenting on *The Last Labyrinth*, Inna Walter says: "Arun Joshi plunges deeper into the depths of the eternal queries that have perplexed man's consciousness from time immemorial"[16] and we agree with the critics since in Joshi the search for identity is spiritual stemming from a rebellion against the degenerating forces of the society. Billy questions "Why this constant blurring of reality? Who am I? Who are my parents? My wife? My child?"[17] This question reveals Billy's spiritual quest for a true identity which has been haunting human minds since eternity. Although critics say that Joshi's *The City and the River* focuses on the aspect of authenticity and is different from his earlier novels, it is difficult to agree with them. Like Joshi's earlier works, *The City and the River* is also based on the individual's search for his true self. Thus, we can conclude that in Joshi's novels the search for identity assumes personal dimension and is related to the growth of the individual's inner self.

References

1. M.R. Dua., "Reply of Joshi," Sep. 3, 1971, qtd. R.K. Dhawan, *The Fictional World of Arun Joshi* (New Delhi: Classical, 1986).
2. Purabi Bannerji, "Interview with Joshi," *The Sunday Statesman*, Feb. 27, 1983, qtd. R.K. Dhawan.
3. Arun Joshi, *The Foreigner* (New Delhi: Hind, 1968), p. 106.
4. Madhusudan Prasad, "Arun Joshi," *Indian English Novelists* (New Delhi: Sterling, 1982), p. 151.
5. Arun Joshi, *The Strange Case of Billy Biswas* (New Delhi: Hind, 1971), p. 23.
6. Arun Joshi, *The Apprentice* (New Delhi: Orient Paperbacks, 1974), p. 20.

7. Arun Joshi, *The Last Labyrinth* (New Delhi: Vision, 1981), p. 107.
8. K.R. Srinivasa Iyengar, *Indian Writing in English* (New Delhi: Sterling, 1985), p. 243.
9. Arun Joshi, *The City and the River* (New Delhi: Orient Paperbacks, 1994), p. 103.
10. Edmund Fuller, *Man in Modern Fiction* (New York: Random House, 1958), p. 3.
11. Lionel Trilling, *The Liberal Imagination* (New York: Doubleday, 1953), p. 205.
12. R.S. Pathak, "Quest for Meaning in Arun Joshi's Novels," R.K. Dhawan, ed., *The Novels of Arun Joshi* (New Delhi: Prestige, 1992), p. 74.
13. O.P. Bhatnagar, "Arun Joshi's *The Foreigner*: A Critique of East and West," *Journal of Indian Writing in English*, 1 and 2 (July 1973), pp. 13-14. Qtd. S.P. Swain, "Sindi Oberoi: Arun Joshi's Alienated Hero in *The Foreigner*," R.K. Dhawan, ed., *Indian Literature Today* (New Delhi: Prestige, 1994).
14. Qtd. Meenakshi Mukherjee, *The Twice-Born Fiction* (New Delhi: Heinemann, 1971), p. 22.
15. Madhusudan Prasad, p. 151.
16. Inna Walter, "Arun Joshi's Vision of Life, Love, God and Death in *The Last Labyrinth*," Balarama Gupta, ed., *Studies in Indian Fiction in English* (Gulbarga: JIWE, 1987), p. 46.
17. Arun Joshi, *The Strange Case of Billy Biswas*, p. 93.

Search for Identity: A Study of Raja Rao's *The Serpent and the Rope*

Raja Rao's *The Serpent and the Rope* is an intricate medley of philosophy, religious systems and cultural history. Like R.K. Narayan's novels, it is not a realistic and humorously ironical portrayal of Indian reality but a philosophical exposition of Indian way of life. Mystifyingly bewildering, it postulates the intrinsic point of the novelist's thematic preoccupation. The novel is not only an assertion and affirmation of Indian values but an acute and melancholic longing for such affirmation which stems from one's being alienated from the core of one's self. The paper aims at a study of this sense of rootlessness and the consequent identity crisis that forms the thematic focus of the novel.

The novel opens with a note of deep anguish. At the very outset, Ramaswamy is delineated as a rootless being, awe-struck at his orphaned existence: "I am an orphan. Am I always going to be an orphan?"[1] It is this quest motif, which leads to his spiritual journey towards the realisation of a genuine Indian identity. Raja Rao is trying to probe the spiritual roots of his motherland through the rootlessness of his protagonist. The quest for the Absolute is portrayed through the psychic and intellectual encounters between an Indian husband and his French wife. Ramaswamy's realisation of his true Indian identity comes through a triangular pattern of relationship between his French intellectual wife Madeleine and his overt spiritual love for the Hindu princess Savitri. Intellectually and academically committed to an Indian interpretation of history, he has frequent recourses to the Vedantic concept of the Absolute consciousness in order to assert and justify the ruthless extermination of medieval heresies.

Ramaswamy is a brahmin who is "never contemporary." (125) Aware of his privileged stance in the Hindu social hierarchy as a Brahman, he struggles for the assertion of his Brahminhood through a metaphysical exploration into the quintessence of it. His quest for identity starts with "A Brahmin is he who knows Brahman" (5) and the quest ends with it too. True Brahminhood is that which "commences when you recognise yourself in your eternity." (215) But Ramaswamy's spatio-temporal involvement in the chronicle of life isolates him from the very purport of his quest. Instead of making a journey to Eternity, Ramaswamy, the Brahmin, makes a journey to the temporal world of "the historical sciences." (231) He oscillates between two polarised modes—of time and timeless, of history and metaphysics.

By profession, Ramaswamy is a historian but by tradition and nativity, he is a Brahmin, who exists beyond historical time: "There never was time, there never was history, there never was anything but Shivoham, Shivoham, I am Shiva, I am the Absolute." (197) There is no harmony between the academic identity of Rama and his religious identity. He feels ill at ease with his Indian identity because of the infrequent incursions of his historical self, which is rooted in the modern Western mode of Judaeo-Christianity and which fails to synthesise with the Indian timelessness. He is a scholar seeking a balance between his existential involvement with life and an intellectual quest for meaning. He is engaged in an intellectual and spiritual journey to reach out to future destinations. But he fails, since the intellect is out of tune with the spirit and the two seldom compromise. He is torn between the concept of timelessness—his Indian identity and a time-bound historical existence—his other identity, that of the historian. The presence of two opposing forces in his psyche—the historical West and the traditional India—keep on waning within his quagmired self. They never reconcile. Hence, his search for identity.

Ramaswamy could never get over the death of his mother—an irreparable and irretrievable loss. The death of the mother becomes a haunting obsession throughout his life, escalating his anguish and alienation: "When I was twenty-two I sat in a hotel—it was in the Pyrenees—and I sobbed, for I knew I would never see my mother again." (6) His anguish issues out of his being a "Being" in the historicity of human existence and his awareness of the laceration of isolation in conceivable time that death is the end and beyond it lurks nothingness, vacuum. He searingly feels the pangs of death: "There is no pain more acute than a pain unnameable, and all the shine of the world is only a prophecy, a shout that death, is, that one loses another." (133) The Vedantic concept that he so assiduously and avowedly cherishes and which crystallises in his mind with self-realisation, is but an intellectual conviction severed from his existential passions and predicaments.

Ramaswamy's attachment to his stepmother, to his sister Saroja and to Savitri, generate in him an awareness of the different facets of the feminine gender—mother, soror and concubine and he feels an inner vacuum. He realises the absence of something significant in his affinity with his French wife Madeleine. His encounter with the feminine principle symbolised in his relationship with little mother and his sister Saroja makes him able to reckon all of a sudden the cause of his alienation from Madeleine. The lack of feminine principle in Madeleine is manifested in her emotional incommunication. Madeleine is an individual feminist more concerned with the abstract concepts of individual human rights and the quest for personal independence, dismissing all socially defined roles. On the other hand, Rama is a relational feminist. An advocate of relational feminism, he stresses on women's rights as women in terms of their nurturing capacities in relation to men. Madeleine falteringly responds in love. She abhors contact: "Touch, as I have said, was always distasteful to her, so she liked the untouching Cathars, she loved their celibacy. . . . The bridge was anyhow there and could not be crossed." (15) Indeed, Rama could never cross the "bridge" between Madeleine and him. But, does the bridge endure? No. it crumbles and eventually topples, when she turns a Buddhist and assumes asceticism which denies "womanhood a right to exist." (170)

Ramaswamy, in contrast to his wife, is free from her emotional ossification. She is self-centred but he is an extrovert and can step out of the self and participate in the ceremonial ritual of life. He is an articulate and imaginative being. When she asks him, "What is it separates us, Rama?" he tells her, "India." (331)

Madeleine, the realist, is different from Rama, the Vedantin. She believes that one cannot transcend the realities one sees and feels. S. Nagarajan aptly affirms that she is a believer in the actual reality of the world and of the human person.[2] Thus, the tryst of Rama-Madeleine is a fusion of two contrary and polarised weltanschauung and hence the note of estrangement in their marital life. Madeleine's failure to form harmonious ties with Rama is on account of her dualism, the assertion that *purusha* and *prakriti* are two separate entities. She gradually drifts away from Rama's life into a state of asceticism. She moves from social communication to divine communion.

The husband-wife have a friend, an expatriate Russian, George, who is beginning to adopt Catholic mysticism. The three of them have prolonged metaphysical and mystical discussions. In the course of their deliberation, Madeleine shows more emotional response to George's feelings than to Ramaswamy's intellectual wanderings. This drives Ramaswamy to the feeling of envy. He feels de trop.

Deficient in feeling and sensation, Ramaswamy fails in emotionally communicating with Madeleine. His concern for the other is an organic need. He reflects: "I need the other in order to realise fully all the structure of my being," (190) and in order to realise, he must be free. For him, Savitri is the true woman, since in her there is an absence of freedom of choice: "For a woman to choose is to betray her biology" and because Madeleine ultimately chooses Buddhism, she is not the right woman for him. She is a centrifugal being whereas he is a "centripetal being." (195) Rama as a man and a husband is incomplete like Narayan's Marco. He is a partial man. This inadequacy of manhood is revealed in his callous attitude to Madeleine's grief over the death of her children. Madeleine's deep love for Ramaswamy goes unheeded and unresponded. He is an emotional stranger to her. The emotional sclerosis of Ramaswamy approximates a state of psychic buoyancy: "I lose you—I know I will lose you. And yet where can I go but to you?" (218) He has no commitments and assurances to offer: "Rama, tell me—tell me, that you love me?" (242) Rama's cold and lackadaisical response indicates his isolation and non-commitment: "I am mine and you Madeleine are a chunk of truth as the sun, the moon, the space or the stars." (242)

Ramaswamy is caught in the grip of an existential anguish. Orphaned, abandoned and impotent, his identity is forever lacerated and the gulf between "the Brahmin and I" (135) is never bridged. Rootless and homeless, he leads a hermetically co-cooned existence of timelessness, outside historicity. Through time, he seeks the timeless and through timeless, the unattainable. Thrown away into the flux of time, he is irrevocably carried away from his native ethos by the stream of existential history. His quest is a means to transcend his own mundane limitations and is an exploration of the essence of traditional values that can be assimilated into the self of an individual to forge a new identity. His obsessive concern for numbers is also an indication of his search for identity. At the end of his encounter with his other identity, he wails out: "There is nobody to go now: no home, no temple, no city, no climate, no age." (402) The pangs of rootlessness strike him with such finality, because of his existential anguish in an intrinsic and fundamental alienation from his native heritage. Time has impinged upon his eternal brahminic self. It has transformed him imperceptibly into a new being, a new entity, that is eternally isolated from the archaic ethos. Som P. Ranchan attributes Rama's alienation from his wife to his anima possession, but to me it is due to his intellectual hubris. The phenomenal reality of India is lost to Ramaswamy. Time has incarcerated him. An alien, even to his nativity, he avers: "I was born an exile and could continue to be one!" (376) Yet the Brahmin desperately struggles to cling to his Brahminic tradition. Severed from the archaic Hindu way of life, he expounds his philosophy, typically Indian, not in the context of the Upanishads but in relation to Plato and Nietzsche. His withdrawal from the traditional Brahmin life suggests a fundamental polarisation. He is stirred by an inscrutable and mysterious force, stronger than the concerted strength of an ancient tradition. A hypostatic call urges him in his quest. He says: "Mother mine, I will go." (149) Drawn into the vortex of existence by historical time, Ramaswamy longs for the Infinite and hence his quest for the Absolute and the Ultimate Reality. He disowns Madeleine's 'dualistic' Buddhism, since it is anti-Indian, the non-dual affirms the truth." (41) To Rama, "there is no world." (336) For him the only reality is the Absolute. Raja Rao has maintained that the meaning of life reveals when the duality resolves into non-duality. But this resolution does not occur in Ramaswamy's encounter with either Madeleine or Savitri. With both of them his affinity is marked by temporal isolation. Rama is the symbol of a mortal paradox. Though he himself declares: "the meaning of life, play," (205) yet he remains forever groping for a meaning, a value: "There must be something that exalts and explains why we are here and what is it we seek." (399)

In him there is a desperately dire need to effect dissociation since he never cherishes the feeling of a rapport between him and the world. He wants to run away, to withdraw from the mainstream of a mundane existence: "Man is a stranger to this earth." (136) "I must leave this world, I must leave, leave this world." (399) Cut off from eternity, Rama the Brahmin is captivatingly entangled in the anguish of time, which he seeks to annihilate. Turned away from his wife, he has an initial feeling of rootlessness but finally sets out on a spiritual odyssey to 'know thyself,' to find his lost self. The painful realisation of his own, spatio-temporal isolation weighs heavily on his soul. He feels dejected and vacant: "There is nobody to go now: no home, no temple, no climate, no age." (402) His agonising sense of alienation reduces him to a mere nothing, a cipher. He becomes a prey to incertitude and anxiety. The traumatic memories of the past crystallisingly creep into his sense and intensify his affliction. Truth prevails over him and on one dreadful night, he leaves for Travancore, searching for a spiritual Guru, a paraclete: "No, not a God but a Guru is what I need." (402)

K.R. Rao observes: "The theme of alienation effects a change of focus in the novel's total design. The deepening of Rama-Madeleine estrangement can be read as symbolic because it illustrates the unbridgeable disparity that exists between the two cultures—the East and the West. Both Rama and Madeleine succumb to the characteristic determinisms of their individual cultures."[4] Despite their efforts to transcend their own cultural limitations and attain a harmony in mutual personal understanding, they fail. Madeleine declines to involve herself in Rama's sense of values, his intuitive world of introspection. She dwells on an intellectual plane and wants to flee from his life. What is real for Rama is but a travesty of the real for her. Her love and fascination for India borders on false romanticism. Madeleine is torn by the conflicting demands of Hinduism, Buddhism and her own Christianity. Without a firm base, she drifts from one self to another. It aggravates her self-alienation, since Rama is a part of her feminine self. Recognizably, a relic of the Western predicament of identity-crisis and isolation, she is a fiasco in achieving a fusion of cultural and ethical values. Her attachment to India is only an infatuation, a snobbery. It is the dramatisation of her neurotic pride. Through the technique of juxtaposition and polarisation, Raja Rao has dramatically portrayed the Rama-Madeleine story of alienation, especially the latter's psychological and spiritual isolation. Madeleine's quest for identity drags her to the fringe of intellectual abstraction and her severance of her ties with Rama, symbolises her withdrawal from Reality, which completes her self-isolation. She realises the utter incompatibility of her views and concerns with Rama's vedantic values and rituals and gradually moves away from him. She even snaps all ties with him to emancipate herself from the bondage of an earthly life. She attains self-identification by equating her Catholicism with Buddhism. *The Serpent and the Rope* is indeed a quest for the Absolute. It can be considered as a novel of pilgrimage of a picaresque saint, Ramaswamy. The pilgrimage culminates in a symbolic and mystical marriage in London. Savitri becomes a "hypostatic presence." She serves as a catalyst to Rama's entry into a transcendental existence. Rama's realisation of his nativity becomes a reality and his search for a Guru becomes a spiritual need.

Ramaswamy, the pilgrim, participates in his metaphysical journeys both at the symbolic and literal plane. He is drawn to a focal point from where he sets out to assert his identity. Member of a specific religio-cultural ethos, he could perceive birth of a new being from his incarcerated self. His spiritual quest is structured around palpable and metaphysically perceptible socio-psychic movements and his inner predicament assumes the form of an internal struggle between antithetical forces and unresolved conflicts. His quest, though without any apocalyptic moment, is nevertheless real. It is self-affirmative and it crystallizes in the need of a Guru and a retreat from the world of illusion to the world of reality, from the serpent to the rope.

Madeleine tries to be other than herself and her world and hence her identity crisis. The genuine 'otherness' in her remains latent. She fails to realise: "We can only offer others what is ours." (123) It is her pseudo otherness which carries her away. She begins to identify more and more with her anti-self. But, Rama is never carried away. He is far from being impervious to the subtler savour of an alien culture. "Otherness" alienates Madeleine but in Rama, it gives vent to forces working towards understanding and assimilation. It makes Rama identify, together with a note of detachment which enables him to see more than "the other" can usually see itself. The Brahmin can be at home in the full-bodied reality of an English pub. Not as one of the crowd but also bringing with him a perspective the crowd has no share in. Rama's is a rootlessness having roots; It is a detachment, which is also an involvement and attachment, that is aware of the Thames flowing with the bear and human warmth and festivity. Hence, the clause—"While the Thames flowed"—brings home to him the realisation of the diverse identities at the pub, in perpetual fission and fusion, strife and strain. His ultimate identification with the cosmic self of a Guru is metaphysically spiritual. Since his real identity lay in his mother i.e. Mother India, from whom he has alienated himself. Alienated from the archaic Hindu existence, he expounds his philosophy not in the context of the Upanishads but in relation to Plato and Nietzsche.

Ramaswamy's quest for identity forms the thematic motif of the novel. His rootlessness leads to the search for identity which to Raja Rao is a "quest for the absolute,"[5]—the Guru Deva, Guru Brahma and Guru Maheswara. His quest for identity is a means to arrive at a value system. It is an assay to forge a new identity to suit his inner urges and drives in a socio-psychically transformed milieu. Besides mirroring an East-West dichotomy, Rama's search for identity symbolises his desire to establish psycho-emotional certainties in psycho-emotionally disturbed milieu. It is a quest to bring about coherence and unity to his socio-historical vision and to assert his time-bound historical self in a metaphysically timeless existence. The intercultural nature of Ramaswamy's being leads to the quest for identity, a leit motif in Indian English fiction. In delineating Ramaswamy's search for identity, Raja Rao lacks sufficient tenacity to push the quest to its natural finale. His quest to strike roots ends in an existential awareness of his spiritual urge manifesting in a symbolic surrender before the paraclete.

References

1. Raja Rao, *The Serpent and the Rope* (New Delhi: Orient Paperbacks, 1968), p. 10.
2. S. Nagarajan, "An Indian Novel," *Considerations*, ed. Meenakshi Mukherjee (New Delhi: Allied, 1977), p. 85.
3. Som P. Ranchan, "Ramaswamy's Dilemma: An Analytical Interpretation of *The Serpent and the Rope*," *Explorations in Modern Indo-English Fiction*, ed. R.K. Dhawan (New Delhi: Bahri, 1982), p. 102.
4. K.R. Rao, *The Fiction of Raja Rao* (Aurangabad: Parimal, 1980), pp. 71-72.
5. Asha Kaushik, "Meeting Raja Rao," *The Literary Criterion*, XVIII, No. 3, 1983, p. 36.

The Theme of Marriage in Raja Rao's *The Serpent and the Rope*

One of the most significant, dominant and sacred institutions, marriage occupies a crucial place in Indian society. It plays a decisive role in human relationships. Portrayal of marriage in Indian English novels is a recurrent feature and it is this element in Indian writing in English which gives it a typical Indian sensibility. In this connection, Meenakshi Mukherjee observes: "Among some hundred and fifty novels published in the last thirty years, one finds hardly two dozen books where a marriage ceremony has not been described."[1] In *The Serpent and the Rope*, marriage has been presented as a pervasive social institution. C.D. Narasimhaiah maintains: "No earthly institution can involve man in the world to the extent that marriage does. Hence the centrality of marriage in the novel. The novelist has drawn our attention pointedly to the pervasiveness of this social institution in the manner he presents human relationships."[2]

Madeleine marries Ramaswamy because she has a desire to understand India, to know India through her identification with the protagonist. Ramaswamy says:

> She loved me partly because she felt India had been wronged by the British, and because she would, in marrying me, know and identify herself with a great people.[3]

The failure of the Rama-Madeleine marriage is on account of their temperamental incompatibility. It is also attributable to Madeleine's successive failures in her life. Shattered by these failures, she takes to Buddhism, its compassion and commiseration casting a powerful spell on her. She finds solace in her self-imposed penance of isolation and subsequently solicits Rama for divorce "in order to free herself from the entanglements that hinder the progress of her spiritual pilgrimage." (70) She writes to Catherine:

> It is all a ghost story—Rama, India . . . and the world. Contemplation is the only truth one has. (394)

Ramaswamy's socio-cultural values exist on the intuitive rather than the intellectual plane but Madeleine's is a self-endorsed world of intellectualism. She fails to extricate herself from her bourgeois virtue, and her circumscribing and stifling intellectual life-style. She declines to be involved in Rama's sense of values, in his intuitive life and hence she fails to participate meaningfully in the rituals through which Ramaswamy seeks to assert his self. Madeleine says:

> Sometimes Rama, I want to run away from you, run far away from you, just to listen to the stupid innocent laughter, like Tante Zoubies; or go to a circus and see the clown make everyone laugh. (135)

She declines to come to India with Rama. She turns down the bride's toe-rings—a sacrilegious attitude in the Indian cultural context. Madeleine is a self-centred, centripetal being whereas Ramaswamy is a man of the world, and can step out of the self to participate in the sacramental ritual of life. Madeleine fails to achieve consonance with the Indian spirit symbolised by Ramaswamy. K.R. Rao holds that "as against Madeleine's escape into the self-denying Buddhist religion, Rama encounters the Vedantic self-expression and affirmation of the world as celebration." In the Rama-Madeleine relationship, Raja Rao sees fissures in the state of matrimony.

Madeleine fails to accept marriage as a sacrament. She even regards mere 'touch' as unholy. She devalues herself by her pseudo-philosophical attitude to sex. She is psychologically and spiritually alienated from Ramaswamy. Such polarisation leads to the failure of her marriage. A typical Westerner, she associates sex with sin and concupiscence. According to Havelock Ellis, "Marriage in the biological sense is a sexual relationship entered into with the intention of making it permanent, even apart from whether or not it has received sanction of law or the church."[4]

Considering this statement of Ellis we can safely conclude that Ramaswamy's sexual relationship with Madeleine is never complete; it hardly attains consummation. Hence Rama's turning to Savitri for love. She fulfils that which Madeleine could not, An amplification of the feminine mystique, in the legendary tradition of Mira Bai, she at length emerges as the veritable heroine of the novel. The Savitri-Rama relationship forms the crux of the story. It is the pivot on which the action of the story rotates. It deals with the feminine principle which is the very ideal and base of a harmonious marital relationship. Raja Rao says:

> Thus marriage as history [Rama-Madeleine] fails, but love as Savitri-Rama succeeds, for in one Madeleine seeks her own God but Savitri her Rama (through whom she sees the whole experience and beyond). . . . The true woman of Rama, therefore, is Savitri, even though she is married to his friend, Pratap.[5]

Ramaswamy's quest for the self culminates in his mystical marriage in London. Savitri thus becomes a "hypostatic presence" which he had been looking for. She becomes a channel of Rama's entry into a state where he transcends the dimensions of the ego idea, and annihilates time and space. Love with Savitri gives a new dimension to Rama's life. It gives new meaning to his otherwise ruffled marital existence with Madeleine.

Walker believes that "marriage is essential to the well-being of human society."[6] He further observes: "The advantage resulting from the states of marriage are that the two sexes may reciprocally satisfy the natural desires which are felt equally by each . . . that they may equally assist each other throughout life by reciprocal affection and cares."[7]

"Marriage and family," according to Cooley, "are the means used by society to control promiscuous sex and dissipation of man's energy."[8] But in *The Serpent and the Rope*, do Madeleine and Ramaswamy maintain fidelity in their conjugal life? Does marriage, in any way, help them in "coming together"? These are the questions which all Rao readers should answer for themselves. Simon de Beauvoir maintains that "the tragedy of marriage is not that it fails to assure woman the promised happiness but that it mutilates her; it dooms her."[9] Madeleine too is mutilated and doomed. She is ruined because of the duplicity of her husband, Rama, "who takes pleasure in his role of a Krishna, a mentor and guide." For Rama, the act of love becomes a sacred orgy. Marriage in the novel often becomes a crisis for both Rama and Madeleine. Ramaswamy remains a "holy vagabond" at heart. Hence the evanescent nature of his passion for Madeleine.

In the novel we have two wholly Western marriages, a "West-East Marriage," symbolised by the Rama-Madeleine tryst and Hindu marriages based on the concept of 'Jati' (Caste) which says that the individual should marry within his 'Jati,' a social situation prevailing in our contemporary society, though now it is gradually disappearing. But endogamy (kinship marriage) still continues to be the prevailing custom among the Hindus. Thus endogamy implies the existence of a caste or kinship area within which one is supposed to look for spouse. In the novel this is illustrated by Subramanya, Little Mother's own cousin's son's marriage with Saroja. In this connection, G.N. Ramu observes: "Gotra (group of people within the caste) considerations played an important role in the marriages of both Brahmins and Vaisyas consistent with the traditional practice. On the contrary Kshatriyas did not regard 'gotra' considerations as important in marriage negotiations."[10]

In the portrayal of Kshatriya marriages in the novel, Raja Rao maintains strict fidelity to facts of contemporary Indian practice by mirroring the proclivity of the Kshatriyas to seek prospective spouses across their caste lines. This is exemplified by the marriage of Savitri to Pratap Singh and on the basis of caste considerations, Jagirdars like Pratap's family members cannot be equal with the royal family of Raja Raghubir Singh, Savitri's father.

On the other hand, we also find that Savitri's sister (a Kshatriya girl) marries a rich 'baniya' (Vaishya) a very reputed politician whose prospects and chance of being a minister was the sole stimulus behind this intercaste marriage.

Occupational status is a deciding factor in the marriage market of the post-Independence India. P.C. Swain aptly maintains:

"Raja Rao's awareness of this recent social trend is amply demonstrated in *The Serpent and the Rope* firstly when the narrator Ramaswamy says, 'an Assistant Resident was still a highly respected party in the marriage-market of North India' and secondly when Savitri writes to Ramaswamy that 'A Delhi diplomat today is worth two private secretaries to an Indian Governor.'"[11]

Further the remarriage of Hindu widows was looked upon with contempt in the pre-Independence India. But widower marriages are now a very common practice. This aspect of the marriage institution is reflected in Raja Rao's novel, in the lives of Rama's father who marries for the third time and Vikram, a Delhiite, who marries for the fourth time a girl of only eighteen.

Marriages in India were, and are still, celebrated with pomp and show. Raja Rao illustrates this realistic aspect of Indian marriage ceremonies by citing the case of Savitri's official engagement with Pratap which is celebrated with great splendour and fanfare, with a lot of jubilation. Raja Rao says, "Altogether it was a splendid occasion for all concerned." (30) Rama's sister Saroja's marriage with Subramanya Shastri is also a grand celebration. The protagonist Rama says: "I found joy in the notes of the serpent-clarionet." (262) He further continues, "The music started, on the other street gunfire went off; the vulgar brass band started playing some military march, with Indian style music being piped amidst." (264)

Marriage is now almost a dying institution. It is hardly a success when girls are now sold in the dowry-market. This once-sacred institution has now badly degenerated. The overall impact that Rao makes on us about the institution of marriage is one of despair and gloom. It is not basically bilateral and there are a lot of deceptions and beguilements in the marital life of the couples. For instance, Georges is cuckolded by his wife Catherine, Tante Zubie has pre-marital sex with Uncle Charles, Little Mother languishes as a widow and takes refuge in her clandestine love for her stepson Rama. Savitri fornicates before her marriage with Pratap. Mrs. Shamsunder (Lakshmi) has a secret liaison with Rama. Raja Rao presents these married women with all their natural follies and foibles. Hence, it would not be erroneous to say that there is hardly a holy and sacred marriage in *The Serpent and the Rope*.

References

6. Meenakshi Mukherjee, "Awareness of Audience in Indo-Anglian Fiction," *Quest* (Winter, 1967), p. 38.
7. C.D. Narasimhaiah, *Raja Rao* (New Delhi: Arnold-Heinemann, n.d.), p. 110.
8. Raja Rao, *The Serpent and the Rope* (1960; New Delhi: Orient Paperbacks 1968), p. 18.
9. A.K. Sur, *Sex and Marriage in India; An Ethno-Historical Survey* (Bombay: Allied, 1973), p. 3.
10. Narasimhaiah, p. 84
11. Alexander Walker, *Women: Physiologically Considered as to Mind, Morals, Marriages, Matrimonial Slavery, Infidelity and Divorce* (New Delhi: Mittal, 1987), p. 78.
12. Narasimhaiah, p. 80.

9. Charles Cooley, *Social Consciousness*, p. 238. Qtd. Pandharinath H. Prabhu, *Hindu Social Organisation: A Study in Socio-Psychological and Ideological Foundations* (Bombay: Popular, 1958).
10. Simone de Beauvoir, *The Second Sex* (London: Pan, 1988), p. 496.
11. G.N. Ramu, *Family and Caste in Urban India: A Case Study* (New Delhi: Vikas, 1977), p. 36.
12. P.C. Swain, "Contemporary Reality in the Indian Marriages in Raja Rao's *The Serpent and the Rope*," *The Mahanadi Review*, 4.2 (April 1985-June 1986).

Myth in Raja Rao's *Kanthapura*

A primitive habit of the mind, myths are the life-blood of contemporary literature. They are living parables which the writers of archetypal vision imaginatively indulge in. For Richard Chase, it is "literature and therefore, a matter of aesthetic experience and the imagination, and as such, it has a fictional character which is imaginatively true."[1] Myth is expressive of the total vision of the human situation, human destiny, human inspiration and apprehensions. It is an aesthetic channel to ventilate, explore and re-create the experience of the self in relation to the past, a mode of expression of the labyrinthine interaction of the self and the society. Most of the myths, whatever they may have meant to the ancient or savage man, are to us meaningless and shocking; shocking by their cruelty, obscenity and by their seemingly silliness—almost what seems to be insane and eerie. The great myths like Orpheus, Demeter and Persephone, the Hesperides, Balder and Ragnarok emerge like elms out of this rank and squalid undergrowth. Even certain stories which are not myths in the anthropological sense have "mythical quality." Such are the plots of *Dr. Jekyll and Mr. Hyde*, Well's *The Door in the Wall* or Kafka's *The Castle*. Extra-literary, the aesthetic pleasure of myth depends hardly at all on such usual narrative attractions as suspense or surprise.

Human sympathy in a myth is at a minimum. We do not project ourselves so vigorously into the characters which are like some mysterious shapes moving in another world. The pattern of their movements has a profound significance to our own life, but we do not imaginatively transport ourselves into theirs. The story of Orpheus moves our pity and sympathy. It makes us sad but we are sorry for all men rather than vividly sympathetic with him. Often fantastic, myth deals with impossibles and preternaturals. Whether a sad or a delightful experience, myth is always grave and solemn. The experience is not only grave but also awe-inspiring. We feel as if "something" very grave and profound has been communicated to us. The incessant and recurrent efforts of the mind to conceptualise this "something" are manifested in the untiring and persistent tendency of humanity to provide myths with allegorical elucidations. Myths are contemplated as well as believed. Dissociated from ritual but based, on them, myths are held up before the fully awake and conscious imagination of a logical and contemplating mind. Since we define myths by their effect on us, it is plain that the same story may be a myth to one man but a fact to another. The value of myth is not a specifically literary value, nor the appreciation of myth a specifically literary experience. The degree to which any story is a myth depends chiefly on the person who reads or hears it. The same book can be merely an exciting yarn to one whereas it may be something of a myth to another. Harry M. Johnson points out that most myths "have to do with the origins—the origin of the gods, of the world, of culture, of certain features of nature. Other myths have to do with the stories of exploits of the gods or exploits or miraculous events in the lives of religious leaders."[2] By living the myths we are transported from "chronological" or "clock-time" to "sacred" or "primordial" time. We move from a definite and concrete plane of existence to an indefinite and abstract world, from the real to the seemingly unreal. Culturally sacred precedents for present actions, myths are necessarily and traditionally believed by many. Max Mueller feels that mythology is the result of a "disease of language,"[3] because the mythical language manifests itself in symbols, fantasies, rituals, metaphors, words, indicators and objects. The binary opposition between the form and the expression gives rise to the myth. A narrative resurrection of a primeval reality, myth caters to our deep religious wants, moral cravings, social submissions, even practical requirements. It is a strong preservative of tradition, not a dogma. Myths are "constantly regenerated; every historical change creates its mythology."[4] Eric Gould maintains: "Myth is a synthesis of values. . . . It is allegory and tautology, reason and unreason, logic and fantasy, waking thought and dream, atavism and perennial archetype and metaphor, origin and end."[5] Whereas to Northrop Frye, "a myth ultimately means mythos—a structural organizing principle of literary form."[6] Myths apparently derive their universal import from "the way in which they try to reconstitute an original event or explain some fact about human nature and its worldly or cosmic context."[7] "The ancient myths," says Rajesh Pallan, "survive in the modern times with all their problematic intensity as they deal with the numinous and the sacred."[8] Thus, myths are the mirrors that reflect man's inner self, thereby discovering the depths of the Unconscious. Products of creative fantasy, they interpret human life in the modern context and make us aware of our existence.

II

Quite a few modern writers have made a deft integration of myths into the thematic fabric of their works. They have emphasised the efficacy of the integrative mythology. James Joyce in *Ulysses*, T.S. Eliot in *The Waste Land*, Eugene O'Neill in *Mourning Becomes Electra* has dexterously and deliberately woven their contemporary material on the mythic parallel. Writers like Thomas Mann, Kafka, James Joyce, Yeats, and Eliot are some of the major writers who have "deployed mythical/ archetypal modes of expression in an age during which man has grown absurd, not quite aware of his identity or destiny and when a transvaluation of all values has become the order of day."[9] The mythical mode of narration consists in manipulating a continuous parallel between contemporaneity and antiquity."[10] The ancient myths and legends are used by these writers to highlight the similarities and contracts between the past and the present. Through the mythic mode of narration as well as a thematic dispensation of it they control, order and give "a shape and significance to the immense panorama of futility and anarchy, which is contemporary history."[11] Myth can be used for compression as well as for expansion. Eliot's *The Waste Land* is an instance of the former and James Joyce's *Ulysses* is an instance of the latter. Use of Myth helps in telescoping the vast canvas of the theme within a short space. Eliot uses the myth as an "objective-correlative" which serves as a mirror reflecting his emotions and ideas. The creative sensibility expresses reality and subjectivity through the creation of myths. Hence myth plays a vital role in the elucidation of human condition and human identity. The modern man reckons a new meaning and design through his mythical experiences. Jung's observations in this context are quite relevant: "Myths have a vital meaning. Not merely do they represent, they are the psychic life of the primitive tribe, which immediately falls to pieces and decays when it loses its mythological heritage, like a man who has his soul. A tribe's mythology is its living religion whose loss is always and everywhere, even among the civilised, a moral catastrophe."[12] According to Richard Chase, writers are attracted to myth primarily because "it is literature itself." (vi)

III

The Indian English novelists have nourished their moorings on their own Indian past. They have dovetailed their mythic experiences with the experience of the immediate present. The ancient culture of India has provided the mythic backdrop to their literary explorations and discoveries. They have harked back to the mythology of their own culture to carve out significant patterns of fiction. But one striking feature of these writers is that they seldom draw their material from the Graeco-Roman or Judaeo-Christian mythical framework. On the other hand, these Indian English writers often and with ease draw on their Indian myths because, as Meenakshi Mukherjee opines: "The Indian people are still closer to their mythology than the modern Irish or British people are to Celtic folklore or Greek legends."[13] The people in India still listen to the *Ramayana* and other recitals with zeal and eagerness. The Indian psyche is moulded and transformed by our mythological and legendary tales. It is conditioned by the stories from the *Panchatantra*, the *Ramayana* and the *Mahabharata*. Hence Pandit Nehru has aptly observed: "I do not know of any books anywhere which have exercised such a continuous and pervasive influence on the mass mind as these two (The *Ramayana* and The *Mahabharata*). . . . they are still a living force in the life of the Indian people."[14]

Why does the Indian novelist in English make a liberal and easy use of the myths and legends? Does he do it for thematic purpose or with certain didactic and ethical point of view? Meenakshi Mukherjee has given a lucid and cogent explanation for the abundance of mythic paraphernalia in Indian-English novel: "If a world-view is required to make literature meaningful in terms of shared human experience, then the Indian epics offer a widely accepted basis of such common background which permeates the collective unconscious of the whole nation." (131)

The "inexhaustible vitality"[15] of our classical mythology has helped the Indian novelists to delve deep into our past experiences and discover a link between it and our contemporary existence. This has also made the delineation of the contemporary reality/absurdity more lucid and more meaningful. Sudhin N. Ghosh holds that the collective psyche or rather the societal psyche/consciousness of any period is reflected in the mythology of those people: "Myths tell us more than bare facts. Men would die for their favourite myths, but not for bare facts and imposing statistics."[16] Myth did not find a much important place in the writings of the earlier Indian English novelists. It is only with the later Indian English novelists like Sudhin N. Ghosh, Raja Rao, Mulk Raj Anand, R.K. Narayan and B. Rajan that myth came to form an integral and corporate part of Indian writing in English. Most modern literature, according to P. Lal, is ignorant of the Indian myths. "The only possible revival" of these myths, according to him, "will take place if one's own myth-values and structures are studied and loved and absorbed and used with creative and critical imagination."[17] Rajesh Pallan maintains: "The use of myth is discernible in Indian-English novel on two planes—the digressional and the structural. In most mythological novels, the use of various myths does not offer a scaffold upon which the modern experience has been erected . . . the myth is simply being used in most cases to offer some kind of looser analogy." (19)

The Indian English novelists do not merely offer myths as analogies, but make them their central thematic or structural principle. In these novelists, the mythological parallel serves as an analogy (as in Anand's *The Old Woman and the Cow*) to the contemporary world which forms the backdrop of the novel and this parallel also forms the thematic motif (as Radha-Krishna motif in Raja Rao's *The Serpent and the Rope*). But Sudhin N. Ghose and Raja Rao make a digressional use of the myths. Their digressional technique is akin to the ancient Indian technique of narration. Their works are replete with (1) Puranic myths, (2) Localised myths which Rao calls "Sthalapurana" and (3) Rites and Rituals. The concept of "matra or the sense of propriety"[17] is another recurring feature of Ghose's works. In Raja Rao, there is the mythologisation of the contemporary reality. Each Indian English novelist casts the myth in his work in his own unique way. Narayan in his *The Man-Eater of Malgudi* (1961) makes a structural use of the myth. In his other novels, he uses it in a digressional manner. B. Rajan makes a rambling and spasmodic use of the myth. Mythical allusions in *The Dark Dancer* (1959) and *Too Long in the West* (1961) are desultory, referential and arbitrary. They hardly integrate into the structural design of the work albeit they do have marginal thematic purport. Tagore too in his *Two Sisters*, *The Wreck* and *The Garden* has made a significant use of the myth, especially thematically. Mulk Raj Anand makes a structural use of myth in *The Old Woman and the Cow*. His use of the myth is from technical point of view. It is a part of the technique. Writers like Anand do not make an imitative or slavish use of the myths and legends. On the other hand, they recreate these myths for themselves and make an imaginative and fictional use of them—by embodying them with new meanings and values. They remould and recreate these myths and legends to fit into the frame of contemporaneity. In fine, the Indian English novelists have made an explorative and innovative use of the myths and legends, thus giving them a new artistic dimension and value. Hence myths impart a new significance to our contemporary existence and "fill the ontological gap between the events and the meaning."[18]

IV

Raja Rao makes a digressional use of myth. Myth meanders through the fabric of his fictional canvas. In the "Foreword" to *Kanthapura*, he observes:

> Episode follows episode, and when our thoughts stop, our breath stops, and we move on to another thought. This was, and still is, the ordinary style of our storytelling. I have tried to follow it myself in this story.[19]

Rao employs three types of myths in his novels: (1) Puranic Myths, (2) Localised Myths and (3) Rites and Rituals. The Puranic myths pertain to the binary opposition of the good and the evil symbolised through the characters of Rama and Ravana. The Rama-Ravana myth appears to be the central thematic motif in *Kanthapura*. The novel is a fictional rendering of a localised myth (such as that of Kenchamma), it is the legendary history of a remote hamlet in the Western Coast of India. In order to create the mythic atmosphere in the novel, Raja Rao has resorted to the depiction of rites and rituals of ploughing, of worship and sacrifice. *Kanthapura* is the legendary history of a place or village, what Rao calls the "sthala-purana." The "rites and rituals," observes Meenakshi Mukherjee, "do not form part of myth but provide a frame of reference." (139) For instance, the offerings of coconut and betel nut at the altar of the deity are frequently found in Rao's *Kanthapura*. Through the telescoping of the past through myths and legends and relating it to modern context or contemporaneity, Raja Rao has presented a viable picture of the Indian reality. He has mythologised contemporary reality. In *Kanthapura*, we have the use of the myths which are inextricably and intimately connected with the religious beliefs and practices of the people and are communicated through symbols. A novel of political resurgence, *Kanthapura* is strewn with many myths which have been deftly woven into the fictional canvas of the story. The Puranic myths have been depicted to dramatise selfless action as expounded in the *Bhagvad Gita*. Murthy becomes the symbol of selfless action, symbol of the Mahatma.

It is again the contemporary Indian reality, the freedom struggle in a tiny hamlet that becomes the cynosure of the action. Taking recourse to various myths, Raja Rao conveys vividly and most lucidly "the whole ethos of Indian villages."[20] In the "Foreword" to *Kanthapura*, Raja Rao stresses the topical significance of the myth:

> There is no village in India, however mean, that has not a rich Sthala-Purana, or a legendary history of its own. Some god or godlike hero has passed by the village—Rama might have rested under this pipal tree. Sita might have dried her clothes, after her bath on this yellow stone, or the Mahatma himself, on one of his many pilgrimages throughout the country, might have slept in this hut. (5)

The village deity Kenchamma has a mythical semblance of the Puranic tales. Her divine presence smacks of the deities in the ancient legends and myths presiding over the fate of the human beings. The Kanthapurians are ardent devotees of Kenchamma. They chant hosannas to her which reminds one of "Durga Stuti":

> Kenchamma, Kenchamma Goddess, benign and bounteous, Mother of earth, blood of life, Harvest Queen rain-crowned, Kenchamma, Kenchamma Goddess, benign and bounteous. (10)

"The story of Goddess Kenchamma settling in Kanthapura," says Rajesh Pallan, "finds a mythical parallel in the *Ganga-Purana*." (26) Like Goddess Ganga, Kenchamma comes down from the Heavens to rescue the Kanthapurians from the draconian rule of the Whitemen, the *phirangis*:

> Kenchamma is our Goddess. Great and bounteous is she. She killed a demon, ages, ages ago, a demon that had come to ask our young sons as food and our young women as wives. Kenchamma came from the Heavens—it was the sage Tripura who had made penances to bring her down. (8)

The fight of Kenchamma with the demon brings to our mind the tale of Goddess Durga killing the brute Mahisasura, as depicted in the *Devi-Purana*. Look at what Achakka says about Goddess Kenchamma:

> And she wages such a battle and she fought so many a night that the blood soaked and soaked into the earth and that is why, the Kenchamma Hill is all red. (8)

The Kanthapurians resign all their problems to the will of Goddess Kenchamma, so much so that they invoke her grace and benedictions to destroy the English in India. Hence we find that Raja Rao resorts to the localised myth of Kenchamma to elucidate the conflict between good and evil. Like Chinua Achebe's *Arrow of God* (1962), the divine power of Kenchamma is omnipresent in *Kanthapura* to direct, control and preside over the life of the villagers. Several myths have been associated with the river Himavathy, the daughter of Kenchamma. Like the Mother Ganga, Himavathy sustains and protects them. Several myths have been woven round this river. People say, "the Goddess of the River plays through the night with the Goddess of the Hill." (8) Range Gowda says: "I drank three handfuls of Himavathy water, and I said, 'Protect us Mother.' (258) "Himavathy" is to the Kanthapurians what "Ganga Mata" is to all Indians. A reality as well as a fiction, a myth as well as a fact. The legend runs that the river Himavathy, while "in high spate, stood silently to allow the last rites of the pious Ramakrishnayya to be performed" and after the last rites were over, it carried away "in fury all that remained of the holy Ramakrishnayya in the form of ash and bone." (146) The other legend associated with the river Himavathy is related to the Chandals of the warrior Rajput clan who lived at Khajuraho. Meenakshi Mukherjee elaborating on the function of legend says, "as soon as the local legend has been narrated and established, its function becomes the same as that of a more well-known myth." (135)

Raja Rao creates the Sthala-purana in projecting the dedicated and selfless deeds of the local Mahatma, i.e. Moorthy. "The impact of Gandhi," observes C.D. Narasimhaiah, "was that of a traditional religion."[21] Moorthy is the "Gandhi incarnate" or you may say a "Mini-Gandhi" who instills the fire of revolution among the Kanthapurians. Like Godot in Samuel Beckett's *Waiting for Godot*, Gandhiji does not appear as a person but his spiritual presence is pervasive throughout the novel. Moorthy, the village Gandhi, is also all-pervasive in Kanthapura and his character has been mythicized. Like the Mahatma, Moorthy leads the Kanthapurians, the little "soldier-saints" (181) of the village, known as "Satyagrahis" who follow "selfless action" (Niskama Karma) as enunciated in the *Bhagvad Gita*. This galvanization of the dormant and slumbering hamlet into action is, to Narsingh Srivastava, "the metaphysic of selfless action expressed through Satyagraha."[22] Moorthy's character is idealized in the novel to the extent of being regarded as a local Mahatma because a myth "necessarily deals with an idealised man or a man larger than life."[23] Moorthy is Jesus Christ to the Kanthapurians. He has come to deliver them from sin and suffering. He is their "Gandhi." (109) They say with exultation, "he is the saint of our village." (135) Range Gowda, the village headman, describes Moorthy as "our Mahatma." (109)

To elucidate and explicate the theme of redemptive suffering in human society, Raja Rao "takes the myth of suffering more directly self-imposed to absorb the evil of others."[24] Like the chief characters in myths which are mythicised by exalting and elevating them above the common rung of humanity, Moorthy too is presented as an exalted and dignified character. In mythicising the protagonist, Raja Rao adheres to the classical tradition. Moorthy is not only mythicised but also idealised. Mulk Raj Anand does not idealise the character of Bakha or Gandhi in *Untouchable*. Even in *Gauri*, in spite of parallel resemblances between Gauri and Sita in regard to the theme of passive suffering, Gauri's character is not mythicised in such an ideal manner. Gauri turns down Sita's lot, her stance in life and explores a new way for herself. Anand uses myth for illuminating and exposing a character like Gauri or for elucidating and projecting the contemporary predicament of woman. On the other hand, Raja Rao almost substitutes the mythical characters with the contemporary ones in Kanthapura in such a dexterous manner that one can hardly discern a difference between myth and reality in the novel. The blending of myth and reality is almost perfect and meticulous in execution. The Rama-Ravana myth has its associations with the 'good' and the 'evil' forces used in the novel in order to portray the struggle for independence from the British rule. The freedom movement is equated with the *Mahabharata Yudha*. There the divine powers of Lord Krishna regulate the war and here the invisible and redemptive presence of the Mahatma control the actions of the Kanthapurians. The illiterate narrator, Achakka, mingles the fact of subtler thoughts of the Mahatma in the contemporary situation with the legends and the myths as embedded in the *Ramayana* and the *Mahabharata*. The legendary heroes are "inextricably mixed, linked up with the historical person." [25] Mahatma Gandhi is thus described as the incarnation of Rama and Krishna, born to liberate Mother India from the draconian rule of the demons, Ravana and Kansa. The Harikatha-man, Jayaramachar, mythically narrates the birth of Mahatma Gandhi on the request of Sage Valmiki to Lord Brahma. Thus Raja Rao harnesses the Puranic style to describe the birth of the Mahatma who was sent to this world by Brahma for destroying evil and restoring good. Srinivasa Iyengar feels that "the style of narration makes the book more a 'Gandhi Purana' than a piece of mere fiction. Gandhi is the invisible God, Moorthy is the visible avatar."[26] By mythicising Gandhiji's character, the freedom struggle has also been consciously mythicised.

Gandhi's character in *Kanthapura* has been highly idealized like that of Rama in the *Ramayana*. Like Rama, Gandhi is described as a reincarnation of the Almighty. His psychological presence in the novel lends a mythical aura around his saintly figure. The exploitation of the Indians in the hands of the Britishers was immense. Like Ravana, the British had come to kidnap our political freedom," i.e. our 'Swaraj.' (257) Gandhi's visit to England to attend the Round Table Conference in 1931 is described in terms of the Indian mythical tradition. It is like Rama's visit to Lanka to save Sita from the hands of Ravana. Sita is our 'Swaraj' and Ravana 'the British.' The ever-present Indian mythos, at length "absorbs the characters and history it has all along been bathing and overwhelming."[27] Gandhi has further been compared with Lord Shiva. The Kanthapurians invoke the grace of Brahma, the Creator, by apprising him of the tyrannous rule of the Britishers. They beseech Brahma to send them one of his Gods so that he may incarnate on earth and retrieve India from the demonic grip of the British rulers. Brahma pronounces:

> Siva himself will forthwith go and incarnate on the Earth and free my beloved daughter from her enforced slavery. . . . The messengers of Heaven shall fly to Kailash and Siva be informed of it. (22-23)

Gandhi's idea of Swaraj has been compared with the three eyes of Shiva: "Siva is the three-eyed, and Swaraj too is three-eyed; self-purification, Hindu-Muslim unity, Khaddar." (20)

The whole situation and characters in the novel are mythicized where the past mingles with the present and the gods mingle with men. K. Ayyappa Paniker feels that "the divine or the supernatural is deeply involved in the human and the natural predicament in *Kanathapura*."[28] Gandhi is also compared with Raja Harishchandra. Raja Rao writes:

> Like Harishchandra, before he finished his vow, the gods will come down and dissolve his vow, and the Britishers will leave India, and we shall be free, and we shall pay less taxes and there will be no policemen. (172)

Gandhi is compared to Harishchandra because he resisted all worldly and mundane temptations as a means to ahimsa.

The battle between the 'suras' and 'asuras' is a recurrent motif in the Hindu mythology and in *Kanthapura* too, we have the fight between the Britishers (asuras) and the Indians (suras). The tussle between the Satyagrahis and the agents of the British Government is symbolic of the clash between the suras and the asuras. The Skeffington Coffee Estate is the world of asuras in miniature. The morally corrupt British officials there let loose a reign of terror and Mahatma Gandhi, the 'Sura' comes to save these people. Alone he doesn't come. He comes with his 'Vanar Sena,' the 'Satyagrahis.' Good and virtue triumph at the end and the whole freedom struggle culminates into a sort of mythological war between Rama and Ravana, 'suras' and 'asuras.'

Through the character of the "Swami," another 'asura,' Raja Rao has sarcastically portrayed the Indian natives joining hands with the British to betray Gandhi's fight against the 'Goras' for attaining freedom. The agents of this Swami act as "agent provocateurs" to subvert the 'Rama-Ravana myth' and exercise their diabolic designs to dissuade the villagers from joining Moorthy's non-co-operation movement. Ironically, the Swami's agent compares the British Government with Rama and Mahatma Gandhi with Ravana.

Alphonso-Karkala rightly opines that Raja Rao's "time module in *Kanthapura* can be easily seen in the life of the living village which, having evolved to Kaliyuga, dissolves towards the end like a Pralaya." (78) Things fall apart and centre cannot hold. Indeed things do fall apart in Kanthapura when people like Bhatta, Waterfall Venkamma and the Swami's agent start fomenting chaos by joining hands with the corrupt British rulers. Anarchy is let loose upon the Kanthapurians. The evil influence of Kaliyuga is evidenced in Satamma's words:

> After all, my son, it is the Kaliyuga floods and as the sastras say, there will be the confusion of castes and the pollution of the progeny. We can't help it, perhaps. (43-44)

The end of the novel is like the end of Kaliyuga with the Pralaya engulfing the whole village. All the villagers leave Kanthapura at the end of the novel to settle down in Kashipura. Range Gowda finds that "there is neither man nor mosquito in Kanthapura." (258) Like Tiresias in Eliot's *The Waste Land*, Achakka, the narrator in Kanthapura, serves as a link between the past and the present. An unlettered woman, she mingles myth and fact in her natural manner of reflection and observation. Achakka reminds us of Shelley's 'West Wind.' Like it, she is a symbol of transformation, of rebirth and resurrection and "the myth becomes so open-ended that dissolving itself continues to live again in another formulation and not definitely concretized."[29] In his interview with Shiva Niranjan, Raja Rao states:

> I like to write like a Purana. I like the Puranic conception, in fact, that is the only conception of novel for me. I don't want to write like a foreign novelist. I am very much an Indian and the Indian form is the Puranic form.

The tale of *Kanthapura* is told in the Puranic style embodying myths and legends. It has also "the breathless garrulity of the Puranas without attempting at formal organization."[31] Raja Rao's purpose of writing in the Puranic fashion is stated in the "Foreword":

> The *Mahabharata* has 214,778 verses and the *Ramayana* 48,000. Puranas there are endless and innumerable. We have neither punctuation nor the treacherous 'ats' and 'ons' to bother us—we tell one interminable tale. Episode follows episode, and when our thoughts stop, our breath stops, and we move on to another thought. This was and still is the ordinary style of our storytelling. I have tried to follow it myself in this story. (6)

Besides this, the prose descriptions of nature, surroundings and happenings are also reminiscent of the 'Puranas': "Kenchamma lies curled up like a child on its mother's lap" (191); the dead body of Ramakrishnayya washed and tied to the bamboo and "behind the jack fruit the sun rose like a camphor . . . and when the waters were still girdling in the gutters, the procession hurried on." (145-46) The description of Ramakrishnayya's death is reminiscent of the account of Nature's response to the death of Karna in the *Mahabharata*:

> when Karna fell, the rivers stood still. . . . The earth uttered loud roars. . . . The mountains with their forests began to tremble and all creatures felt pain.

In *Kanthapura*, Ramakrishnayya's death is also described in mythical tones:

> And that night sister, as no other night, no cow would give its milk . . . and calves pranced about their mothers and groaned. . . . Lord may such be the path of our outgoing soul. (101)

T.S. Eliot uses the mythical technique in *The Waste Land* to interpret and criticise the present-day world but Raja Rao uses this technique to glorify the present, to laud it and impart to it the dignity and grandeur of the 'Puranas.' The novel is replete with rituals especially in relation to the celebration of festivals like 'Sankara-Jayanthi,' 'Rama-festival,' 'Krishna-festival' which lend a mythical halo and fervour to the novel. Achakka says that the festival of lights (Dipavali) is celebrated in the month of Kartik "so that when darkness hangs drooping down the caves, gods may be seen passing by, blue gods and quiet gods and bright-eyed gods." (118)

Long poetic descriptions of nature, evocative and symbolic are a feature of the Puranas, especially the *Bhagvad Purana*. *Kanthapura* too has such lyrical and poetic descriptions which are prose-poems. The advent of 'Kartik' is described thus:

> Kartik has come to Kanthapura. Kartik has come with the glow of lights and the unpressed footsteps of the wandering Gods. . . . Kartik is a month of the gods, and as the gods pass by the Potters' Street and the Weavers' Street, lights are lit to see them pass by. (118)

The performance of various rituals lends a mythical frame of allusion to the novel. The Kanthapurians offer goddess Kenchamma 'saree' and 'gold-drink' to ward off the malefic influences. During the ploughing time, the villagers wait for the 'Rohini' star to 'yoke their bulls to the plough.' (151) Ploughing is considered to be fruitful only if the omen of the Eagle, the vehicle of Goddess Kenchamma, shows itself. The villagers light bonfires and sing and dance in Kenchamma's honour. When Moorthy is in prison, the Kanthapurians sing 'bhajans' with "cymbal, conch and camphor, clapping hands and droning drums, the perfume of the sandal paste, flowers in the hair and in our eyes, Shiva's eyes." (156) Fasting as an important ritual is undertaken by the villagers to gain divine grace and appease the gods. Moorthy undergoes fasting several times. The congregational worship ritual for appeasing Kenchamma is another instance of the mythic fashion and style. Ratna offers "ten coconuts and a kumkum worship" (98) to Kenchamma for the recovery of Moorthy. Satamma feels that "it was our Kenchamma, she tore a rag from her saree fringe, and put it into a three piece bit, and a little rice and an areca nut, and hung it securely to the roof." (79) Rice and coconuts are to the Kanthapurians, traditional symbols of fertility, of prosperous marital status of a lady, a shaven head without kumkum, i.e. a widow, is considered inauspicious. Besides creating a mythical ambience, rituals in the novel are "a device for concretising the point-of-view."[33] Deeply steeped in local chores, the narrator, Achakka, assimilates the contemporary reality into a mythical frame of structure.

The time bound dispensation of myth in relation to the contemporary predicament in *Kanthapura* serves as a parallel to the concept of the timeless. The interweaving and dovetailing of the myths, legends and rituals transforms contemporaneity into the eternal histrionics between virtue and vice; good and evil; gods and demons and the time and the timeless. Through Achakka's narrations, Raja Rao achieves a deft and artistic blending of the mythical and the real. As a result, the novel becomes a "glorious myth . . . as profound as a shastra, and as prolific as a 'purana,' yet in its brevity and verbal economy, it excels in capturing excessive critical imagination."[34] Srinivasa Iyengar calls *Kanthapura*, a "Gandhi-Purana," as it echoes the high majesty and grand dignity of the Puranas. Myths and symbols in the novel occur as an artistic and creative mode of conveying "a meaningful world-view of human reality in terms of shared human experience."[35] Thus, there is a perceptible mythical pattern in *Kanthapura*. The use of Indian myth, like the *Ramayana*, lends a fairy tale charm, a romantic aura to the novel and stimulates our imagination. These myths transport us to the remote times in the past when gods, demi-gods and superhuman beings played a vital role in our lives, the days when myths regulated our emotional and intellectual actions.

References

1. Richard Chase, "Foreword," *Quest for Myth* (New York: Greenwood Press, 1969), p. vi.
2. Harry M. Johnson, *Sociology: A Systematic Introduction* (New Delhi: Allied, 1980), p. 405.
3. Qtd. Chase, p. 140.
4. Chase, p. 79.

5. Eric Gould, "Mythical Intentions," *Modern Literature* (Princeton: Princeton University Press, 1981), p. 28.
6. Northrop Frye, *Anatomy of Criticism: Four Essays* (Princeton: Princeton University Press, 1971), p. 136.
7. Gould, p. 6.
8. Rajesh K. Pallan, *Myths and Symbols in Raja Rao and R.K. Narayan* (Jalandhar: ABS, 1994), p. 8.
9. B. Das, "Myth, Criticism and its Value," *The Indian Journal of English Studies*. Vol. XV, 1974, p. 162.
10. T.S. Eliot, *The Sacred Wood* (London: Methuen, 1964), p. 16.
11. *Ibid.*
12. C.G. Jung, "Archetypes of the Collective Unconscious," *The Modern Mind*, ed. Ellmann and Feidelson (London: OUP, 1965), p. 645.
13. Meenakshi Mukherjee, *The Twice-Born Fiction* (New Delhi: Arnold Heinemann, 1974), p. 131.
14. Jawaharlal Nehru, *The Discovery of India* (New Delhi: OUP, 1974), p. 99.
15. R.K. Narayan, *Gods, Demons and Others* (New Delhi: Hind Pocket Books, 1979), p. 15.
16. Sudhin N. Ghose, *Cradle of the Clouds* (London: Michael Joseph, 1951), p. 90.
17. P. Lal, "Myth and the Indian Writer in English: A Note," *Aspects of Indian Writing in English*, ed. M.K. Naik (Delhi: Macmillan, 1979), p. 16.
18. Rajesh K. Pallan, p. 21.
19. Raja Rao, *Kanthapura* (Delhi: Orient Paperbacks, 1971), p. 6.
20. Harish Raizada, "Point of View, Myth and Symbolism in Raja Rao's Novels," *Perspectives on Raja Rao*, ed. K.K. Sharma, (Ghaziabad: Vimal, 1980), p. 197.
21. C.D. Narasimhaiah, *Raja Rao* (Delhi: Arnold Heinemann, 1973), p. 43.
22. Narsingh Srivastava, "The Image of India in the Novels of Raja Rao," *Indian Scholar*, Vol. 2, No. 1, 1980, p. 58.
23. Mukherjee, p. 141.
24. John B. Alphonso-Karkala, "Myth, Matrix and Meaning in Literature and Raja Rao's Novel, *Kanthapura*," *Perspectives on Raja Rao*, ed. K.K. Sharma (Ghaziabad: Vimal, 1980), p. 79.
25. Rao, *The Fiction of Raja Rao* (1980), p. 55

26. K.R. Srinivasa Iyengar, *Indian Writing in English* (New Delhi: Sterling, 1984), p. 291.
27. Richard R. Guzman, "The Saint and the Sage: The Fiction of Raja Rao," *The Virginia Quarterly Review*, p. 39.
28. K. Ayyappa Paniker, "Man and God in Indian and African Fiction: A Study Based on *Kanthapura, Arrow of God* and *Mookajji's Visions*," *Commonwealth Literature: Problems of Response*, ed. C.D. Narasimhaiah (Madras: Macmillan, 1981), p. 109.
29. Alphonso-Karakala, p. 80.
30. Shiva Niranjan, "Myth as a Creative Mode: A Study of Mythical Parallels in Raja Rao's Novels," *Commonwealth Quarterly*, Vol. 4, No. 13, 1980, p. 50.
31. Pallan, p. 38.
32. P.C. Roy, trans., *The Mahabharata* (Calcutta, 1956), rev. ed., Vol. VII), p. 283.
33. Mukherjee, p. 142.
34. Alphonso-Karakala, p. 82.
35. Raizada, p. 176.

Khushwant Singh's *Train to Pakistan*: A Thematic Analysis

A short story writer, novelist, historian and journalist, Khushwant Singh has established himself as a distinguished Indian writer "with an individual status in modern Indo-Anglian literature."[1] This individuality in his writings is on account of his anger and disenchantment with the "long-cherished human values in the wake of inhuman bestial horrors and insane savage killings on both sides during the partition of the subcontinent between India and Pakistan in August 1947."[2] The harrowing and spine-chilling events of 1947 had shaken the faith of the people in the innate nobility of human beings. It had driven them into a state of wonder over what man has made of man. To Khushwant Singh, this was a period of great disillusionment and crisis of values, a distressing and disintegrating period of his life. The beliefs he had cherished all his life were shattered. Giving vent to his inner struggle and agony, he says: "the division of India had been accompanied by the most savage massacres known in the history of the country. . . . I had believed that we Indians were peace-loving and non-violent, that we were more concerned with the matters of the spirit. . . . After the experience of the autumn of 1947, I could no longer subscribe to these views. I became an angry middle-aged man, who wanted to shout his disenchantment with the world. . . . I decided to try my hand at writing."[3]

The sinister and venomous impact of partition and the indignation it spawned in him has been realistically expressed in a scathing irony in *Train tò Pakistan*. Originally entitled Mano Majra, the novel portrays with a bold and unrelenting realism, the brutal story of political hatred and violence during the turbulent and fateful days that preceded and followed the partition of British India when the spirit of communal frenzy and a passionate zeal for self-expression were fuming and fumbling within the mass. Khushwant Singh's objective in this novel is to expose and explore the world around him and to present it in all its naturalistic setting. The socio-political theme he takes up in this novel is intrinsically a journalistic tour de force chiming in with the artistic tenets of sincerity and truth.

The novel relates the story of Mano Majra, a tiny village which becomes the microcosm of the communal strife and inhuman violence in the wake of Partition. But in the teeth of such ghastly violence we do have people who maintain a dignified stoicism—people who encounter the existential buffets of destiny with equipoise and fortitude. Jugga, the romantic deviant, is one such man. "The heroic spirit of man," observes Harish Raizada, "is revealed in the novel not by men who are considered religious and respectable in the public and supposed to have innate goodness but by a man like Jugga who is treated as a confirmed ruffian." (127) A "budmash number ten,"[4] Jugga is an invincible person whom neither darkness can blind nor death scare. With his indomitable courage and unconquerable will, he becomes the symbol of self-sacrifice and goodness that humanity basically stands for. He redeems himself by saving the lives of thousands of Muslims in a thrilling climax. But all is not lost. Jugga does everything he can to assert the nobility of his self. Thus an idealistic and affirmative tone pervades the novel which imparts a silver lining to the encircling gloom in which all humanity is enmeshed. The avenger's plan to cause a gruesome accident on the train and massacre its passengers bound for Pakistan is averted by Jugga, a confirmed ruffian with a human heart. Khushwant Singh's Jugga is a character "stuffed with the so-called innate goodness of man and he is the only character which is entirely fiction."[5] The novelist thus invests a common man like Jugga with tragic grandeur in order to show "the dignity of man for all helpless littleness in the face of the universe, for all his nullity under the blotting hand of time."[6] But a deeper reading of the novel reveals that Jugga's sacrifice is an assertion of his love for an individual, not all humanity. He averts the accident because he wanted to save the life of his Muslim beloved, Nooran. Realising the danger the revenge might mean to his beloved, he manages to slash at the rope with his Kirpan: "He went at it with his knife, and then with his teeth. "The engine was almost on him. There was a volley of shots. The man shivered and collapsed. The rope snapped in the centre as he fell. The train went over him, and went on to Pakistan." (158)

The train of Muslim refugees passes over to Pakistan safely but Jugga is shot by his co-religionists. His heroic death is a sacrifice, an act of self-immolation that unveils the hypocrisy and duplicity on which the so-called civilized society thrives. Khushwant Singh's genial comic irony manifests itself in his unmasking the sham pretension of the much-acclaimed and glorified values of human life symbolized by the assassination of Juggut Singh. The murder of Jugga in another way symbolizes the culmination of the novelist's vision of life which is positive. This vision of life in the novelist expresses itself through love and dedication. With his intuitive understanding, he depicts things as they are and not as they ought to be. This transcription of life brings out the note of verisimilitude to life since literal transcription of life is well nigh impossible.

Khushwant Singh's is a plausible interpretation of life. R.K. Narayan and Mulk Raj Anand portray the photographic reality, a reality that is artistic but Khushwant Singh is interested in the stark and naked realism of life and thus comes closer to the French socialist realists like Balzac. Like the socialist realists, Khushwant Singh's approach is positive—not negative—inasmuch as he views the socialist order as an independent entity. Unlike a critical realist, his approach is definitely concrete, since he looks at the society from the inside, not from the outside. Like Balzac's characters, his Juggut Singh alias Jugga is a man endowed with formidable will power and individuality. The theme of the novel with all its emphasis on partition does not become a political propaganda like Raja Rao's *Kanthapura*. On the other hand, it is a tale of the fate of the individuals in Mano Majra, a small village on the river Sutlej. Sikhs and Muslims are enmeshed in a fratricidal conflict. Everywhere there is mass madness and Mano Majra too reels under the opprobrious and ghastly scene of communal frenzy. Muslims are evacuated to a refugee camp for departure to Pakistan later. As the preparation for the departure of the Muslim refugees to Pakistan is in full swing, religious fanatics are busy with vindictive activities in their underworld. They plan to blow up the bridge and the train which is to carry the Muslim refugees to Pakistan in retaliation for what Pakistani Muslims have done to Hindus on their way to India. When Jugga comes to know that his beloved Nooran is going to leave India by the train to Pakistan, he immediately rushes to the rescue of Nooran and ultimately falls a prey to the bullets of the Hindu saboteurs and is killed. With this bare outline, Khushwant Singh is able to build up a novel portraying the hard and bitter facts of life against the harrowing tale of India's partition.

In its dexterous anatomization of the real and its penetration beneath the inhuman bestialities of life to the human factor of love and sympathy, *Train to Pakistan* is a unique artistic rendering of the gruesome and vile. To Khushwant Singh, love in spite of its concomitant frustrations, "is the greatest, the most exhilarating experience of life."[7] A moving story of people in turmoil, the novel is an idyllic tale of "a village led to a moral action through its own apathy and indifference."[8]

Besides the horrors of partition and the self-sacrifice of Jugga, the novel has a deep symbolic concern. The first symbol is Mano Majra which is representative of the spirit of India herself—India, the land of Ahimsa. Here, in this idyllic village in the remote confines of the line, half a mile away from the river Sutlej, we get a picture of unity in diversity. Here the Hindus, Sikhs and Muslims lived peacefully together as they had been living since times immemorial. Though the frontier between India and Pakistan turns into a gory scene of riot and massacre, everything is calm and quiet in Mano Majra. Partition does not ruffle the normal tenor of life there. Mano Majrans are unaware of the political situation of the country. They even do not know that the British have left India and that India has been partitioned and is ruled now by the popular Congress ministry. Mano Majra's tranquil milieu reminds one of the famous lines of Thomas Gray's poem "Elegy Written in a Country Churchyard":

> Far from the madding crowd's ignoble strife,
> Their sober wishes never learned to stray,
> Along the cool and sequestered vale of life,
> They kept the noiseless tenor of their way.

Mano Majra is in fact a symbol of staticity, of immobility and passivity. The harmonious atmosphere and the idyllic tranquillity of this tiny village is a veritable oasis of peace. The villagers remain unruffled by the frantic acts of murder, plunder, arson, abduction and rape:

> Mano Majra is a tiny place. It has only three brick buildings, one of which is the home of the moneylender Lala Ram Lal. The other two are the Sikh temple and the mosque. . . . The rest of the village is a cluster of flat-roofed mud huts and low-walled courtyards which front on narrow lanes that radiate from the centre. . . . There are only about seventy families in Mano Majra, and Lala Ram Lal's is the only Hindu family. The others are Sikhs or Muslims, about equal in number. . . . But there is one object that all Mano Majrans—even Lala Ram Lal—venerate. This is a three-foot slab of sandstone that stands upright under a keekar tree beside the pond. It is the local deity, the Deo to which all the villagers—Hindu, Sikh, Muslim or pseudo-Christian—repair secretly whenever they are in special need of blessing. (2)

Deo, the local deity, becomes the symbol of communal harmony like the goddess Kenchamma in Raja Rao's *Kanthapura*. The Kanthapurians rise to the call of Gandhiji and involve themselves in the independent movement but the Mano Majrans remain passive spectators to the whole scene of pre-Independence struggle. They have heard the name of Gandhiji but remain unmoved by the call of the Mahatma to oust "the firangi from our soil." Their passivity and staticity to the violence in the wake of Partition has been very vividly described by Khushwant Singh:

> The summer before communal riots, precipitated by reports of the proposed division of the country into a Hindu India and a Muslim Pakistan, had broken out in Calcutta, and within a few months the death toll had mounted to several thousand. . . . By the time the monsoon broke, almost a million of them were dead, and all of northern India was in arms, in terror, or in hiding. The only re-

> maining oases of peace were a scatter of little villages lost in the remote reaches of the frontier. One of these villages was Mano Majra. (1-2)

As a contrast to the tranquil and static environs of Mano Majra, the train serves as an important symbol of mobility. It stands for all that is dynamic. Though at the outset of the story, it acts as an almanac and a regulator for the people of the hamlet, later on it acquires a sinister and formidably horrific dimension when its swift and placid tenor of life receives a shocking jolt in the wake of the bloody partition: "Trains became less punctual than ever before and many more started to run through at night. Some days it seemed as though the alarm clock had been set for the wrong hour. On others, it was as if no one had remembered to wind it." (92) The irregularity of trains symbolizes the disturbance in the smooth flow of life in Mano Majra. It presages chaos and disorder, riot and violence. The odd arrival of a train from Pakistan in the morning with heaps of mangled and mutilated corpses lets loose a reign of terror. Bestiality manifests in violence, revenge, mass rape of women in public, arson, infanticide and carnage. All this leads to the massacre of Mano Majran Muslims leaving for Pakistan by a train. The train to Pakistan reveals the humanity in Jugga, his sense of integrity in love and self-dedication. The train to Pakistan thus becomes a unique symbol in the novel. It is a symbol of motion in contrast to Mano Majra which is a static point in space. V.A. Shahane observes: "The use of the word 'train' is significant in other ways too. The train signifies groups or multitudes of people who are on the move . . . the train implies the movement of vast communities, torn from their links of nativity, from their places of birth and upbringing and areas of traditional growth in search of a new 'Jerusalem.' It indicates the harrowing process of this change, the awful and ghastly experiences of human beings involved in a historical, objective and almost dehumanised process. The train suggests the fate of the individuals, the destinies of two newly formed dominions. . . . Secondly, the train is also a symbol of the machine age. . . . Modern mechanistic, materialistic age has caused severe destruction of humanistic values." (347-48) Further the train is symbolic of the rhythmic pattern of the novel. It is at the heart of Mano Majra, a village which has "always been known for its railway station." (3) The villagers' activities are patterned by the to and fro movement of the train. It fills the villagers with the very pulse of life.

The arrival of a ghost train at Mano Majra stuns the villagers. They are awe-struck at the sight of the train being loaded with dead bodies giving out the acrid smell of searing flesh. The bestial scene is too terrible for the innocent villagers. It unveils the horrible and ghastly drama of communal violence—the sinking and erosion of human values. The sight of the geckos pouncing on the moth and catching it fluttering is symbolic of the genocide (since there is mass killing of Hindus and Muslims), a common feature of Partition. It points to the extermination of not only people but the annihilation of human values under the garb of religious fanaticism. Even the magistrate's fear of spending the night all alone in his room is symbolic of terror and apprehension leading to insecurity and indecision.

The summer sun going "on, day after day, from east to west, scorching relentlessly" (79) is also a very significant symbol. It suggests the "disillusioned, dejected, thirsty and sweating" (90) people of the time. The comforting and cheerful rain after the parching heat of the summer turns into a series of experiences, pertaining to death and destruction. Serpents, centipedes, scorpions and the moths fluttering around the lamps, mosquitoes and flies made life awfully irksome. The monsoon, giving a boost to the tempo of life and death, is symbolic of the inhuman acts done by the people as a result of communal violence. Life everywhere was chaotic. Man had to move on the razor's edge. Retaliation became the talk of the day and the law of retaliation the philosophers say is the law of necessary evils. Hence the Hindus and Muslims sported themselves with the lives of one another. There was no end to it. The train to Pakistan and the train from Pakistan became the symbol of man's inhumanity to man, man preying upon man. But the Mano Majrans still had some amount of sanity and wisdom, humanity and fellow-feeling. "What have we to do with Pakistan? We are born here. So were our ancestors. We have lived amongst you as brothers," (14) says one of the Muslims amidst a crowd of Sikhs. The Sikh lambardar replies forthwith: "Yes, you are our brothers. As far as we are concerned you and your children and your grandchildren can live here as long as you like. If anyone speaks rudely to you, your wives or your children, it will be us first and our wives and children before a single hair of your heads is touched." (30) The peasant folk of Mano Majra, especially the Sikhs cannot deny shelter to the terror-stricken refugees. To them "hospitality was not a pastime but a sacred duty." (9) People of Mano Majra live in amity. They are god-fearing and religious. Friendship and philanthropy was the be-all and end-all of their life. But for how long? Soon their amity and integration is going to be shattered by the train to Pakistan when they will be alienated from their near and dear ones for ever. Violence in the human world is symbolised by violence in the natural world. The flashing crash of lightning and thunder symbolize murder and looting of the people after Partition.

The swelling Sutlej presented a terrifying sight. Flood in the river suggested and foreshadowed the flood of violence. The lambardar "had never known the Sutlej to rise so high in so short a time." (121) The river's appearance in the night like a sheet of paper symbolized the black beastly acts of violence. The new American engines wailing "like someone being murdered" (123) also symbolized the diabolic deeds of horror and the degeneration of long-cherished socio-moral values. The cries of the jackals symbolized predatory craving. It thickened the atmosphere of awe engendered by the sight of the carcasses floating on the water and kites and vultures hovering in the sky.

Khushwant Singh does not arraign any particular party or community. He finds both the Hindus and the Muslims equally responsible for the inhuman deeds. He puts the blame squarely on both the racial factions. He feels the Mullahs actively participating in the frenzied butchery of human beings and human values. These mullahs instigate the people to mutiny and murder: "Mullahs roamed the Punjab and the Frontier Province with boxes of human skulls said to be those of Muslims in Bihar." (1)

Still further, Singh's attack is on the nonchalant politicians in Delhi whiling away their time in political gossips and commitments. "Nero fiddled upon the harp, when the Roman empire was burning." This is exactly what these politicians did when the entire nation was reeling under the pangs of the two-nation theory. Partition had brought about estrangement to the lives of the people who believed in one India. They were utterly broken by the people in power sitting in Delhi making "fine speeches in the assembly" (153) in the midst of lovely foreign women. The outgoing rulers dragged the nation to utter chaos and confusion. The crazy fallacy of the two-nation theory has been fully exposed and exploited. The quest for a safe homeland had uprooted the masses of humanity. Non-violence was thrown to the winds. Religion now was found to be hollow and shorn of all moral values. Iqbal, a philosopher and social worker, says, "Ethics, which should be the kernel of a religious code, has been carefully removed." (149) But God-consciousness still haunts the minds of the people undergoing the pain of suffering and misery with their emphatic and searing realisation: "God is punishing us for our sins." (107)

Despite the note of utter despair bordering on nihilism, the novel is a message of hope and compromise. The most basic of all human instincts, i.e. man-woman love, sustains the sympathetically bitter tone of the novel. Jugga's sacrifice is an act of self-redemption, it is an identification in alienation. To William Walsh, *Train to Pakistan* "is a tense, economical novel, thoroughly true to the events and the people. It goes forward in a trim, athletic way, and its unemphatic voice makes a genuinely human comment."[9] Khushwant Singh's *Train to Pakistan*, with its realistic and touching portrayal of characters, chiefly round, lays bare the grimly tragic situation of the human context in which Khushwant Singh's fictional people march towards the altar of self-immolation. To Shahane, "The concept of common man as a tragic hero is an interesting aspect of the theme and symbol in *Train to Pakistan*." (350)

The novel is a tragedy of human situation. "There is no tragedy without transcendence"[10] and true to this Jugga transcends himself. Jugga's sacrifice is the inner dynamics of tragedy since "the tragic feeling is invoked in us," observes Arthur Miller, "when we are in the presence of a character who is ready to lay down his life to secure one thing . . . his sense of personal dignity."[11] *Train to Pakistan* is a tragedy written in a mock-comic tone, criticising the celebration of freedom with mass murder and bestiality and ingeniously delineating the pity and horror of the two-nation theory. It is "a nightmare with an exciting finish, one closes the novel with a sense of relief."[12]

References

1. V.A. Shahane, "Khushwant Singh: An Artist in Realism," *Critical Essays on Indian Writing in English*, ed. Naik et al (Madras: Macmillan, 1977), p. 344.
2. Harish Raizada, "*Train to Pakistan*: A Study in Crisis of Values," *Khushwant Singh: The Man and the Writer*, ed. R.K. Dhawan (New Delhi: Prestige), p. 126.
3. Khushwant Singh, "Guest of Honour Talk," The Australian Broadcasting Commission's Guest of Honour Programme, broadcast on 5 April 1964.
4. Khushwant Singh, *Train to Pakistan* (London: Chatto and Windus, 1956), p. 54.
5. John Thompson, "Indian Accent," a programme of interviews with Indian Writers broadcast by the Canadian Broadcasting Commission in 1961.
6. Bonamy Dobree, "Thomas Hardy," *English Critical Essays Twentieth Century* (London: OUP, 1942), p. 328.
7. Khushwant Singh, Address to Expo 1967, Auditorium, Montreal, Canada (1967).
8. Review in *The New York Herald Tribune Book Review*, 12 April 1956.
9. William Walsh, *Commonwealth Literature* (London: OUP, 1973), p. 18.
10. Karl Jaspers, "Basic Characteristics of the Tragic," *Tragedy Is Not Enough* (Beacon Press, 1952), p. 41.
11. Arthur Miller, "Tragedy and the Common Man," *The New York Times*, 27 February 1949.
12. K.R. Srinivasa Iyengar, *Indian Writing in English* (Bombay: Asia, 1973), p. 501.

The Novels of R.K. Narayan and Indian Reality

The fictional world of R.K. Narayan appears to be a transcription of the actual world in which we live. His novels float as gently as a lily pad on the surface of Indian life and yet suggest the depths beneath. He has dealt neither in fashionable modes of fiction writing nor in themes of eye-catching topicality. In almost all his novels, he chooses matters of ordinary everyday life. A part of the national life, his novels are universal in their appeal. They please the one and the many.

The term realism has two meanings. First, it may mean depiction of things as they really are, or as they appear to be; secondly, it means the art of making the unreal appear real. A writer may make the impossible appear as probable. To some scholars, realism is the fidelity observed in the transcription of life as it is whereas to some others, it is a plausible interpretation of life. Percy Lubbock defines it as verisimilitude to life because literal transcription is well nigh impossible.

R.K. Narayan does not portray the photographic reality; he rather represents reality which is artistic. In this, he differs from the French realists and naturalists who were interested in the stark and naked realism of life. Narayan depicts a kind of realism which is something more than reportage; he grabs the Indian mind fully with all its superstitious comprehension of life, its gullibility, its bewildering contradictions and its sarcastic comic irony. How far Narayan is realistic in the manner of his narration can be seen from the harmony which his narration acquires in the blending of theme and the style.

In keeping with the middle class milieu of his novels, Narayan adopts a pedestrian style. His is not the vigorous, sensational and colourful style of Manohar Malgonkar. His simple diction mirrors the daily rhythm of life of the middle class people of Malgudi. In this connection Philip Rahv says: "All that we can legitimately ask of a novelist in the matter of language is that it be appropriate to the matter in hand. What is said must not stand in a contradictory relation to the way it is said."[1]

Often preoccupied with the oddities and eccentricities of individuals, their incompatibilities rather than possibilities of human predicament, his art flourishes, as it were, on the use of the commonplace. He limns out the common rhythm of Indian life. The Malgudi of his novels is India in microcosm. Like Hardy's Wessex, Malgudi is a recurrent locale of his novels. It is the symbol of Indian reality. What happens in Malgudi, is in fact what happens to the Indians in general. The landscape in Narayan embodies structural solidity of Indian reality pervaded by the customs and traditions which control human identity and its spatio-temporal continuum. He delineates the ambivalence and the incongruities of life. His novels are an intricate alliance of the serious and the comic, tuned to a series of realistic experiences and encounters. They reflect the typical India. They are a lively and realistic rendering of the interaction of character and a typically Indian situation. The characters dwell in the reality of our existence and the events narrated are like the occurrences of real life. His people take after people we meet in real life. Their world is a replica of the actual and the real. Narayan frequently draws on ancient Indian religious themes, like renunciation, incarnation, re-birth, ahimsa and the law of karma. To him, the Indian myth is a reality. So also to all of us. He invariably resorts to an ancient myth or legend to give vent to his vision of modern life. In *Mr. Sampath*, there is an allusion to the burning of Kama by Lord Shiva. *The Guide* is based on the traditional Hindu belief that Gods can be propitiated and rains can be brought about through fasting and prayer. Vasu, the protagonist of *The Man-Eater of Malgudi*, is modelled on Bhasmasura. In his novel, *A Tiger for Malgudi*, the theme of the oneness of the soul of all living beings—tiger and man alike—has been stressed. Myth in Narayan figures as the ultimate vision of Indian reality. William Walsh holds: "The religious sense of Indian myth is a part of Narayan's grip of reality."[2] But the central mythical idea of the works never mars or bedims the realism of the novels. Narayan is an avowed realist. Basically tales of Indian life, his novels portray individuals who are deeply rooted in the Indian social order. Indian reality in his novels is reflected in the perpetual clash between tradition and modernity. The novelist's spatio-temporal consciousness makes his works more real and genuinely artistic. "Malgudi," observes C.D. Narasimhaiah, "is the microcosm of traditional Indian society."[3] What happens in Malgudi, happens all over India with regional nuances and shifts. The underlying situation in the novels of Narayan is real to all Indians and it is intimately linked to their immediate psychic awareness and social experience. They are not confined to local political and social issues but are concerned with the changing socio-political and socio-cultural influences affecting the daily life of an Indian. Cynthia vanden Driesen holds: "Malgudi reflects a quality of the larger world."[4] Narayan's personages are human types and their problems are universal problems. What is true of Malgudi is true of India. Though a fictional creation, Malgudi breathes the aroma of Indian life.

It is quite evident from *Swami and Friends* that there is hardly any 'ragging' in our schools, and the dreadful tyrants are not senior boys as in Tom Brown's school days or David's experience at Salem House but teachers and headmasters. Ebenezer's denunciations of Krishna is a common feature in Missionary schools in our country. The chapter on Broken Panes describing a strike in the school on the occasion of the Non-cooperation Movement has a historical as well as an intrinsic interest. In fact what happened in India several years ago is recounted realistically. The varied experiences of Swami, the protagonist and his friends Mani and Rajan at Albert Mission School, have been realistically rendered. The final chapter of the novel brings a lump to the throat but scenes in the school are replete with rollicking humour entirely natural and convincing, delineating a lively picture of Indian schools.

Chandran in *The Bachelor of Arts* reads in a college, which is like many other colleges up and down the country. In this novel, Narayan portrays the whole set up of administration with a touch of sarcastic humour. Aziz, the Principal's peon, won't let

Chandran into the Principal's presence. But on Chandran's promising to give him an old coat he has, all obstructions vanish and Chandran is let in. The circumstances in which Chandran meets Malati on the sands of Sarayu and falls instantly in love with her are the stuff of life. Such an accident could happen to anyone at anytime and it does happen. The slavish adherence to the ancient dogmas and doctrines prevailing even to this day has been vividly described. The most striking of these traditional practices is the consultation of horoscopes. Chandran cannot marry Malati because the horoscopes do not tally. Is it not an aspect of Indian reality? It seems as if everything was pre-ordained for an Indian. Through the mental flux of Chandran, Narayan portrays the hackneyed caste system that has generated the crisis of conscience and values, leading to social compartmentalisation and alienation, and individuation of the self. Chandran feels that a marriage would not be tolerated even among sub-sects of the same caste. "If India was to attain salvation, these water tight divisions must go—community, caste, sects, sub-sects, and still further division. He felt very indignant."[5] The novel presents a first-hand account of Indian life from within.

The Dark Room, a tragedy of domestic life and disharmony, attempts a new technique, dexterously real and exquisite, with all the paraphernalia of trivial and familiar confrontations, a common feature of the Indian soil. Like his earlier novels, here too, Narayan sets down a fragment of life as he actually sees it. Bullying husbands like Ramani, and patient wives like Savitri are the stuff with which he weaves the web of his story. Savitri is not patient like the numerous puranic women not because the husband is the lord and the master and it is a sin to flout him but simply because she has no right of exercising her choice in any matter. P.S. Sundaram maintains: "The bully who will bring guests into the house without notice and expect them to be fed, is hardly thought of as a bully by anyone. It is the Indian tradition to honour the guest as God, to share whatever one has with the stranger."[6] The nagging and bullying which Savitri got used to is akin to the hapless plight of many of the Indian housewives of the lower middle-class family. Freedom is certainly a fine concept for women when one is reminded of the "Women's Lib," but persons like Savitri can do only one thing with it—commit suicide. Here is the sort of thing that happens in thousands of households in our country: a few Savitris hang, burn or drown themselves. The great majority dare not do it. It is only suggested of course that every Indian is a tyrant and every Indian wife is obliged to put up with tyranny. Mari and Poni take pity on Savitri and give her shelter. But whereas women of the lower classes like Poni can at a pinch shift for themselves by doing manual work, the Brahmin girl of the middle classes is completely desperate save as a housewife. *The Dark Room* depicts a story, which is the sort of thing that takes place in every society where the double standards are still valid and the women are economically so desperate that they just have to endure what they detest and scorn.

Narayan's novels mirror the real India through living and breathing characters and not through cascades of Sanskrit slokas as in Raja Rao's *The Serpent and the Rope*. His is the India where the frustrated and the forlorn give up themselves to Sanyasa like Krishnan in *The English Teacher*. Susheela, his wife who gives foremost importance to her family and her domestic obligations, is the symbol of a devoted Hindu wife. Krishnan's satirical comment on Indian education is a veritable echo of the contemporary Indian reality: "This education had reduced us to a nation of morons; we were strangers to our own culture and camp followers of another culture, feeding on leavings and garbages."[7]

Margayya, the hero of *The Financial Expert*, begins as a petty moneylender doing business under a banyan tree right in front of the Central Co-operative Land Mortgage Bank in Malgudi. He is typically representative of our money-lending class who amass money by hook or crook. "If the purpose of the Co-operative Movement was the promotion of thrift and the elimination of middlemen, these two were the objects that were defeated here under this banyan tree."[8] And this is what Indian life is where government strategies and steps for progress are obstructed by people like Margayya for selfish interests. But persons like Arul Doss and Balu come in Margayya's way, shatter all his prospects and then Margayya, like any frustrated Indian, consults the astrologer. The astrologer advises Puja and Margayya goes through the rituals of the Puja for good luck and for the propitiation of the adverse stars and planets. This is how men prosper on Indian soil. Pujas and recitation of mantras and slokas becomes their magic wand for luck and prosperity. An aspect of Indian mysticism indeed. The relationship between Margayya and his brother highlights the bonds of kinship in an Indian family. Margayya's assault on Dr. Pal takes the form of "shoe-beating," a typical Indian mode of assaulting. Would a European commit such a nuisance? No.

Waiting for the Mahatma is more suggestive in its portrayal of Indian reality. It is *Kanthapura* distorted. The religious aspect of Indian reality is mirrored in the doings of Granny who, being a pious Hindu, refuses to touch the canvas chair, made out of the skin of dead animals. Even now there are many crones in India who, like Granny, are piously orthodox and traditionally modern.

In *The Guide*, the vicissitudes of Raju's fortunes provide an excellent opportunity to the novelist to satirise the nouveau riche of post-war independent India. The story of a sinner like Raju, an impresario becoming a saint, is a story that has the magnanimity and grandeur of the Indian scene and is a tragedy wholly of it. The novels of Narayan have a unique Indian rural setting like this: "an ancient temple, surrounded by hills, the river Sarayu flowing in front of it, whose very name, if not the river carried its obvious implications for a reader of the *Ramayana*, even as the name of the village—Mangala—has its rich overtones and evocative power."[9] Raju, who malingers to be a mahatma and goes on fast to bring rain to the drought-stricken wasteland is peculiarly Indian. India, too, has many 'Sadhus' and 'Dharmatmas,' practising hypocrisy and fraud in the name of religion and at length meeting their tragic doom, like Raju. The continued absence of rain evokes fantastic speculations from the villagers. One villager wants to know if the rains fall because the movement of the aeroplanes ruffle the clouds while the other seeks to know if the atom bombs are responsible for drying up the clouds. This reveals a humorous and funny aspect of Indian reality—the remarkable co-existence of science and superstition; prescience and nescience; mythology and weather forecasts. Allusions to *The Bhagvad Gita* and Indian legends in *The Man-Eater of Malgudi*, spawn out a peculiar Indian setting.

The conductor of Mempi Bus Transport Corporation Limited has been presented in a humorously fascinating manner. He lectures to the passengers every now and then as though he was a headmaster dealing with school-children: "I am not stopping for more than five minutes; if any one is left behind, he will be left behind, that is all I warn you all, don't blame me later."[10] And in reality, he stays half an hour at each teashop. "The seat of honour has to be reserved for the 'Circle,' the Police Inspector who will not pay for his seat and if the 'seat of honour' is not immediately vacated when he approaches, he will impound the entire bus with all its passengers at the next stop for overcrowding. With the 'Circle' inside, the bus will crawl at twenty miles an hour."[11] Such instances of flexibility in duty and nepotism prevails even in the present bureaucratically dogged social set-up. When a complaint is sent to the Sanitary Inspector of Malgudi to make arrangements for removing the dead animals from the terrace, all that he does is to send a printed form to say that the matter is receiving attention. The Chairman of the Municipality has a sweet-mart with a top storey housing an elementary school—a rickety terrace, which would come down any day, but has been certified safe, because it is the Chairman's building. What did the lives of hundred schoolchildren and six or eight teachers matter? Narayan exposes the stark reality of India with an undertone of sarcasm and banter. He humorously satirises such a faulty system that is eating into the vitals of our society. The patriotic spirit of the then Indians against the despotic and draconian rule of the Britishers is revealed through Jagan in *The Vendor of Sweets*. Unlike Jagdish in *Waiting for the Mahatma*, he is a genuine Gandhiite, who had his skull cracked while trying to pull down the Union Jack from the flag-post in the Collector's bungalow and consequently spent some years in goal. This is true for almost all the revolutionaries of the time. A true Gandhiite, Jagan uses only "non-violent footwear," chappals made out of animals dying a natural death and not butchered for the purpose. A faddist and believer in the profound wisdom of our ancients, the margosa is to him an ambrosial plant, its leaves and fruits always to be preferred to aspirin. Twigs of trees made ideal toothbrushes, not bristles made out of pig's tails. Beef-eating to him is a sin. It is the five deadly sins according to our Shastras. Though the joint family is breaking up all over India, the sense of kinship is strong in a Narayan novel. In *The Financial Expert*, Margayya and his brother, though for most of the time not on speaking terms, are yet next-door neighbours, sharing a well, and in moments of special joy or sorrow simply cannot do without each other.

Ved Mehta maintains: "R.K. Narayan . . . manages by a miracle of perception and choice of detail to convey the Indian without a single false feeling or gesture."[12] Writing under the impact of the growing industrialism and technology, the gross materialism of the age could not shut his eyes to the socio-economic realities of the Indian society. Narayan is a writer whose sympathies and ideals do not isolate him from his socio-historical moorings.

William Walsh observes: "Narayan's fastidious art, blending exact realism, poetic myth, sadness, perception and gaiety, is without precedent in literature in English. . . . It is kind but unsentimental, mocking but uncynical, profoundly Indian but distinctively individual. It fascinates by reason of the authenticity and attractiveness of its Indian setting." (169)

The image of India, which Narayan projects in his novels, has a universality of vision. *The Times Literary Supplement* comments: "What is true of Malgudi is true in the whole world."[13] "Malgudi is an image of India and a metaphor of everywhere else,"[14] observes William Walsh. But this is not all. Cynthia vanden Driesen goes still further to affirm: "Despite the Indian colouring of Narayan's novels . . . we become aware of universal human nature." (57)

Despite all the universal acclaim, Narayan "does not dwell upon the garish and the bizarre features on which Naipaul and Nirad C. Chaudhuri seem to thrive."[15] He depicts Indian reality in all its simplicity and not in its metaphysical ambiguity, as does Raja Rao. His fictional rendering of Indian reality is richly human as that of Dickens but never caricatured. Narayan's novels are a curious blending of the eerie and the commonplace. The extreme simplicity and ingenuousness with which he has portrayed the Indian scene restrict the appeal of his novels both for the native and the alien. V.S. Naipaul maintains: "He operates from deep within his society. The India of Narayan's novels is not the India the visitor sees."[16]

Anthony Thwaite offers a similar observation: "Unlike E.M. Forster's India [Narayan's] is seen from inside."[17] His use of English as a medium of expression to delineate the social reality appears dim and inadequate and it is a literary pitfall. Had he expressed it through his vernacular, he could have portrayed a more genuine and authentic picture of Indian reality. Akhileshwar Jha maintains that it is an "inadequate means of apprehending social reality."[18]

From *The Dark Room* (1938) to *A Tiger for Malgudi* (1983), one clearly perceives the steady encroachment of modernity into our traditional tempo of life. One becomes aware of a profoundly tradition-bound society giving in to the flux of a modern Western way of life. His novels echo the socio-cultural influences on Indian life. Ramani, the protagonist of *The Dark Room*, works for the Englandia Insurance Company and enjoys tennis at the club, Chandran in *The Bachelor of Arts* seriously considers higher education in England while Mali in *The Sweet Vendor* considers the United States as the only apt place for higher studies. *The Guide* chronicles the arrival of the railway in Malgudi. His characters do enjoy a night out at "The Palace," where film featuring Dietrich, Garbo and Laurel and Hardy are regularly screened. Thus the features of modernity are a part of the Indian reality as delineated in the novels of R.K. Narayan. This reality to some critics is the "everyday reality" of an Indian scene. Narayan's is the traditional Indian way of perceiving reality. For him, reality is a unity where there is no intrinsic and fundamental schism between its constituent parts. Accordingly he finds a semblance of unity between the consciousness of a tiger and a man's consciousness in his novel, *A Tiger for Malgudi*. His vision of Indian reality is a harmonious blending of the old and the new, the impulsive and the wary, the rational and the irrational. India, in his novels, becomes the arena of the traditional rhythm of life and the intrusion of modernity into it. Margayya in *The Financial Expert* is temptingly vexed by the thought of purchasing a Western automobile. Dr. Pal induces Margayya to accept the semi-pornographic *Bed Life* for publication. Mali, the son of *The Sweet Vendor*, frantically longs for America and has the hope of writing western fiction. Shanta Bai, the adulterous heroine of *The Dark Room*, complains to Ramani: "A wretched Indian film! I'd give my life to see a Garbo or a Dietrich."[19]

Narayan seems to suggest the disintegrating effect of the West on Indian sensibility and the distortion of traditional social values. He fails to portray the simmering discontent, squalor and poverty of the Indians as does Mulk Raj Anand. What about the socio-political and socio-psychic aspects of Indian reality? Save for *Waiting for the Mahatma* and *The Dark Room*, one doesn't find allusions to any of these aspects of Indian reality. The novelist is humorously obsessed with the socio-comic aspect of Indian reality which accounts for the immense readability of his novels. It is not that he deliberately drags in what is typically Indian—these things are there in the story. Allusions to Indian habits and customs are functional and not informative. It would be wrong to infer that Narayan depicts Indian reality in toto. He is chiefly concerned with the ethos of the then India and not the modern India as we see it now. His is the Hindu India. Rarely had he portrayed any Muslim or Christian character in his novels. However, he has made these characters neither specifically medieval nor ancient but typically Indian. In his book, *Indian Novel in English*, R.S. Singh calls Narayan "a writer of surface realities." Narayan's depiction of Indian reality is not profound. He does not make a liberal and felicitous use of local and regional dialects as does Anand. Hence, the note of realism is thin and foamy. Nevertheless they are a delectably ironical depiction of Indian reality. In fine, they are the comedies of Indianness.

References

1. Phillip Rahv, *Fiction and the Criticism of Fiction* (New York: 1965), p. 58.
2. William Walsh, *R.K. Narayan: A Critical Appreciation* (New Delhi: Allied, 1983), pp. 166-67.
3. C.D. Narasimhaiah, *The Swan and the Eagle* (Simla: Indian Institute of Advanced Study, 1969), p. 136.
4. Cynthia vanden Driesen, "The Achievement of R.K. Narayan," *Literature East and West*, Vol. XXI, Nos. I-4 (Austin: Texas Press), p. 61.
5. R.K. Narayan, *The Bachelor of Arts* (Mysore: Indian Thought Publications, 1937), p. 38.
6. P.S. Sundaram, *R.K. Narayan* (Indian Writers Series, Vol. VI (New Delhi: Arnold-Heinemann, 1973), p. 43.
7. R.K. Narayan, *The English Teacher* (Mysore: Indian Thought Publications, 1945), p. 171.
8. R.K. Narayan, *The Financial Expert* (Mysore: Indian Thought Publications, 1952), p. 2.
9. Narasimhaiah, p. 137.
10. R.K. Narayan, *The Man-Eater of Malgudi* (Mysore: Indian Thought Publications, 1962), p. 48.
11. Sundaram, p. 104.
12. Ved Mehta, *Saturday Review*, XLIV (March 11, 1961), p. 29.
13. Ashis Nandy, *At the Edge of Psychology* (Delhi: 0,U.P., 1980), p. 58.
14. William Walsh, *A Manifold Voice* (London: Chatto and Windus, 1964), p. 22.
15. D.S. Phillip, *Perceiving Indian through the Works of Nirad Chaudhuri, R.K. Narayan and Ved Mehta* (New Delhi: Sterling, 1986), p. 97.
16. M.M. Mahood, *The Colonial Encounter* (Totowa, New Jersey: Rowman and Littlefield, 1977), p. 94.
17. Anthony Thwaite, "*The Painter of Signs*," *Times Literary Supplement*, Jan. 20, 1976, pp. 6-7.
18. Akhileshwar Jha, *Intellectuals at the Cross-Roads: The Indian Situation* (New Delhi: Vikas, 1977), p. 81.
19. R.K. Narayan, *The Dark Room* (London: Macmillan, 1938), p. 90.

Nirad Chaudhuri's *The Autobiography of an Unknown Indian*: A Critique

A monument to "the creative clash of two civilizations,"[1] *The Autobiography* tells the story of the early period of Nirad Chaudhuri's life, of the condition "in which an Indian grew to manhood in the early decades of this century."[2] It is in the nature of an intellectual acrobatics interpreting Indian history from a nonconformist standpoint. Chaudhuri exhibits his critical acumen and insight by his elucidatory and subjective approach to the problems of Indian history, society, politics and culture. He says: "The story I want to tell is the story of the struggle of a civilization with a hostile environment, in which the destiny of British rule in India became necessarily involved. My main intention is thus historical. . . . The book may be regarded as a contribution to contemporary history." (vii) Highly informative and reflective, *The Autobiography* is an Indian self-portrait, mirroring the tortured and asserting spirit of a scholar extraordinary: "I never developed a true religious and spiritual life. . . . I had no religious culture." (125) But it is more of a national than personal history.

The Autobiography gives us a coherent and imaginatively unified picture of India's past history since all the chapters focus on our socio-cultural aspects. Chaudhuri says that it is our "unity in diversity" which has urged the British to look at Indians with esteem and regard. Chaudhuri says that ours is a civilisation with past achievements and we are a single community despite being endowed with a multi-racial and multi-lingual culture. As human beings, they transcend these narrow conscriptions and barriers:

> the Indian people crossed the line which divides primitive peoples from civilised peoples. They could now be said to belong to the same species as the Homosapiens historicus of Europe. (442)

In this connection, Srinivasa Iyengar observes: "Chaudhuri's real aim is to write history, and the autobiographical exercise is merely a means to get the history started. Early in his college days he had fallen in love with history."[3]

The Autobiography is not only Chaudhuri's verdict on the British Raj but it is also a virulent criticism of the Indians being poor imitators of the Western materialist culture. It delineates through concrete images the alien society's superior material culture that transforms us into what Naipaul would have called 'mimic men.' The author cities an instance of the steam-powered vessel of Mr. Stapleton on its maiden arrival near Kishorganj:

> As the house-boat stood moored a little stand-offishly, we . . . gaped at it in wonder. It seemed to be a palace in comparison in spite of its beautiful lines, its red, white and green paint, and its essentially aquatic presence it was not . . . quite in keeping with the surroundings. (5)

Cultural collision between the natives and aliens occurred even at the mundane level of existence. In 1916, Chaudhuri reports that the boys of the matriculation class bowed down to locomotives as if to gods. We are also apprised of the English steel trunks which Chaudhuri's father purchased two or three a year. Even the catalogues of British departmental stores were regularly pursued in the Chaudhuri household for the items that might improve domestic convenience. Chaudhuri's interaction with the West was chiefly concerned with the spiritual realm of existence:

> My Westernization is of the older pattern, concerned more with the mind than material things.[4]

The West had a tremendous impact on his mind. He acutely felt it like the other Indians of the time but these occidental influences were "felt mainly in the higher centres of consciousness and manifested themselves in the sphere of culture."[5] Chaudhuri says that the British Empire conferred subjecthood on us and at the same time it withheld citizenship. Cultural contact was sensibly felt by him. It was a psychic and imaginative experience. In the Prefatory Note (Book I, Early Environment) Chaudhuri says:

> My first account will thus be of the little country town in which I was born and lived till my twelfth year, my second, of my ancestral village; and my third, of the village of my mother's folk. These three accounts will make up the first three chapters of this book; but as England, evoked by imagination and enjoyed emotionally, has been as great an influence on me as any of the three places sensibly experienced.

In Chapter IV of Book I, he has very deftly and superbly captured the spell of England. He says, "the chiaroscuro of our knowledge of England was extremely sensational . . . so that what we knew gripped us with immeasurably greater power." (101) In this context, Raghavendra Rao observes: "Chaudhuri had also built up the physical image of England as a place, churning out a whole mytho-geography out of books read and pictures seen. The England thus conjured up was 'a country which possessed not only beautiful spots but also place names which sounded beautiful.' England was always seen as a sea-girt."[6]

Chaudhuri refers to Shakespeare, Webster, Charles Lamb and even to the characters of Jane Austen. His approach to the English works of men of letters is elucidatory and comparative. Speaking of Shakespeare's *Julius Caesar*, he says:

> Our familiarity with the name of Julius Caesar was only a byproduct of our knowledge of Shakespeare, and the first idea we formed of the great Roman was in the image of Mr. Rames Roy, a top-form boy of Kishorganj High School, who in a black English suit had taken the part of Caesar in a performance of Act III, Scene 1, given by the senior students. (103)

Again about Homer's *Iliad* and the Indian epic *Ramayana*, he says that it was the obvious parallelism which deceives us:

> In both cases there was an abducted woman. Sita in the *Ramayana* and Helen in the *Iliad*. In both cases there were two rescuing brothers, Rama and Lakshmana in the Indian epic and Menelaus and Agamemnon in the Greek. (103)

Speaking of John Milton's magnanimous personality, Chaudhuri says:

> Milton stood before us in solitary and somewhat awe-inspiring grandeur. His claims upon us were manifold. In the first place, he was the author of the bright volume in the glass-fronted cupboard. Secondly, he was the model of Michael Madhusudan Dutt. Thirdly, he was the writer of a most striking line which my father was fond of repeating and which ran as follows: 'Better to reign in hell than serve in heaven.' Lastly, it appeared he had something to do with the execution of Charles I, who had tried to deprive the English people of their liberties. (104)

But Chaudhuri's lucid prose at times degenerates into bold and airy exaggerations exhibiting his parochial sentiment, when he says:

> If any wholehearted Bonapartists were to be found anywhere in the world at the end of the nineteenth century and the beginning of the twentieth they were to be found in Bengal. (105)

He further makes a verbal display of his deep-seated love for the Bengalis' intellectual and literary calibre: "I do not know if any other country or people in the world has ever made one author the epitome, test, and symbol of literary culture as we Bengalis did with Shakespeare in the nineteenth century. . . . It was a cult which we had made typically Bengali." (197) Even he goes to the extent of contrasting a Tudor chest, with the native wooden box made by the native craftsman.

Chaudhuri talks about our curiously mixed feelings of love and hate towards the English people. Articulating his ambivalent attitude towards the English in his critique of a war in which England was a participant, he observes: "One half of us automatically shared in the English triumph, while the other and the patriotic half wanted the enemies of England to win." (108) Nirad Chaudhuri, the historian, gives an account of European history as a symbol of man's struggle for freedom: "European history was a series of struggles for freedom, as a result of which the ambit of a beneficent and fertilizing freedom had been enlarged in ever widening circles, in the course of modern history." (111)

Look at the caustic remarks of Niradbabu, the anti-Indian, on an Indian's lack of balance, proportion and psychic equilibrium. He says that an Indian is impulsive by nature:

> to ask an Indian to be balanced among a number of things, each good in its way, is to ask him, not to be effective in his varied loyalties, but to be futile in all of them. He has neither the vitality nor the will-power which springs from that vitality to observe proportion in his pursuits. He is and can be driven only by his impulses and emotions, fixed into impulsive and emotional habits, and these impulses and emotions cannot be checked in their natural course without bringing about . . . an atrophy of the whole motive power of effort. (222)

The most unique, single discursive work, *The Autobiography* is concerned with Chaudhuri's fascination with himself. "Here," says William Walsh, "Chaudhuri sees himself as an object in a landscape or as an impulse in a more inclusive and controlling rhythm, and the whole presentation of the self is impressively tranquil and objective." (45)

Chaudhuri's intellectual self was shaped and moulded by the classical ideals of Greece and Rome. Reading of the classical texts brought him enlightenment and through these textbooks he acquired "a feeling of oneness with Athens." (477) Despite his closeness with the Athenian culture and the classical texts, Chaudhuri humbly confesses that he "never became a scholar." (336) "A small number of books, which even yet I have not seen and about which I had only read," says Niradbabu, "stirred my imagination so deeply in my early college days that they may be reckoned as very powerful influences on my intellectual growth." (340)

About the role of the historian, Chaudhuri says that he is an impartial judge of men and events. He is a man speaking to man. Ideas which are truths in religion and politics are forces in history and the task of a historian is to reflect these ideas and facts with utmost sincerity, fidelity and detachment:

> The historian must be content to state facts as they happened, or, to use a modern phrase, to show a development without intruding his opinions and predilections into the narrative. His position is not

> among the fellowmen of whom he is writing. He does not share their joys and passions nor mingles in their affairs. His position is that of a spectator who stands on a balcony and watches a crowd street under him. (353)

To Chaudhuri "objectivity is a distinct advance in the direction of the historical point of view" and that the "fundamental idea of history is the idea of change." (354)

Dedicated to "The Memory of the British Empire in India," *The Autobiography* describes all that was noble and ideal within us being moulded and transformed by the British rule in India. The view of history that Chaudhuri projects is highly unorthodox. He says at the end of "An Essay on the Course of Indian History" that "from the personal standpoint, the historical thesis has emancipated him from a malaise that has haunted me throughout my life." (526) Speaking of his alienated plight during his educational career, he further says, "During the years of my education I was becoming a stranger to my environment . . . in the next ten years I was oppressed by a feeling of antagonism to the environment." (526) Despite having aped all the appurtenances of Westernization, India has remained a static entity. Hence, Chaudhuri bemoans the Indian endeavour to carve out a modern culture out of an East-West cultural synthesis. There was an all-out effort by Indian intellectuals for taking in the West. Michael Madhusudan Dutt, Raja Ram Mohun Roy and Bankim Chandra were the pioneers in bringing about an East-West cultural tryst. But extreme Westernization in some cases led to nativization, as with Michael Madhusudan Dutt who having begun his literary career being inspired by Western literature had at length to return to his native Bengal. Not only that, even he had to return to his native language after carrying out his literary pursuits in the English language. His "early poetry was written in English, but after once going over to Bengali he never came back to English for literary expression." (196) Bankim Chandra, too, wrote his very first novel in English, but "came over to Bengali permanently after that youthful misfire." (196) Chaudhuri sarcastically points out that the English were more hostile than the most bigoted Hindu orthodox to the modern Indian culture based on East-West cultural fusion. As pointed out by the critics, Chaudhuri cannot be dubbed as an anti-Indian for he entertained no ambition of hobnobbing with the English in India. "As long as I lived in Calcutta," says Chaudhuri, "I wore no article of English clothing and had none. In general, I disliked and despised the local English." (376) Chaudhuri was never an adherent of the British Empire, its ideas and ideals. He was out and out an Indian, a true Bengali babu:

> The British Empire in India has 'perished without my ever coming into intimate personal contact with Englishmen. . . . I do not regret it for with all the Anglicanism of my spirit I should have felt a total stranger in the English society of Calcutta. (377)

Nirad Chaudhuri, the Anglophile, had a special fascination for the beauty associated with English life. Such a beautiful life had left an indelible romantic impression on his mind:

> However, scrappy and simple our ideas of English life and society might have been, they could not exist at all without the accompaniment of some visual suggestion. Everything we read about the British Isles or in English evoked pictures of the external appearance of the country. . . . Taken together, these gave us the impression of a country of great beauty . . . a country which possessed not only beautiful spots but also place-names which sounded beautiful . . . their beauty of appearance produced a vivid effect on me. (113)

Despite such romantic fascination that the English way of life had on Chaudhuri and despite the magic spell it had cast on his psyche, Chaudhuri "could never think of England," as he "thought of Bengal and of India, as a stretch of land alone." (115) Very humorously does Chaudhuri talk about the Indianization of English textbooks in order to make them easily comprehensible to the average Indian student: "when I was young the educational authorities had a sudden inspiration that it was too much of a burden for young Indian boys to have to cope with English ideas in an English background in addition to having to master the intricacies of a foreign language. In pursuance of this theory our English textbooks were being Indianized as the administration of India was Indianized later." (116) Chaudhuri attributes the cause of the fall of the British Raj to "the bankruptcy of European civilization, its spiritual poverty, and its moral iniquity." (323) Another factor that precipitated its sudden fiasco was the inefficiency and the "declining calibre"[7] of the Viceroys sent to India:

> But India had no Viceroy of genius after Lord Curzon. Hardinge, Reading, and Willingdon were clever men, who succeeded in stealing a few marches on the nationalist. . . . They may be compared to very experienced old foxes. . . . But they were not the grand animals to scatter the pack with a roar and rush. Not for a single moment between 1905 and 1945 did the British Government in India succeed in wresting the initiative from the nationalists, although at quite a number of junctures that could easily have been done. (326)

The unique trait of Chaudhuri's critique is that he represents India as a static and moribund culture. He debunks the Hindu culture. To him, the Hindu civilisation is "dead forever, and cannot be resuscitated, and to hope to create a second civilization of the same order is for us today a superannuated piece of folly." (521) "In the eighteenth century," says Chaudhuri, "on the eve of the establishment of British rule, the Hindus had no recollection of their real past, nor any idea of the true character of the classical Sanskritic civilisation. Their Hinduism was a broken-up and simplified version of the Hinduism of ancient India. It was unorganised in space and unsupported in time." (442) He further adds, almost derogatorily and disparagingly:

> Hindu society does not teach its youth to face life bravely. The phrase 'courage of life' is unintelligible to a Hindu, who accepts the first wail of birth as the leitmotif of existence and manages quite successfully to lead a mock-turtle's life during the whole of it. (369)

One of the most controversial and difficult writers of the age, Chaudhuri sounds a bit anti-Indian in *The Autobiography*, especially in his criticism of Hindu culture. Hence, it won't be erroneous on the part of the patriotic and orthodox Indian readers to describe the book as "The Autobiography of a Known Anti-

Indian." This is not all. He even goes to the extent of saying: "Hinduism appears to be swimming against the current . . . it is a retrograde and out of sympathy with reality" (439) and with Alberuni he agrees that "Hindus are haughty, foolish, vain, self-conceited and stolid. They are by nature niggardly." (416) It seems Nirad Chaudhuri's love for the Hindus is only skin-deep. But such seemingly pessimistic appearance of this great man of letters is only a wild guess for he is very judicious in his critical remarks. He appears to be an anti-Hindu but in reality he is not so. He is all praise for Hinduism's moral virtues: "Hinduism," he says, "cannot justly be charged with having let down moral conduct . . . it has safeguarded the operative part of morality through a method peculiar to itself." (222)

Chaudhuri says that all endeavours of the Indians to imitate the West and be Europeanised has been a failure and what one sees today is nothing but "an immense expense of debased Europeanization mottled here and there with Hindu or Muslim traits." (508) This dilution is transparent in every sphere of our cultural activity. We have been barbarized. About the Western education, Chaudhuri says that it was received only outwardly and superficially. We have not imbibed the spirit of Western education in us. In spite of our aping the Western culture, we are still not modern in spirit and temper. Our "Westernization" is by and large sartorial and cosmetic. Our 'Secondrateness' has made us a poor travesty of all that is Western and European. We have missed the reality beneath the surface of our sham and hypocritical existence. This is our predicament, something uniquely conducive to our sedimented and fossilised feelings and ideas about the West. Our attempts at Westernisation are limited to the adoption of Western dress, food and manners which does not necessarily mean the acceptance of occidental ideas and values.

Chaudhuri's extremist thesis in *The Autobiography* that Indian history comprises three cycles during each of which "a strong and creative foreign influence provided the primary motive force viz., the mid-European Aryan, the Muslim and the British respectively . . . appears very much like an intellectual extension of the wish-fulfilment of a self-confessed Anglophile, alienated from his own culture."[8] The invasion of India by the Europeans, especially the British was a blessing to the Indians. It aroused in us our feelings of nationalism and made us what we are today. Chaudhuri seems to acquiesce with Vivekananda who said that "one of the great blessings of British rule in India was that the days of exclusive privilege and exclusive claims were gone forever from the soil of India. . . . Even to Muhammadan rule we owe that great blessing, the destruction of exclusive privilege. . . . The Muhammadan conquest of India came as salvation to the downtrodden, to the poor." (qtd. 434) While speaking at a public meeting on religion, Vivekananda said, "Had it not been for the power of the Anglo-Saxons, we should not have met here today to discuss the influence of our Indian spiritual thought." (*Ibid.*)

With a relish for the specific and a refined perception, Chaudhuri eulogises the Britishers' love for the actual, the concrete and the substantial, something which was lacking in Indian civilisation which is manifest in Hinduism with its love for the illusory, the unreal, the abstract and the unsubstantial. Hinduism is not with the current, it is against the tide of life. As said earlier, it is retrograde and out of tune with reality. Chaudhuri also focuses on the influence of the English language on our men and manners. He says that the linguistic basis of modern Indian culture is made up of a combination of English, a denatured vernacular, and a mixed, colloquial language. And it is this fact which testifies to the basically alien character of modern Indian culture. Even our literatures today are alien in spirit, since what we write today hardly has the stamp of originality. It is but an idea of an idea, an imitation of an imitation. It is an absorption of all that is a lien without any assimilation. Our use of the English language and literature is just a mechanical process. This is because we "never know the Englishmen properly."

The socio-cultural and socio-historical facts of *The Autobiography* are supported by "a massive fund of anthropological and historical learning and penetrated by sensitively intelligent sociological speculation."[9] Basically melancholic and nervy, the tone of *The Autobiography* is less cordial and almost humorously solemn. The attitude that Chaudhuri exhibits is arrogant and antagonistic. His historical vision is catholic but at times it becomes myopic and hyperbolic. Hence, I do not agree with William Walsh when he says that Chaudhuri is "faithfully Indian and saltily himself." (51) But Walsh is certainly right when he says: "He fiercely cherishes what most people would find intolerable, the identity of the alien" and the most tragic of all, Chaudhuri makes "half the population of Indian foreigners in their own country." (51) Truly indeed, an Indian, especially a Hindu, after reading *The Autobiography* becomes an alien in his own soil since the cultural attire which he puts on today is a mask. It is a borrowed garment which smacks of all that is occidental, all that is second-rate and an imitation of the West.

References

1. William Walsh, *Indian Literature in English* (New York: Longman, 1990), p. 52.
2. Nirad C. Chaudhuri, *The Autobiography of an Unknown Indian* (Bombay: Jaico, 1973), p. vii.
3. K.R. Srinivasa Iyengar, *Indian Writing in English* (Bombay: Asia, 1973), p. 591.
4. Nirad C. Chaudhuri, "The Western Influence on India," *The Atlantic*, March 1964, p. 71.
5. *Ibid.*, p. 72.
6. Raghavendra K. Rao, "An Epitaph for the British Raj," *Critical Essays on Indian Writing in English*, ed. Naik et. al. (Madras: Macmillan, 1977), p. 395.
7. *Ibid.*, p. 398.
8. M.K. Naik, *A History of Indian English Literature* (New Delhi: Sahitya Akademi, 1992), p. 265.
9. Walsh, p. 46.

The Quest for Meaning: A Study of Amitav Ghosh's *The Shadow Lines*

Basically a memory novel, Amitav Ghosh's *The Shadow Lines* presents a dexterous blending of private lives and public events into a desultory mosaic of history. The narrator's story unfurls itself through fragmentary streams of consciousness where the private turmoil of the individual is reflected in the public chaos and crises. It is through the stories narrated by Tridib that the narrator, a young boy, validates his experiences: "Tridib had given me worlds to travel in and he had given me eyes to see them with."[1]

The question that Amitav Ghosh raises or seems to ask to his readers is that whether or not one can draw a demarcating line between imagination and reality and the implied response that he offers is "No." There indeed cannot be a dividing line between imagination and reality. Ghosh seems to suggest that there can only be a "shadow line" between imagination and reality, since reality is too vast and complex a concept to be circumscribed within historical chronology or geographical contours. A place is more than its geographical and historical features. It carries a deep imaginative meaning. The narrator disapproves of Ila's down-to-earth perception of reality. He says:

> I could not persuade her that a place does not merely exist, that it has to be invented in one's imagination; that her practical bustling London was no less invented than mine, neither more nor less true, only very far apart. (21)

The interpretation of reality in mundane terms, as does Ila, is a falsification of it, since such a perception of reality is shorn of its true meaning. It lacks imaginative perception of feeling. It is gross. But Ila is obsessed with such feelings and hence the narrator's failure to persuade and convince her to a meaningful imaginative interpretation of reality. Amitav Ghosh seems to say that it is imagination alone which can portray a lucid and enduring picture of reality. Hence, he gives more emphasis to the creative role of imagination, in delineating the uncoiling of memories through the stream-of-consciousness of Tridib and other characters in the novel like the grandmother: Exploration of meaning occurs at two planes—the private and the public. In the first section of the novel, "Going Away," the novelist focuses on London on the eve of and during the war. London is vividly portrayed through the narrator's deft dispensation of his historical imagination. The significance of war is explored both at the personal and the human level. At the personal level there is a feeling of pity and sympathy, of fellow-feeling brought about by the shadow of an impending death and at the national (public) level, there is a feeling of masked and counterfeit exhilaration across national borders, and both in England and in Germany. Sharmila Guha Mazumdar opines that this sense of exhilaration is "the defence mechanism that people developed to combat the sense of doom."[2] The personally experienced reality of Tridib colours the imagination of the storyteller. It is through Tridib and the grandmother that the narrator views reality and lends meaning to his meaningless infantile fancy. The title "The Shadow Lines" becomes an ambivalent symbol. It suggests the dichotomy of one's mind, the shadow lines that pervade the minds of the people. Grandmother's son says:

> This is the modern world. The border isn't on the frontier; it's right inside the airport. You'll see. You'll cross it when you have to fill in all those disembarkation cards and things. (151-52)

In the absence of any clear-cut division, the meaning of nationalism as described in the novel becomes quite blurred and vague. The narrator unable to vividly comprehend "these physical equivalents of the division"[3] says: "They had drawn their borders, believing in that pattern, in the enchantment of lines, hoping perhaps that once they had etched their borders upon the map, the two bits of land would sail away from each other like the shifting tectonic plates of the pre-historic Gondwanaland." (233)

Amitav Ghosh aims to drive home the meaning of nationalism, in the minds of the readers, through the characters in the novel. The narrator's grandmother thinks nationalism a holy and sacred word which has become the focus of political thinking in the nineteenth and twentieth century. It suggests everything that is anti-British. Sharmila Guha Mazumdar observes: "In her desire to win political freedom she dreamt of killing English officials. She even considered war as a necessary evil which inspired the idea of nationalism and thus strengthened the foundation of a nation." (146)

Nationalism in the late twentieth century degenerated into political animosity between the Indians and the Englishmen. Such was the narrow-mindedness of the grandmother that she viewed nationalism as a belligerent and recalcitrant attitude held by the Indians towards the Englishmen. She failed to have a proper grasp of nationalism in her mind. Not only the grandmother but also Irishmen like Mike thought that "for a person to be rightfully Indian, it was necessary to kill Englishmen." (Mazumdar) Such is the individual enmity between the Indian and the Englishman that they fail to form a meaningful interpretation of nationalism. In the section "Coming Home" Ghosh explores the meaning of political freedom. Indian nationalism, a manifestation of political freedom, fails to guarantee the territorial integrity of the country. The historic event of Partition gave a jolt to the Indian's sense of nationalism, Mazumdar holds that "nationalism in the Indian context changed its meaning to exclude people on the other side of the border but could not include everybody on this side of paradise." (146) But I would suggest that the characters fail to form a cogent picture of nationalism because of the lack of an inner harmony, or rather the lack of a mutual sense of love and regard for each other. After all what is nationalism and political freedom without the element of love and regard for oneself as well as others? But the grandmother, with her perspicacity and clarity of vision gives her own views of nationalism. She thinks that the sentiments of nationalism can only develop through war and bloodshed. Her feelings of nationalism are related to the ideals of self-esteem and national power. The grandmother tells the narrator:

> It took those people a long time to build that country . . . years and years of war and bloodshed. Everyone who lives there has earned his right to be there with blood. . . . War is their religion. That's what it takes to make a country. (77-78)

In a bid for political freedom, people have frenziedly and madly given themselves to terrorism and communal violence. "Even characters like the grandmother and Ila who do not indulge in violence are on the fringe of it."[4] Her willingness to run errands for the Bengal terrorists and kill the English magistrate at Khulna depict her love of violence and war. If in the grandmother the quest for political freedom manifests in her belligerent and violent motives, then in Ila it manifests in her personal freedom, her breaking away from her family for a cosmopolitan way of life in London. It is this quest for freedom—personal and political—that imparts a realistic touch to the novel. With a dialogic narrative approach Ghosh reveals the motive behind everyone indulging in violence and mutual hatred. Robi, the IAS officer, philosophies to Ila and the narrator:

> You know, if you look at the pictures on the front pages of the newspapers at home now, all those pictures of dead people—in Assam, the North-East, Punjab, Sri Lanka, Tripura—people shot by terrorists and separatists and the army and police, you'll find somewhere behind it all, that single word: everyone doing it to be free. (246)

Amitav Ghosh does not describe to elaborate the meaning of concepts and ideologies. On the other hand, he insinuates the readers into the world of history through the mind of characters, their painful and nostalgic recallings and recollections and it is these psychic intrusions that destroy the narrative sequence of the story. The novel, therefore, becomes a series of random reflections, for it reflects "reality itself in the process of its unfolding . . . the tendencies of a new world still in the making."[5] Personal histories, family histories and the history of the nation are weaved into a thin and transparent gossamer of imagination.

They are restructured in a quest for meaning, of quest for knowledge since what the characters reminiscence has the touch of inaccuracy. Hence, Tridib is not sure as to the accuracy of his memory: he didn't know whether it had really happened or he had imagined it." (26) He gives meaning to his reminiscences through his imagination and tells the narrator to "use imagination with precision" (29) to make it sensible and. meaningful. It is through imagination that the "I" narrator experiences much of his life in the process of knowing through a search for meaning:

> I shook my head violently. . . . You're lying I shouted at her. That can't be a staircase because it's flat, and staircases go up, they aren't flat. And that can't be upstairs because upstairs has to be above and that isn't above; that's right beside the drawing room. I dropped to my knees and began to scrabble around in the dust, rubbing out the lines, shouting: You're lying, you're mad, this can't be a house. (70)

This is nothing but the travesty of a quest by the half-knowing young narrator who makes a fancifully naive approach to validate materiality. But the narrator, despite his imaginative skill, fails to comprehend the real when his childhood hero, Tridib, falls a prey to the "seamless silence," (270) that meaningless violence in Dhaka. It was May Price who finally recounted the incident that gobbled Tridib. K. Damodar Rao observes: "The silence that preceded and followed the revelation was a moving statement on the actualization of internal violence. The search and the revelation together cause a harrowing experience for the narrator." (65)

In fact the search for meaning amidst communal frenzy and political chaos is motivated by the awareness of a need, that is the need to know the cause and nature of silence that premeates the life of the inquisitive young narrator:

> Every word I write about those events of 1964 is the product of a struggle with silence. It is a struggle I am destined to lose, have already lost—for even after all these years, I do not know where within me, in which corner of my world, this silence lies. . . . It is simply a gap, a hole, an emptiness in which there are no words. (218)

The silent quest of the narrator for meaning in life, for filling up the inner void in him with words forms the focus of the novel and it is this search for words, the need to articulate silence, that "throws the notions of secularism, nationalism and freedom into disarray."[6] But could the narrator fill up the gap, the silence in him with words and voice? All voices seem to be stifled in that traumatic psychic state where uncertainty and horrific apprehensions make our otherwise peaceful existence on this earth meaningless, futile. Look at Ghosh's graphic account of the communal situation in the sub-continent where all forms of quest for meaning are rendered futile:

> It is like the fear of the victim of an earthquake, of people who have lost faith in the stillness of the earth. . . . It is a fear that comes of the knowledge that normalcy is utterly contingent that the spaces that surround one, the streets that one inhabits, can become, suddenly and without warning, as hostile as a desert in a flash flood. (204)

Such a psychological situation alienates man from and even sets apart the sub-continent from the rest of the world. It is this that has "the special quality of loneliness that grows out of the fear of the war between oneself and one's image in the mirror." (204) Such meaningless absurdity of our shaky existence where, in the words of Matthew Arnold, "ignorant armies clash by night," ("Dover Beach") where incertitude rules our life, man's quest for meaning and value turn into a cry in wilderness.

The novel urges the reader's involvement in actively constructing for himself an interpretive framework that runs parallel to the characters' traumatic and anguished recounting of the past. Especially the grandmother's remembrances of her painful and haunting past have been vividly and dramatically presented. They give validity to her existence, meaning to her chaotic and tense life. The grandmother, the narrator, Tridib, Ila and many other non-Indian characters present a multiplicity of voices characterised by variegated discourse and language to recount their experiences. This is nothing but a striving after meaning and reason for the stifled thoughts of the past tormenting their psyche.

Replete with interpretive potential, an appealing aspect of the novel is its multivocal dimension, and a structure fragmented and episodic, successfully leading to a conclusion that the historical events of the past, political rivalry, religious and communal strife and even personal trauma and nostalgia are beyond objectification. Through multivocal narrative, Ghosh lends meanings to social and political chaos reflected in the individual's search of a meaningful existence personified in memory as a relived experience.

The meaning of political freedom in the modern world is for Ghosh a complicated and intricate one. It is without a clear solution. In land where culture and communities thrive on mutual hatred and antagonism, the quest for meaning is liable to end in failure. The journey motif which runs through the fabric of the story like the grandmother's journey to Dhaka, in the second part of the novel,`and the narrator's journey backwards in time is symbolic of the quest for meaning in life. It is the quest for wholeness, an attempt to impose a pattern to our otherwise chaotic experience. It is a shadow line. The novel which depicts violence and crude barbarity through the recounting of riot memories seems to convey the message that man's running after self-esteem, his search for an authentic selfhood through freedom to act the way he likes, is a mirage. It would only come to a point of no return. Hence, the futility of the quest for the validation of one's existence. Hence, it is difficult to say why Tridib gave up his life, why did he throw himself to his own death. Louis James maintains that he was "drawn by the 'shadow-line' of imaginative sympathy."[6] But the question that crops up in our mind is why he did it. It is a mystery. Ghosh does not give any clear answer to this and so Tridib's death, though a real sacrifice, becomes a mystery, an absurdity for the common man who fails to find any meaning in it. The quest for meaning thus continues without finality.

References

1. Amitav Ghosh, *The Shadow Lines* (New Delhi: Ravi Dayal Publisher, 1988), p. 20.
2. Sharmila Guha Mazumdar, "Amitav Ghosh's *The Shadow Lines* and *In an Antique Land*: Some Thematic Considerations," *Indian Literature Today*, ed. R.K. Dhawan (New Delhi: Prestige, 1994), Vol. I, p. 145.
3. Damodar K. Rao, "Silence as Possible Mode of Response in Amitav Ghosh's *The Shadow Lines*," *The Indian Journal of English Studies*, Vol. XXXIII, 1994-95, p. 63.
4. Novy Kapadia, "Imagination and Politics in Amitav Ghosh's *The Shadow Lines*," *The New Indian Novel in English*, ed. Viney Kirpal (New Delhi: Allied, 1990), p. 205.
5. Mikhail Bakhtin, "Epic and Novel," *The Dialogic Imagination*, ed. Michael Holquist, trans. Caryl Emerson and Michael Holquist (Austin: Univ. of Texas Press, 1981), p. 7.
6. Damodar Rao, p. 65.
7. Louis James, "Shadow Lines: Cross-Cultural Perspectives in the Fiction of Amitav Ghosh," *Indian Literature Today*, p. 160.

Gandhi and Indian Novel in English

Indian novel in English owes far more to Gandhiji than is generally recognised. With the Gandhian revolution in our socio-political life, there came also a revolution in our writing. The themes developed by Gandhian novelists are but theoretical applications of what the Mahatma preached. In Indian Writing in English Gandhiji figures more as a powerful force that brings about a moral change in, the mass than as an ideal simply to be cherished. Before Gandhi came, Indian English novelists had lost touch with contemporary social reality. They lived in ivory towers built on the life of landed aristocracy or fairy tales or historical romances or religious scriptures or medieval knight-errantry. Novelists like Bankim. Chandra Chatterjee in *Rajmohan's Wife* (1864), Sirdar Jogendra Singh in *Nur Jehan* (1909), S.M. Mitra in *Hindupore* (1909), A.S.P. Ayyar in *A Historical Romance of Ancient India*, A. Madhavish in *Clarinda* (1915) and Dwijendranath Neogi in *Sacred Tales of India* (1916) etc. wrote under the influence of Anglo-Indian women novelists like G.H. Bell, Charlotte Cameron, Maud Diver, A. Ursula Becket, Flora Anne Steel etc.

It is only when Gandhi appeared that Indian English fiction took a different and distinct turn with Mulk Raj Anand, Raja Rao, R.K. Narayan and Bhabani Bhattacharya in the 1930s and 1940s. With his love for the lowliest and the lost, Gandhi played a catalytic role. He provided a new literary possibility. He inspired creativity on a scale surpassed by none. Under his influence Tarashankar Banerjee in *Dhartidevata* and Satinath Bhaduri in *Jagari* depicted the life of the masses. The emphasis shifted from the high to the low, from the learned to the illiterate, from the vociferous to the voiceless. To quote M.K. Naik, "The 'Three Musketeers' of Indian Fiction in English—Mulk Raj Anand, Raja Rao and R.K. Narayan—started writing during 1930s, and the first of the novels of the first two demonstrate the Gandhian impact convincingly."[1]

Gandhiji appears as a character in Anand's *The Sword and the Sickle* and *Untouchable*, R.K. Narayan's *Waiting for the Mahatma*, K.A. Abbas's' *Inquilab*, Nagarajan's *Chronicles of Kedaram* and Venu Chittale's *In Transit*. He appears as a pervasive influence in Raja Rao's *Kanthapura* and K.S. Venkataramani's *Kandan, the Patriot*.

One may ask what was it in Gandhian ideas that left so abiding an impression on Indian English novelists? Gandhian ideology lent their novels a frame of reference. It linked them to the soil. It took them to the roots of Indian culture. It created in them a social awareness and helped them to creatively interpret the social reality. It made them look at man as a social animal, an individual with his responses and reactions. It sent them searching for a national identity. It enabled them to share their intellectual journey through modern Western ideas back to the reinterpretation and renewal of the life of Indian traditions. Thus, Gandhi helped not only to recharge the political life of India but also to reorient Indian literary values.

Each of these writers adopted Gandhi according to his own intellectual inclinations and artistic compulsions. Yet there was a common thread of thought. The freedom struggle of India under the indomitable stewardship of Gandhi gave these novelists a common platform. It was an exciting emotional experience, a Renaissance of nationalist feeling, a new experience of seeing this lone man moulding and manipulating the destiny of India, making history. It revived their interest in the cultural heritage of India they had lost touch with through Western education. It gave them their themes. It gave them their thoughts. It turned them into political novelists. Mulk Raj Anand based *Untouchable* on casteism, Raja Rao's *Kanthapura* on village reconstruction, R.K Narayan's *Swami and Friends* on Gandhian Non-cooperation Movement and Bhabani Bhattacharya's *So Many Hungers* on Quit India Movement.

Venkataramani's Murugan in *Murugan, the Tiller* is an exponent of Gandhian economics, whereas Kandan in *Kandan, the*

Patriot is a proponent of Gandhian politics. Even Venkataramani's *Jatadharan*, a collection of stories, and *The Next Rung*, a critique of modern civilisation, bear the stamp of the Mahatma's influence. Civilization in *The Next Rung* has been looked at and sketched from a Gandhian point of view. It was during 1931-32 that his second novel, *Kandan, the Patriot*, appeared serially in the *Swarajya*, then a Daily edited by the Andhra patriot, T. Prakasam. With the Second Round Table Conference in London rendered fruitless, the year 1932 witnessed a revamping of the Civil Disobedience Movement. Repression led to popular discontent and nervous excitement and it was at this time that *Kandan, the Patriot* saw the light of day. It was enthusiastically received all over the country. In the words of K.R. Srinivasa Iyengar: "If all roads ultimately lead to Murugan, to the tiller's way of life in rural surroundings, in Kandan, all roads lead at least to Satyagraha, to a defiance of the 'satanic' government through the power of suffering and love."[2]

Influenced by Gandhian idealism, Kandan is beyond doubt a moral force of vast dimensions, a sharp and symbolic portrait of the Gandhian age. The individual will and the national perspective coalesce into creative art without actually introducing the Mahatma as a character. Though Gandhian philosophy and idealism goads Kandan to take the cudgels against the alien rulers, yet Gandhi himself remains behind the arras. The Mahatma is, at the most, a pervading spirit in this novel

Anglo-Indian novelists like Rudyard Kipling and Edward Thompson sang the glory of the British Empire in the novels they wrote. They gloated over British imperialism, its economic exploitation, its political dominations, its cultural colonisation. But Raja Rao sends Moorthy 'back to the village' to fight the Gandhian non-violent battle against the British authority, Bhattacharya makes Rahoul see the futility of English education and jump into the fray in order to shatter what Shamsul Islam[3] calls the 'mystique of the Raj' in his *Chronicles of the Raj* and Anand makes Bakha abandon his ambition to be a gentleman for the life of a freedom fighter.

Kamala Markandaya's second novel, *Some Inner Fury*, depicts the later phase of the Gandhian age covered by the 'Quit India' movement of the early Forties. It "dramatises the lives of young people lost in political confusion of the Independence struggle."[4] The fury of love, which consumes Mira, has been set against the fury of Govind and his associates. Mira's fury fizzles out into the larger fury of the national struggle for independence spearheaded by the Mahatma, who, here remains an invisible spiritual influence upon both Mira and Govind. Though Gandhiji is not a character in the novel, yet the personages inspired by his ideology plunge into the fire of revolution against the aliens. Roshan travels ticketless to demonstrate his civil disobedience, while Govind incites his followers to violence. (One doubts whether Gandhi himself would have approved such steps!) This "socio-political novel of modern India," observes A.V. Krishna Rao, "is symbolically significant on two levels: first the emotional inner fury of Mira is completely quenched when her love for Richard results in an ecstatic experience of the 'sweep and surge of love'; secondly, the wider inner fury of the nation at large is finally vented, culminating in the violent demonstration of national indignation at the alien rule, Govind being the focal figure."[5] *Some Inner Fury* is politically a war cry against the British rule in India, though O.P. Bhatnagar does not include it in his account of the political novels in Indian English literature.[6]

Khwaja Ahmad Abbas's *Inquilab* (1955) introduces many prominent personalities of the Gandhian era besides the Mahatma. The novel covers the earlier period commencing with the Rowlatt Act and Jalianawala Bagh tragedy to the Salt Satyagraha and the Gandhi-Irwin Pact of 1931. Abbas projects the Gandhian revolutionary age in its entirety with Motilal, Jawaharlal, C.R. Das, Subhas Chandra Bose, Sardar Patel, Rajgopalachari, Sarojini Naidu, Dr. Ansari, Muhammad Ali, Maulana Azad, Ghaffar Khan and Pandit Madan Mohan Malaviya. All these characters serve as a foil and a contrast to Gandhi. The protagonist of the novel is the illegitimate Anwar, whose mother was a Muslim and father, a Hindu merchant. A 'character' novel, *Inquilab* shows Anwar irretrievably involved in the political cataclysm of the age. He meets Gandhi for the first time in Dr. Ansari's place "a thin, spindly-legged man in coarse dhoti and kurta, plying a charkha. He had a white cloth thrown over his head and from a distance Anwar had taken him to be a woman."[7] Anwar's interview with Gandhi at Muhammad Ali's house is emotionally gratifying:

> Now he knew why they called him Mahatma—a Great Soul. On his face was a look of suffering, kindness and pity, as if he personally felt the misery of every single human being. But there was also infinite calm and serenity and the boy's spirits revived as he looked into those gentle eyes. (111)

The novel recounts Anwar's romantic odyssey throughout the politically ruffled and violently agitated India and closes on the political plane with the Gandhi-Irwin Pact. *Inquilab* lacks "the sweep of comprehension," and "the creative potentiality of execution" of Venu Chitale's *In Transit* (1950) which mirrors the Zeitgeist a little more faithfully, more cohesively. It is a study of Hindu joint family life in Maharashtra silhouetted against the Gandhian Age.

Zeenut Futehally's *Zohra* (1951) presents through the heroine the blend of a vague adolescent romanticism with Gandhian idealism. Inspired by a selfless love for the country and by the saintly philosophy of Gandhi, she stands romantically idealised. She falls in love with her brother-in-law Hamid, a melancholy romantic and a perennial outsider. The disagreement between the brothers over the Gandhian method is meant to indicate a more intrinsic difference of temperaments. Zohra's faith in the Gandhian idealism is second hand. But still she cherishes her trust in the Mahatma. She echoes the words of Hamid: "But is not Mahatma Gandhi doing that? Only his is a new way of Revolution. But it will surely lead to the regeneration of India."[8] Hamid's involvement in the Satyagraha movement is a means of sublimating his love for Zohra. He is not a political hero like Lal Singh in Mulk Raj Anand's *The Sword and the Sickle*.

In *Chronicles of Kedaram* (1961), K. Nagarajan sets the Iyengar feud against the backdrop of a South Indian district town during 1930s. The Mahatma alone can annul this tension and bring spiritual solace. The two Iyengar factions are reconciled with the timely intervention of Gandhiji. Nagarajan does not directly look at Gandhi. He sees him through his protagonist, Koni. In fact, Koni is Nagarajan objectified. Koni attends a meeting of the Mahatma but is unable to hear him clearly:

> So far as I could see, nobody did. The din was terrific. Stray words floated on the air. India's right to govern herself, Swaraj, Khaddar, Vanchinatha Sastri; Harijans, Devadasis, and so on, so that one could guess what he was saying.[9]

Thus, Nagarajan does not give a lucid picture of Gandhi. He only gives a glimpse. And his stance towards the Mahatma is so unclear. He neither commends nor condemns him. He only adopts an ambivalent posture. Gandhi is overtly introduced into the story. The foreground drama of the novel concerns the romantic love between Vasu and Nirmala Chari. Disappointed in love and marriages, Nirmala seeks sanctum in the Mahatma's Ashram at Sabarmati. It is here that Gandhiji's personality is revealed more clearly and elaborately than at Kedaram. Nirmala becomes the symbol of the myriad lovelorn and forlorn Indians languishing in their own private woes and painful frustrations, reckoning in the Mahatma's love the panacea for their personal privations. In most Indian English novels Gandhi emerges a saviour out of the interaction in love between the hero and the heroine.

Manohar Malgonkar's *A Bend in the Ganges* is an epic rendering of India's struggle for freedom from the late Thirties to the partitioning of the country in 1947. It explores Gandhiji's ideology of non-violence vis-a-vis man's volcanic urge for blood. The opening chapter, 'A Ceremony of Purification,' describes the ceremonial burning of foreign cloth. Gandhiji appears on the platform, but does not speak, since it is his day of silence. The cries of Mahatma Gandhi-ki-Jai!, Bharat-Mata-ki-Jai! rend the air. In the closing chapters of the novel there is more burning, this time of civilization and not of cloth. Is this a ceremony of purification? The following epigraph from Gandhi sets the tonal modality of the novel:

> This non-violence, therefore, seems to be due mainly to our helplessness. It almost appears as if we are nursing in our bosoms the desire to take revenge the first time we get the opportunity. Can true, voluntary non-violence come out of this seeming forced non-violence of the weak? Is it not a futile experiment I am conducting? (Epigraph).

Yes, it is a futile experiment borne out in the last three chapters of the novel. People do not accept Gandhi's ideals in the true spirit of Satyagrahis, they make a travesty of it.

A Bend in the Ganges paradoxically exhibits Gandhi, an upholder of the Hindu-Muslim unity, an apostle of non-violence, an inspiration behind the partition of India. Shafi, Debi and Basu—the three important male characters belonging to different communities and political allegiances—unanimously agree on this. Shafi's irate outburst and debunking of Gandhi is worth noticing: "A million shall die, I tell you . . . a million! For each man who should have died in the cause of freedom, Gandhi will sacrifice ten. That is what non-violence will do to this country."[10]

Raj Gill's *The Rape* bitterly blames the politicians for the vivisection of the country and the violence in the wake of India's independence. Even Gandhi is castigated for his sheer perfidy to the cause of the Hindu. Dalipjit, the protagonist, who fires in his dream an oneiric shot at the Mahatma, fails to accept the fact of Gandhi's assassination:

> How could Gandhi be shot dead? He was not living. He had shot Gandhi long back, years ago. They could not shoot a dead Gandhi. It was non-sense. He chuckled to himself in his unchallenged superiority over the men around him who were gullible enough to believe in some one's claim, who just craved the credit that he already held. He chuckled again and swam around gleefully in his ocean of warmth.[11]

Thus, Gandhi looks more imaginary than real in this novel.

In Bhabani Bhattacharya's *So Many Hungers* (1974), Gandhi occurs as an indirect presence. We see him through the aged nationalist leader, Devesh Bose, so deeply involved in the Civil Disobedience movement, so willingly incarcerated for the courage of his conviction, for the strength of his soul! *So Many Hun-*

gers describes against the backdrop of hunger for money, hunger for sex, hunger for freedom, the Quit India movement and the political storm raging in Calcutta when "India spoke in the voice of a volcanic outburst in the fateful mid-August days."[12] This voice spoke to Devesh Basu, 'Devata' of Baruni, a prototype of Gandhi who on his way to jail told the villagers whose faith in human values stood unshaken by centuries of hardship and strain: "Do not betray yourselves, there is violence in your thoughts; that is evil enough. Do not make it worse by violence in action." (72) The voice of Basu is the voice of Gandhi. This voice spoke to Kajoli, the peasant girl of Baruni, the image of the new woman heralded by Gandhian thought, Kajoli who reminds us of Mohini in *Music for Mohini* (1952), Meera in *Goddess Named Gold* (1960), Suruchi and Sumitra in *Shadow from Ladakh* (1966), Lekha in *He Who Rides a Tiger* (1954) and Devjani in *A Dream in Hawaii* (1978). Intimidated by the storeman and the grocer, the villagers sell their crops. Kajoli marries Kishore who is killed by the imperial police while crossing the railway line in Calcutta where he had gone to earn for his family. The 'dehydrated sticks of humanity' (135) march towards Calcutta. The women are enticed into Calcutta's brothels. Kajoli is raped. The unborn child is killed. She sees her mother and brother licking food from the garbage. Kajoli moves towards the brothel to sell her body in order to be able to give them food when she hears the hawker shouting:

> Prisoners start hunger strike. 'Devata' had started hunger strike. Why can't she? Devata's mantra rang in her ears: Be strong. Be true. . . . She could earn her living by selling newspapers. 'This way,' said Kajoh, and her feet hurried. 'Which way? The woman scowled. 'Hindustan,' said the girl briefly. (191)

This voice spoke to Rahoul, an astro-physicist of Calcutta university who had heard his grandfather say: "Why should you fight the people of England. They are good people. The people are good everywhere. Our fight is with the rulers of England who hold us in subjection for their narrow interests." (21) Sitting in the laboratory, he had seen the huge non-violent demonstrations in their thousands passing by the college street, the policemen insulting the tri-colour flag and lathi-charging the peaceful processionists. He hears the voice of that one personage whom India knew to be her man of destiny.

Rahoul goes to jail. He was indifferent towards himself, indifferent even to his captors, and his mind was without hate, without anger, in 'a nirvana of passionlessness.' (204) Rahoul wonders if the new dawn will 'break into boom, growing out of the seeds of the spirit' in the 'vast swamp of suffering and struggle.' (205) And yet one asks with Iyengar if these characters are mere 'algebraic symbols.' (412)

Edwin Gerow calls Bhabani Bhattacharya 'a socially programmatic novelist'[13] who borrowed his socialistic approach to life from Gandhi's experiments with truth. In the ordinariness of Gandhi's life presented in his *Autobiography* in an unpretentious, uninhibited way which reveals with relentless candour the dark recesses of the author's career, Bhattacharya finds a 'human interest' which pervades all his writing. His characters are cast in the Gandhian mould. While Satyajit in *Shadow from Ladakh* (1966) follows Gandhi in sexual abstinence, Jayadev in *Music for Mohini* (1952) is a Gandhian who transforms village Behula into a place where there is no casteism, no superstitions, no exploitation..

Gandhian ideas and ideals continued to dominate the Indian English novelists even beyond the 1940s. In Kamala Markandaya's *Nectar in a Sieve* (1954) and *A Handful of Rice* (1960), we see the Gandhian concern for the lowly and the lost. In Nayantara Sahgal, Gandhian values are more pervasive and less explicit. *A Time to be Happy* (1957) embodies India's starry-eyed optimism after independence. *This Time of Morning* betrays symptoms of disillusionment, while *Storm in Chandigarh* depicts the deterioration of the political situation around the beginning of the 1960s. If Gandhi is represented in *A Time to be Happy* as the fine flowering of Hindu heritage, the assumption is contested in *This Time of Morning*, although finally it is Kailash the Gandhiite who wins the day. Lastly, in *A Situation in New Delhi*

(1977) Gandhian values of non-violence are vindicated through the Vice Chancellor of Delhi University—Usman.

Chaman Nahal in *Azadi* (1975) explores the meaning of India's independence accompanied by the tragedy of partition. He shows Gandhi as the architect of freedom and as a martyr of communal harmony. And in *The Crown and the Loincloth* (1981), Nahal fictionalises the life of Gandhi from 1915 to 1922, from Gandhi's arrival in India from South Africa to his launching of the first Non-Cooperation Movement. The novel is an epic delineation of the first phase of the Indian freedom movement under the charismatic leadership of the loinclothed Gandhi, which shook the century-old pillars of British rule in India.

Gandhi's anti-mechanisation, anti-casteism and non-violence had a profound influence on Mulk Raj Anand. Like Gandhi, Anand finds in the 'gadget-mongering civilization of the West,' 'a ferocious man-eater of the profit system.' He finds in the Hindu social structure 'man's inhumanity to men,' which lends *Untouchable* (1935) its coherence and shape.

Anand's Bakha is an archetypal image of the untouchable, He meets Gandhi in the last section of the novel when he is driven out of home, taken out of himself, unconsciously forming a part of the crowd rushing towards Gandhi: "And like Bakha, they had not stopped to ask themselves why they were going. They were just going. The act of going, of walking, running, hurrying occupied them."[14] To them Gandhi was the enemy of the old and the harbinger of the new: "It seemed as if, in trampling on the blades of green grass, they were deliberately trampling on a part of themselves which they had begun to abhor." (153) Bakha in Khaki uniform was different from the white-clad crowd. But Gandhi united them. He united one age with another. To the villagers Gandhi was a tradition, an oracle, a legend. To the city, a symbol of anti-colonialism and anti-imperialism. Bakha looks at Gandhi 'with a mixed feeling of wonders reverence and fear.' (157) A part of him seemed to have flown, to have evaporated. He felt he had lost something of himself. He had gained something. He had been liberated. Bakha, Anand's untouchable, is thrilled by Gandhi's compassion for the outcasts.

He is attracted by what the poet says about the closet. He returns home with a tentative decision:

> 'I shall go and tell father all that Gandhi said about us' he whispered to himself, 'and all that poet said. Perhaps I can find the poet on the way and ask him about his machine.' And he proceeded homewards. (97)

Here again Gandhian idealism is pitted against our craze for machines. The poet's speech at the end of the novel is an expansion of what Gandhi had said. "He [Gandhi] is, by far, the greatest liberating force of our age says the poet and adds that Gandhi is "fundamentally sound." (167) Thus, the poet's speech and his views fall within the ideological framework of Gandhism. Gandhiji's speech electrifies Bakha's consciousness and his message has a tremendous impact on him. It brings him self-realisation, self-revelation.

In *Untouchable*, Anand is probably giving vent to his anti-Congress attitude. His physical description of Gandhi is vicious and venomous: "There was quixotic smile on his thin lips—something Mephistophelean in the determined little chin immediately under his mouth and the long toothless jaws resting on his small neck." (120) Though Bakha's meanderings and protests come to an end, "the conflict in his soul was not over. . . He was torn between his enthusiasm for Gandhi and the difficulties in his own awkward naive self." (133) Thus, the presence of the Mahatma in the innermost recesses of his being makes him psychically tense and physically tired.

While *The Old Man and the Cow* (1960) projects a picture of the resurgent Indian womanhood under Gandhi's leadership, *Coolie* (1936) presents 'a Gandhian critique of industrial civilization,' the 'many-headed and many-armed machine,' 'the jig-jig-jigging of its pistons, the fickle-tick-ticking of its knobs, the furious motion of the broad conveyor belts across its wheels' (168) run by workers with their faces assuming 'the sinister horror of unexpressed pain.' (195)

Two Leaves and a Bud (1937) reflects the reality of the Gandhian non-violent, non-resistant movement when the passivity is vigorously alive with the deep warm 'togetherness' of the Assam tea planters with whom Gangu lives and faces the rapacious brutality of the British.

Like Munoo in *Coolie*, Lalu in *The Sword and the Sickle* (1942) undergoes Gandhian suffering that makes him fit for the national struggle for freedom. He makes the Gandhian sacrifice that leaves him fit for the service of the country: "We have to give, give, give of ourselves, for he who gives himself to the service of others is blessed, enriched". (*Coolie* 392).

The Big Heart (1945), as Anand calls it in a letter of Nov. 1971 to Saros Cowasjee, is 'a drama of machine wrecking'[15] enacted through Hans Raj opposed to 'the evils of Vilayat'[16] under the influence of Gandhi whom he calls 'the mysterious God who is greater than all petty considerations of want and family demands.' (115) Ananta, the protagonist is another Gandhian whose passions are stirred to see in Bombay the ruin of a man 'utterly naked, his buttocks wrapped in a paste of sweat and dung and urine, rolling about on the edge of a ditch in a hissing agony, lifting his neck with an aching stupor and then slipping into his filth.' (56) Ananta must remove this evil with Gandhian non-violence, with a big heart. But ironically it is he who dies a violent death in the hands of Rallia who, while angrily smashing the machine, inadvertently batters Ananta's head against it. As Cowasjee rightly observes, "The novel shows the difficulty of applying this knowledge of non-violence in a world torn by hatred and suspicion."[17]

While Margaret Berry discovers Marxist aestheticism, Saros Cowasjee Marxian humanism and Meenakshi Mukherjee radical socialism in Mulk Raj Anand, K.R.S. Iyengar in *Indian Writing in English*, C.D. Narasimhaiah in *The Writer's Gandhi*[18] and M.K. Naik in *Mulk Raj Anand* see in him streaks of Gandhian humanism.

Raja Rao's *Kanthapura* (1938) microscopically concentrates and mythically interprets the Gandhian revolution of the 1930s. Tenets of Gandhian thought, which remain otherwise incomprehensible to the folk imagination "so deeply rooted in age-old customs and traditions suddenly come alive when explained and enacted in the language of religion."[19] Rao views the Gandhian revolution through "mythical moorings."[20] While Narsinga in "The Cow of the Barricades" sees Gandhi as Sita, the village narrator in *Kanthapura* views him as Rama who vanquished the Ravana of England or as Krishna who killed the "serpent of the foreign rule" (22) or "as Shiva with the three eyes of self-purification, Hindu-Muslim unity and Khaddar." (20)

Anand takes up untouchability, anti-mechanisation, ahimsa, colonial and racial subjugation as his themes while Rao deals with the spiritual regeneration which the Gandhian revolution brought about. Through the major incidents of India's freedom struggle—the Dandi March, Civil Disobedience, Satyagraha, Non-Cooperation, Nehru's social progressivism, Gandhi's untouchability, prohibition, spinning etc. are scattered over the white canvas of the novel, yet *Kanthapura* is "an integrated vision of Gandhi."[21] Though Gandhi appears nowhere in the novel, the very idea of Gandhi revitalised and revolutionised the "peasant sensibility"[22] of the Kanthapurians by arousing their traditional religious consciousness. Gandhi's campaign against untouchability sends shock-waves throughout the village. The female narrator Achakka is shocked to see Moorthy in Pariah quarters:

> and I closed my ears when I heard he went to the Pariah quarters. We said to ourselves, he is one of these Gandhimen, who say there is neither caste nor clan nor family . . . only they say, too, . . . a brahmin might marry a Pariah and a Pariah, a brahmin.[23]

Bhatta, the village moneylender, finds this "Gandhi business nothing but weaving coarse handmade cloth, not fit for a mop, and bellowing out bhajans and bhajans and mixing with the Pariahs." (40) This lucidly brings out the violent reaction Gandhi's radical thinking about untouchability must have created in the average Indian minds deeply and firmly rooted in the conservative conventions of the past.

Moorthy's conversion into the Gandhian creed is brought about quite mystically. He sees Gandhi in a dream. The Mahatma's voice—"There is but one force in life and that is Truth, and there is but one love in life and that is the love of mankind and there is but one God in life and that is the Good of all" (52-53) —goes through "the hair and the nails of Moorthy into the very limbs." (52)

Bakha in Anand's *Untouchable*, too, experiences this therapeutic influence of Gandhi. But while Bakha was an uneducated untouchable, Moorthy is a learned brahmin whose mystical experience transforms him from a ritualistic brahmin into a humanist of the Gandhian order. It shows him "the sheathless being of his soul." (54) The Skeffington Coffee Estate like the Assam Tea Plantation in Anand's *Two Leaves and a Bud* throws up the economic exploitation and sexual violence of the white masters. The scenes of Moorthy's visit to the Estate, the resistance and obstacles he encounters, the lathi charge by Bade Khan, the violence by the coolies against the police and Moorthy's "no beatings, sisters. No beatings in the name of the Mahatma" (80)—are all modelled on Gandhian non-violent passive resistance. Moorthy, like Ramakrishna in *Cat and Shakespeare* (1965), like Ramaswamy in *The Serpent and the Rope* has "the fright of gun and sword."[24]

Moorthy who takes to fasting on Gandhian lines as a panacea against violence, feels: "were he full of the radiance of ahimsa, such things should never have happened." (90) He takes the entire responsibility upon himself: "the fault of others, Rangamma, is the fruit of one's own disharmony." (90) When Waterfall Venkamma and Seethamma denounce him, he invokes inner strength: "The great enemy is in us, Rangamma." (96) Another Gandhi is born.

But the illiterate Kanthapurians find it difficult to mouth this Gandhian faith in man's innate goodness: "Rangamma did not understand this, neither, to tell you the truth, did any of us," (96) comments the narrator. Yet they follow Moorthy. The indispensable Range Gowda is persuaded to join the Congress: "and if the Mahatma says what you say, let the Mahatma's word be word of God," (103) he tells Moorthy. Even the Kanthapurian women feel a stray force released within them and their temporary hesitation ('mad we were, daughters, mad to follow Moorthy,' [230]) is swept away by something deeper and more irresistible: "and we forgot the pariahs and the policemen and Moorthy and the Mahatma, and we felt as though we were some secret brotherhood in some Himalayan Cave." (221) Some strange fever "rushed up from the feet, it rushed up . . . and something powerful shook us from hand to foot, and we rushed back home, trembling and gasping with the anger of the gods. Moorthy forgive us! Mahatma forgive us! Kenchamma forgive us! We shall go. Oh, we shall go to the end of the pilgrimage." (230-31) And they go to the end of the pilgrimage with unfaltering steps. The Mahatma is "a holy man, and freedom struggle, a pilgrimage, and the Kanthapurian women, soldiers of the Mahatma." (192) Such was the hypnotic impact of the Gandhian Movement on the Indian mind, which reminds one of what Nehru said in *The Discovery of India* in connection with Gandhi's appearance in the contemporary Indian political scenario: "He was like a powerful current of fresh air, a beam of light that pierces the darkness, like a whirlwind that upsets many things." (327)

Rao's Moorthy goes the Gandhian way after his mystical communion and conversation. But Narayan's Swami is an ordinary schoolboy swayed by the current of Gandhian movement. In *Kanthapura*, Moorthy bears the lathi of Bade Khan without a word. He resorts to fasting as a panacea against violence. But in *Swami and Friends* (1935), Swami boycotts the class, stones the school building, pits himself against the police whom he calls "nefarious agents of the Lancashire thumbcutters."[25]

In Raja Rao's *Kanthapura*, the perennial strife between good and evil, exemplified in Rama and Ravana, is used to describe the Gandhian struggle against the brute force of the Englishmen. Here the impact of Gandhiji is seen as mythological. He remains behind the screen but his presence is always felt through the transformation he brings about in Kanthapura. Gandhi is present in the novel through report and not in person. This unseen, invisible influence of the Mahatma guarantees the halo of myth around his saintly personality.

Against the holy figure of Gandhi, we have the sacrilegious presence of the Swami's agent, who regards the British King as the protector of faith and rails derisively: "All this Gandhi and Gandhi who cannot pronounce even gayatri!" (102) Gandhi is Rama, Gandhi is Krishna. Just as Krishna killed the serpent Kaliya who had created havoc with the lives around, Gandhi crushed the unmitigated tyranny of the British Raj in India, himself remaining miraculously safe in the prevailing chaotic conditions.

Gandhi is Harishchandra, symbol of truth, piety, justice, dedication and sacrifice. Like Raja Harishchandra, he left his lucrative legal profession and love for money. Dressed in a very simple dhoti or loincloth, he was ever ready to sacrifice himself for upholding the principle of truth: "Like Harishchandra before he finished his vow, the gods will come down and dissolve his vow, and the Britishers will leave India, and we shall be free, and we shall pay less taxes, and there will be no policemen." (135) Moorthy is a Kanthapura Gandhi. "He is the Mahatma's physical presence in Kanthapura—a mini Gandhi. Moorthy is spoken of by the villagers as "our Gandhi," "Our Mahatma." (89) He is the messiah of the Mahatma, a pragmatic Gandhiite, spreading the Gandhian ideal and philosophy throughout Kanthapura. But he is Gandhi with a difference. He is a travesty of the real Gandhi. He dislikes to be with the pariahs. He hates to enter their huts. He would always speak to the pariahs from the gutter slabs. He hesitates when requested by a pariah woman to enter her house: "No, no, no, and he looks this side and that and thinks surely there is a carcass in the backyard . . . and his hands steal mechanically to the holy thread, and holding it, he feels he would like to say, 'Hari-Om, Hari-Om.'" (83) Though Gandhi has been given a mythological colouring in the novels yet the character that personifies him (i.e. Moorthy), has failed to bring out the real Gandhi in him. He has rather made a holy and mythopoeic mockery of the Mahatma. His is an apotheosis of the Gandhian idealism. Srinivasa Iyengar rightly regards Kanthapura as the "grammar of Gandhian ethics," though Anand looks another way. "The bardic narrative in *Kanthapura,*" says Anand, "is fused with the speaking-acting-dramatic flow of speech of the novel, recording the crisis of change in every character through the impact of Gandhi."[26] Anand sees the Gandhian vision transforming the characters and elevating them to a higher spiritual plane of existence.

While Anand explores man's relationship to the society, Rao exposes man's relationship to the ultimate duality (within the matrix of Gandhian thoughts). Anand's disillusionment with the Marxian dialectic materialism led him to Gandhian secular humanism. But Rao's intellectual propensities propelled him to the metaphysical world of Gandhian thought.

Anand and Bhattacharya relate man to the society, Rao to the spirit, Narayan to education which is an instrument of cultural, spiritual and personal liberation. Narayan's ambivalent approach to Gandhi distinguishes him from Anand, Rao and Bhattacharya. In *Waiting for the Mahatma*, Sriram looks askance at the Mahatma even though he is eager to follow him. So do Bakha and Moorthy and Rahoul. But while "Anand, Rao and Bhattacharya are committed" observes Rama Jha, "Narayan is comic" (179)

In R.K. Narayan's *Waiting for the Mahatma*,[27] Gandhi's Quit India movement paves the path for the protagonist Sriram's intellectual and emotional growth. Here Gandhi is a character. Sriram is an incarnation of the Gandhian spirit. To Narayan, Gandhism is a sort of humanism. Narayan's grasp of the quintessence of Gandhian idealism transcends the bare conscription of character delineation. The novelist views Gandhi as the nexus of polarities of existence. Gandhi appears intermittently in this novel. He features as a minor character. Narayan unpretentiously and unsentimentally presents him a symbol of the novelist's racial and spiritual wisdom. Gandhi is both a man and a god. A persuasively human figure, Gandhi's presence has great spiritual import. A thoroughly pictured character, he becomes a striking symbol—the symbol of truth, non-violence and freedom. Sriram's lyrical love for Bharati is juxtaposed with his slack grasp of the Gandhian doctrines. The movement of these two parallel themes—love for the beloved and love for Gandhi—makes the presence of the Mahatma markedly romantic and sentimental. In the words of K.R. Srinivasa Iyengar:

> In *Untouchable*, Anand gives the Mahatma a part towards the end. Other novelists, whether writing in English or in the regional languages have likewise exploited the magic of Gandhi's name and presence, but seldom is the Gandhian role subsumed in the fiction as a whole. Gandhi is too big to be given a minor part: on the other hand, he is sure to turn the novel into a biography if he is given a major (or the central) part. The best thing for the contemporary novelist would be to keep Gandhi in the background but make his influence felt indirectly. In *Waiting for the Mahatma*, the theme is apparently the Bharati-Sriram romance which, however, gains a new dimension in the background of their common allegiance to the Mahatma. Since the stress is not merely on Gandhi's influence but on Gandhi himself—we see him in Malgudi stationed in Nellappa's Grove and we see him, years later, in Delhi on his way to prayer on the fatal day of 30 January, 1948—the novel develops a duality of interest which is not wholly resolved by the compulsion of art. (372-73)

Narayan's picture of Gandhiji is complimentary. To quote M.K. Naik:

> the novel is the ironic portrayal of the response of various Indians to Gandhiji's thought and philosophy. The irony in the Municipal Chairman's ridiculous attempts to bask in the borrowed limelight of the Mahatma is, of course, too obvious to be missed. What seems, however, to have generally been missed is the subtle irony which underlines the picture of the impact of Gandhiji on the hero, Sriram—a blind follower of a leader whose methods and policies are too subtle for his limited comprehension. He indulges in terrorist activities against all Gandhian principles. Narayan is perhaps hinting at the fact that a large section of the Indian public did not understand Gandhi properly at all. (377)

It would be worthwhile to note that in many of the Indian English novels, the Gandhian issue dies away due to sentimentalisation of Gandhian philosophy or to the prominence given to the protagonist's involvement in love or to the overlapping of the stock theme of East-West confrontation. Yet as Meenakshi Mukherjee observes: "No discussion of Indo-Anglian fiction dealing with the independence movement would be complete without an assessment of the function of Mahatma Gandhi in these novels."[28] And how does Gandhi function? He functions as "an idea, a myth, a symbol, a tangible reality, and a benevolent human being." (*Ibid.*) Gandhi seems to have had a profound impact upon the philosopher-novelist Raja Rao. The two symbols—'the cow' and 'the prince'—coalesce in Rao's fictional imagination. The cow represents compassion and gentleness, while the prince stands for reverence and hero-worship. These two symbols blend in the Mahatma. Gandhi in Raja Rao's *Kanthapura* figures as a God-like presence, invisible yet indomitable, operating in everyone's deeds and thoughts. R.K. Narayan, on the other hand, presents Gandhi as a person and not as a symbol or a myth. In his *Waiting for the Mahatma*, Gandhi appears in flesh and blood and transforms the idyllic life of a young couple—Sriram and Bharati. Without losing track of the Mahatma's historical authenticity, Narayan sketches him with delectable, rollicking and tolerant humour. But the picture of the Gandhian way of life becomes an emotional flop. It neither evokes nor provokes.

In Abbas's *Inquilab*, Gandhi is portrayed through the emotional reverence of a young boy, overwhelmed by his physical presence before him. Gandhi in Abbas symbolises the public psyche. Mulk Raj Anand does not defy or glorify Gandhi. Anand's hero, Lal Singh, never holds the Mahatma in high esteem. He fails to respond to Gandhian principle:

> The Mahatma seemed full of himself, of his spiritual struggles. And Lalu felt himself lapsing into listlessness as if he were being suffocated by the deliberate simplicity of the egoistic confessional talk of self-perfection.[29]

Michael Pousse observes: "Gandhian novelists have done nothing but shroud in Indian clothing what basically remains a Western form of literature."[30] These novelists have given an artistic shape to the 'eternal' and the 'enduring' in Gandhian philosophy. Be he a symbol or a myth or a tangible reality, Gandhi basically remains a human figure. Emotionalism of the later novels mars their leitmotif. The presence of Gandhi, besides making the work crudely national, gives it a spatio-temporal historical identity. To the characters in these novels, Gandhi becomes the source of strength, unity and purity. And yet does not this preoccupation with the Gandhi theme contribute to the sharp decline in the creative powers of these novelists? Rama Jha rightly observes: "Gandhi gave a new insight to the Indian intelligentsia . . . and added a new dimension to their imagination. . . . Indo-Anglian novelists learned to discover their own country." (40)

References

1. M.K. Naik, "Gandhiji and Indian Writing in English," *Critical Essays on Indian Writing in English*, ed. M.K. Naik et. al (Madras: Macmillan, 1977), p. 375.
2. K.R. Srinivasa Iyengar, *Indian Writing in English* (Bombay: Asia, 1973), p. 281.
3. Shamsul Islam, *Chronicles of the Raj: A Study of Literary Reaction to the Imperial Idea towards the End of the Raj* (London: Macmillan, 1979).
4. S.C. Harrex, "A Sense of Identity: The Novels of Kamala Markandaya," *Journal of Commonwealth Literature*, Vol. V, 1, June 1971, p. 65.
5. A.V. Krishna Rao, *The Indo-Anglian Novel and the Changing Tradition* (Mysore: Rao and Raghavan, 1972), p. 59.
6. K.A. Abbas, *Inquilab* (Bombay: Jaico, 1955), p. 63
7. Z. Futehally, *Zohra* (Bombay: Hind Kitabs, 1951), p. 8.
8. O.P. Bhatnagar, "The Indian Political Novel in English," *Nagpur University English Teacher's Journal*, 1981.
9. Qtd. Iyengar, p. 287.
10. Manohar Malgonkar, *A Bend in the Ganges* (New Delhi: Orient Paperbacks, 1964), p. 16.
11. Raj Gill, *The Rape* (New Delhi: Sterling Paperbacks, 1974), p. 288.
12. Bhabani Bhattacharya, *So Many Hungers* (New Delhi: Orient Paperbacks, 1978), p. 40.
13. Edwin Gerow, "The Persistence of Classical Esthetic Categories in Contemporary Indian Literature: Three Bengali Novels," *The Lit-*

erature of India: An Introduction, ed. Edward C. Dimock, Jr. (Chicago: Univ. of Chicago Press, 1974), p. 230.

14. Mulk Raj Anand, *Untouchable* (1935; rpt. New Delhi: Orient Paperbacks, 1970), p. 50.
15. Saros Cowasjee, *Letters of Mulk Raj Anand* (Writers' Workshop, 1973), p. 121.
16. Mulk Raj Anand, *The Big Heart* (1945; rpt. Bombay: Kutub Popular, 1945), p. 115.
17. Saros Cowasjee, *So Many Freedoms* (New Delhi: O.U.P., 1977), p. 128.
18. C.D. Narasimhaiah, *The Writer's Gandhi* (Patiala: Punjabi University, 1967).
19. Rama Jha, *Gandhian Thought and Indo-Anglian Novelists* (New Delhi: Chanakya, 1983), p. 94.
20. L.S.R. Krishna Sastri, "Raja Rao," *The Second Literary Reader*, ed. P. Lal (Calcutta: Writers' Workshop, 1973), p. 50.
21. Jha, p. 95.
22. Atma Ram, "Peasant Sensibility in *Kanthapura*," K.K. Sharma, ed., *Indo-English Literature* (Ghaziabad: Vimal, 1977), p. 194.
23. Raja Rao, *Kanthapura* (Delhi: Hind Pocket Books, n.d.), p. 19.
24. Raja Rao, *The Serpent and the Rope* (1960; rpt. New Delhi: Orient Paperbacks, 1968), p. 7.
25. R.K. Narayan, *Swami and Friends* (1935; rpt. Mysore: Indian Thought Publications, 1977), p. 99.
26. Mulk Raj Anand, "Roots and Flowers: Content and Form in *Untouchable* and *Kanthapura*," *Littcrit*, 14, Vol. 8, No. 1, June 1982, p. 55.
27. R.K. Narayan, *Waiting for the Mahatma* (1955; rpt. Mysore: Indian Thought Publications, 1978).
28. Meenakshi Mukherjee, *The Twice Born Fiction* (New Delhi: Heinemann Educational Books India, 1971), p. 61.
29. Mulk Raj Anand, *The Sword and the Sickle* (Bombay, 1955), p. 207.
30. Michael Pousse, "Narayan as a Gandhian Novelist," *The Journal of Indian Writing in English*, Vol. 19, No. 2, July 1991, p. 8.